The Cosmic Hierarchy

A Christian Cosmology,

dedicated to the honor of

Pope St. John Paul II

in the year 2020,

the centenary of his birth

A CHRISTIAN COSMOLOGY

by

Richard J. Pendergast, SJ

Edited by

Valerie Miké

Dates on Volumes 1–5 indicate year of completion of the book manuscript.

Volume 1.   **THE COSMIC HIERARCHY:**
  God's Plan for the Evolution of the Universe (**2012**)
  Introduction to a Christian cosmology, an integration of modern science and divine revelation, with the aim of achieving a coherent view of the universe. The focus here is on the key scientific issues.

Volume 2.   **THE COSMIC HIERARCHY:**
  The Universe and Its Many Irreducible Levels (**2007**)
  A Christian cosmology, the integration of modern science and divine revelation. Analysis of scientific issues in the full context of insights offered by philosophy and theology.

A CHRISTIAN COSMOLOGY

Volume 3. ***A VISION FOR OUR TIMES:***
In the Sadness of the Modern World **(1988)**
Response to the need for a cosmology that incorporates modern science into a religious view of the world and offers meaning. Use is made of new concepts of physics (quantum mechanics) and philosophy (process thought).

Volume 4. ***THE LIVING UNIVERSE:***
An Organic Theory of Mind and Matter **(1990)**
An interpretation of quantum mechanics with the synthesis of Aristotelian and Whiteheadian concepts results in a process cosmology. The relationship of the cosmos to the transcendent reality of God.

Volume 5. ***CREATION, EVIL, AND THE TRINITY:***
A Christian Process Theology **(1990)**
Integration of the new cosmology into a wider theological synthesis shows Christian revelation on this process basis to illuminate the fundamental nature of reality in a fresh way.

Volume 6. ***THE MASS ON THE WORLD:***
A Modern Theory of Transubstantiation **(2008)**
Reprint in three languages (English, German, and Spanish) of the author's study concerning the teaching of the Catholic Church on the real presence of Christ in the Eucharist.

Richard J. Pendergast, SJ
1927–2012

The Cosmic Hierarchy

God's Plan for the Evolution of the Universe

by
RICHARD J. PENDERGAST, SJ

Edited by
Valerie Miké

A Herder & Herder Book
The Crossroad Publishing Company
New York

A collaboration with The Ethics of Evidence Foundation, Inc.

A Herder & Herder Book
The Crossroad Publishing Company
www.crossroadpublishing.com

Copyright © 2020   The Ethics of Evidence Foundation, Inc.,
             with consent of the USA Northeast Province of the Society of Jesus

Crossroad, Herder & Herder, and the crossed C logo/colophon are registered trademarks of The Crossroad Publishing Company.

All rights reserved. No part of this book may be copied, scanned, reproduced in any way, or stored in a retrieval system, or transmitted, in any form or by any means, electronic, mechanical, photocopying, recording, or otherwise, without the written permission of The Crossroad Publishing Company. For permission please write to rights@crossroadpublishing.com.

In continuation of our 200-year tradition of independent publishing, The Crossroad Publishing Company proudly offers a variety of books with strong, original voices and diverse perspectives. The viewpoints expressed in our books are not necessarily those of The Crossroad Publishing Company, any of its imprints or of its employees, executives, or owners. Although the author and publisher have made every effort to ensure that the information in this book was correct at press time, the author and publisher do not assume and hereby disclaim any liability to any party for any loss, damage, or disruption caused by errors or omissions, whether such errors or omissions result from negligence, accident, or any other cause. No claims are made or responsibility assumed for any health or other benefits.

Cover design by George Foster after the original of John Miké
Hubble Telescope image of a star formation region in jet HH 901 of the Carina Nebula

Library of Congress Cataloging-in-Publication Data
available from the Library of Congress.

ISBN   cloth 9780824598136
ISBN   ePub 9780824501976
ISBN   mobi 9780824501983
ISBN   Tradepaper 9780824503673

Books published by The Crossroad Publishing Company may be purchased at special quantity discount rates for classes and institutional use. For information, please e-mail sales@crossroadpublishing.com.

*Receive, O Lord, this all-embracing host,
which Your whole creation, drawn by Your magnetism,
offers You at this dawn of a new day.*

*This bread, our toil, is of itself, I know, but an immense
fragmentation; this wine, our pain, is no more, I know,
than a draught that dissolves. Yet in the very depths
of this formless mass You have implanted—and this
I am sure of for I sense it—a desire, irresistible, hallowing
which makes us cry out, believer and unbeliever alike:*

Lord, make us one!

Pierre Teilhard de Chardin
THE MASS ON THE WORLD

Contents

Foreword: A Man with a Mission
    by Valerie Miké xiii
Preface xxvii

Part One: Some Basic Concepts

Chapter
1 • The Call for a Christian Cosmology 3
2 • Theories of Matter: The Cosmic Hierarchy 19
3 • Various Attempts to Explain Away Human
    Consciousness 37

Part Two: Quantum Mechanics

4 • Past Interpretations of Quantum Mechanics 61
5 • Entanglement 76
6 • The Nature of Time 86
7 • A New Interpretation of Quantum Mechanics 98

Part Three: Biological Evolution

8 • Modest and Ambitious Darwinism 113
9 • The Intelligent Design Movement 132
10 • The Nature of Evolution 147
   • Excursus: Editor's Update on Intelligent Design 160

Part Four: Theology and Evolution

11 • Evil, Original Sin, and Evolution 169
12 • The Future of Mankind 188

Appendix: Essence and Existence 195

Reference List 205

Preview 1: Contents of Volume 2 227

Preview 2: Synopsis of Volume 2 233

Curriculum Vitae: Richard J. Pendergast, SJ 237

Index 239

About the Author 261

About the Editor 263

About the Publisher 265

Foreword

A Man with a Mission

Richard J. Pendergast, SJ, was my friend. Although we were both New Yorkers, our meeting in the summer of 1984 was not a chance encounter. Quite the contrary, it was for me the end result of a targeted search.

A native of Budapest, Hungary, I had lived through the Second World War as a child, and come to the United States in my teens with my family in the subsequent wave of refugees from East Central Europe. I attended public high school, and my early love of mathematics was joined by a growing interest in philosophy as I completed a broad liberal arts program on scholarship at Manhattanville College. Further support was provided by Bell Labs, where I worked in systems engineering while studying for a doctorate in mathematics at the Courant Institute of New York University. Readings in the history of science led to the desire to participate in the introduction of mathematical techniques in medicine.

By this time, I had been engaged in medical research and education for nearly two decades at a large medical center on the Upper East Side of Manhattan, where I also lived. My work was engrossing and meaningful, but I sensed with increasing intensity the absence of a dimension in the totally secular framework of my professional life: issues upon issues that cried out for exploration and analysis in the full context of our rich traditions that include the world of the spirit. I kept buying books, I kept reading. There was the recurring thought that perhaps I need not be alone, perhaps there were others somewhere, others I could join in a common quest. The two authors whose work had made a special impression on me were Teilhard de Chardin and Karl Rahner. Since both were Jesuits,

I thought I should find out what the Jesuits were doing. But I did not know any Jesuits. Then one day, browsing in the literature rack in the vestibule of St. Ignatius Jesuit Church near my apartment, I came across the announcement of a one-week directed retreat to take place shortly at Loyola Retreat House in New Jersey, not far from Manhattan. I had no idea what a directed retreat was; I knew only about preached weekend retreats that I had attended. But it said here that participants had their personal director with whom they met for an hourly session each day. Speak with a Jesuit for an hour every day for a week? That seemed perfect for me, and I signed up. Under comments, I added that I would like an older director and I wanted to discuss my work.

My director was Father Harvey Haberstroh, a kind, gentle man in his early seventies. He listened intently as I told my story, then said that he would think about it. He suggested that in the meantime I enjoy the week ahead. And I did just that. It turned out that I was the only lay member of the group. The others were priests and nuns making their annual one-week retreats, and many seemed to know each other. But I was rapidly drawn into the spirit of the event. The beautiful setting of thirty acres of lawns and gardens, the open, friendly environment, the intimacy of daily Mass with the community gathered in the small chapel—a new experience for me, used to large city churches—contributed to a peaceful, joyous stay.

The day before the end of the retreat, Father Haberstroh returned to the subject of my visit. He said that he had been praying about it, to discern how to help me in my search. The best advice he could offer was that I should meet another Jesuit priest, Richard Pendergast, who had been on the staff here and had just been assigned to St. Ignatius in Manhattan. A few years older than I, he had a doctorate in physics and had published a book called *Cosmos* that was available in the retreat house library. "You should meet Dick Pendergast," Father Haberstroh said, "because you are soulmates." I did find a copy of *Cosmos* in the library. Its dedication read: "To Karl Rahner and Pierre Teilhard de Chardin, masters and older brothers in Christ."

When I called Richard Pendergast shortly afterward, he had already heard about me from Father Haberstroh. We agreed to meet at St. Ignatius at one o'clock on a day later that week. He was waiting for me when I arrived at the rectory and we sat down in the parlor. The conversation flowed easily and became absorbing. So much so, that the next time I looked at my watch, I was surprised to see that it was six o'clock. He understood and responded to the issues I raised, and I in turn was familiar with concepts and titles he mentioned, books I had read on my own over the years. He spoke of the significance of *The Cloud of Unknowing*, the fourteenth-century English classic of mysticism, a work that I knew and owned. When I got home, I took the little book off the shelf and read it again that evening.

Although the circumstances and settings would vary, that first meeting set the pattern for the next twenty-eight years: five to six hours of rambling conversation, about anything and everything. We would generally meet every few weeks, with phone calls in between.

I asked him at the start what he was doing. He explained, and this I also knew, that the best exposition of Catholic doctrine was held to be that of St. Thomas Aquinas, based on the philosophy of Aristotle. But the latter has a static worldview, whereas science today thinks in terms of process, of evolution. An approach especially suited to properly modify the expression of Church teaching was the process philosophy of Alfred North Whitehead, who had important insights that had not been developed from a Catholic perspective. Making use of these to seek a modern synthesis of Thomistic thought based on reality as process was Richard Pendergast's aim. I already knew of Whitehead as a major figure in mathematics, and all this made a lot of sense to me. People try to find the meaning of life as experienced in their own culture, and the eternal message of the Church is clearly most meaningful if proclaimed in the framework of a compatible cosmology.

In fact, to reconcile modern science and Christian faith was the reason Richard Pendergast became a Jesuit. He had served in the Navy, was an electrical engineer, had a girlfriend. In the end, the desire to devote his life to seeking a resolution of conflict between science and religion became decisive, and he felt that he could best do that as a member of the Society of Jesus. By the time we met, however, he had been a Jesuit for over three decades and had a realistic picture of the situation. This was not an age of syntheses, he said; there was virtually no interest. The focus was entirely on science, its stunning feats and promises. His own hope now was to develop the synthesis outlined in his 1973 work *Cosmos*,[1] publish his insights in a book and leave it for posterity, for the Lord to make use of it at the proper time as he willed.

Zachary Hayes, OFM, devotes a section of his book *What Are They Saying about Creation?* to a review of *Cosmos*. "Perhaps the most sustained attempt to map out the contours of a new theological model is the little-known study by R. Pendergast entitled *Cosmos* (Fordham University Press, 1973).... Throughout he expresses the implications of the basic conviction that dynamic process is a fundamental feature of cosmic reality which theology ignores only at a great price."[2]

The Cosmic Hierarchy, the title of Volumes 1 and 2, reflects the primary roles of the nature of time and of teleology in Richard Pendergast's crystallized vision. He saw evolution as the progressive, step-by-step actualization of the successive levels of what he called the cosmic hierarchy (six or more levels from the smallest particles to living beings), with progress in terms of ontological value. He did not see aimless wandering through the space of all possible configurations of inanimate matter. An early draft of his manuscript was already in existence when we met. He gave me a copy to read, and I had the opportunity to see and discuss later versions as his material continued to develop.

An author significant in Richard Pendergast's work who would become central to my own thinking about scientific activity was the scientist-philosopher Michael Polanyi. Challenging positivist concepts of objectivity with his theory of personal knowledge, Polanyi argued that all explicit knowledge relies on tacit knowledge, a vast domain of tacit assumptions, perceptions, and commitments of the persons who hold them. Science is a more formalized type of knowledge, but not distinct in kind from other human knowledge. It is an affirmation of our beliefs; these must be responsible beliefs consistent with the evidence, but the ultimate commitment is that of personal judgment.

Polanyi's thought complemented in my own mind the revolutionary insight of twentieth-century mathematics concerning the intrinsic limitations of scientific knowledge, achieved by Kurt Gödel's incompleteness theorem. According to this theorem, any consistent mathematical system that includes even as little as the arithmetic of whole numbers contains statements that cannot be proved either true or false within the system. No mathematical system can encompass all truth; there will always be some truths that are beyond it. This means that science will never be able to explain all of reality.

My main focus was on issues of uncertainty and evidence in medicine, and I sought an approach that could be meaningful to all in our pluralistic culture. I called it the Ethics of Evidence.[3] Why ethics? The aim of evidence is to promote some belief or action, and thus it has an intrinsic moral dimension. Evidence is complex and fragile, with standards that vary by discipline. Developed initially for medicine, the approach has since been seen to be widely applicable to other areas of decision making in human affairs. Summed up in two simple rules or imperatives, it calls for (1) the creation and use of the best possible evidence in each relevant field, and (2) increased awareness and acceptance of the extent and ultimately irreducible nature of uncertainty—scientific and existential uncertainty. The desired outcome is a conscious act of personal judgment.

After a year's assignment at St. Ignatius, Richard Pendergast served for six years as chaplain at a retreat house on Long Island. In 1991, he suffered a major stroke, from which he recovered almost completely, but an existing heart condition turned more serious, and he became a permanent resident at Murray-Weigel Hall, the Jesuit infirmary on the Fordham University campus. He engaged in pastoral ministry nearby and continued his scholarly work. He had taught physics in college in his early years as a Jesuit but had left academic life by the time we met. Pastoral ministry combined with his own research and writing was what he wanted to do. His closest friends were devout Catholic couples with large families who welcomed him into their homes. His parents were deceased. He had a younger sister, a Dominican nun, whom he brought over to meet me on her next visit to New York; sadly, she died of cancer not long afterward. He had three cousins in New Jersey with whom he kept in touch. Through him I met other Jesuits, mostly at conferences we attended together.

When he came to Manhattan, at times we would go to see an exhibit at the nearby Metropolitan Museum of Art. When I visited him at Murray-Weigel, we attended the community Mass and had lunch with the community, then spent the afternoon at the New York Botanical Garden adjoining the Fordham campus. He enjoyed walking in the Garden and visited it almost every day.

When, calling him about something in the evening, I asked what he was doing, nearly always he was saying the Rosary. I asked him once how much time he spent in prayer each day, and he said three hours. During the 1995 papal visit to New York, when Pope John Paul II celebrated Mass in Central Park for 125,000, Richard Pendergast was one of two hundred priests concelebrating with the Holy Father and distributing Communion to the faithful.

On occasion we spent a weekend at my widowed mother's home in New Jersey, where he celebrated Mass for us. Early risers both, they would engage in wide-ranging conversation at the kitchen table, as she offered him a rich menu for breakfast. He also enjoyed her fine Hungarian cuisine at the holiday dinners he came to share with us. He visited my mother regularly at Memorial Sloan-Kettering during her final illness, and he was with me at the hospital on the day she died.

In his 2012 autobiography, the distinguished German Catholic philosopher Robert Spaemann makes the statement that, in his view, the most significant work of metaphysics of the twentieth century was *Process and Reality* by Alfred North Whitehead.[4]

But the situation was far from clear in America. A rejection letter Richard Pendergast received from a well-known Catholic publisher states, "I think that the topics covered are extremely important." But … "we are not quite ready to stake out a claim in the hylomorphism wars." There had been similar responses to previous attempts to have his book published. It may be, although I cannot of course be sure, that the reticence of Catholic publishers to get involved was based on the perceived conflict between modern physics, with related process thought, and Aristotle's theory of matter, of substance as matter and form (hylomorphism), used in the philosophical formulation of the teaching of the Catholic Church on the Eucharist.

This important, highly specific theological topic did not appear in the Pendergast manuscript. He published a separate, long essay on the subject in a peer-reviewed journal of philosophy and theology. Titled "The Mass on the World," this essay presents a comprehensive historical review and sketches a modern theory of transubstantiation that is consistent with Church doctrine.[5]

Briefly, it involves the cosmic hierarchy, a form of holism discussed by Richard Pendergast, and his use of the original Hegelian term *aufheben*, translated into English here as "to sublate." (Hegel introduced this German word with its diverse contradictory meanings in everyday use, exemplified by "to cancel" and "to preserve," into philosophical terminology. It has been employed by other scholars whose interest was in the word itself, unrelated to Hegelian philosophy.) When entities are sublated to a higher level of ontological value of the cosmic hierarchy, their own properties are preserved, while they themselves are integrated into the entity on the new level. In consecration, the Eucharistic bread and wine are sublated from their natural level to the highest level of the hierarchy and become the incarnate Word. The real presence of Christ in the Eucharist is a sign and promise of the final transformation of the world, and the essay here recalls the mystical prayer of Teilhard de Chardin reflected in its title.

Richard Pendergast had already published a study on his Thomistic-process theory of the Trinity,[6] a process theory of Creation,[7] and a process Christology,[8] with two more studies to follow.[9,10] At this point he decided on a radical revision of his manuscript. His primary aim had always been to reach a wide audience, the general public, readers seeking meaning in their own lives amid the fragmentation and noisy claims of the secular world. Retaining the main title of the book, he changed the subtitle from "The Universe and Its Many Irreducible Levels" to "God's Plan for the Evolution of the Universe."

This new, condensed version focuses on the important current concerns of science—the nature of matter, the problem of human consciousness, the interpretation of quantum mechanics and of biological evolution—and with extensive review of the literature offers a coherent view that is compatible with scientific findings as well as divine revelation.

But since every conclusion is based on a philosophy, there is an appendix on philosophy, where the author describes his own position. His early training had been in the Aristotelian-Thomistic tradition, as it was understood by Etienne Gilson and other neo-Thomists of the day. He had also been influenced by the ideas of Karl Rahner, Michael Polanyi, Alfred North Whitehead, and others. He explains some of the concepts that are accepted by most, or at least many, contemporary Thomists, with certain modifications of his own. He was basically a Thomist.

My brother John, also a physicist, offered to prepare a prepublication edition of this new version, and Pendergast gladly accepted. He did not see the cover, designed by my brother using an image of a star formation region from the Hubble telescope, until the carton of books arrived by mail at Fordham. It was meant as a surprise, and he loved it.

They had begun working together on the index when he died. He called me late one evening to ask about the results of some tests concerning my deteriorating eyesight. His death was sudden, due to a heart attack or stroke, and appears to have occurred shortly after we spoke. His last words to me were words of consolation and hope.

Always an optimist brimming with ideas, my brother insisted that we could continue on our own, and plans to get the book published were our top priority in the months that followed. Then John himself, having completed a manuscript of his own in physics, suffered a massive stroke. He survived for three years but was totally incapacitated.

Out of this, for me, devastating situation emerged a thought that has become reality—a foundation to carry on our work, mine and theirs. It is the Ethics of Evidence Foundation, a not-for-profit corporation incorporated in the State of New York. Funded initially by my personal resources, it has been approved by the Internal Revenue Service as a 501(c)(3) tax-exempt corporation, so that others can contribute to support its mission of research and education. Richard Pendergast's work pertains to cosmology: integrating notions from science, philosophy, and theology to yield a coherent view of the universe.

The Pendergast Series

The Church does not have a formal teaching on evolution at this time. But in 1981 Joseph Cardinal Ratzinger preached a series of homilies in the Liebfrauendom, the cathedral of Munich, on the subject "In the Beginning: A Catholic Understanding of the Story of Creation and the Fall," in which the future Pope Benedict XVI offered a symbolic interpretation of the Bible narrative.[11]

Richard Pendergast distinguishes between "ambitious" Darwinism, the theory that random variation and natural selection are sufficient to explain the evolution of the universe, and "modest" Darwinism, which includes the third factor of purpose. Examples of the latter are the cosmic vision of Teilhard de Chardin, with his by now classic essay on the interior life, *The Divine Milieu*,[12] and the intelligent design (ID) movement of recent years.

In his 1996 address to the Pontifical Academy of Sciences, Pope John Paul II stated that "new knowledge has led to the recognition of the theory of evolution as more than a hypothesis. It is indeed remarkable that this theory has been progressively accepted by researchers, following a series of discoveries in various fields of knowledge." But he added that there are in fact several theories, and he rejected those of the first category above, because they "are incompatible with the truth about man. Nor are they able to ground the dignity of the person."[13]

Summing up this book, the first volume of the Series: With the theme expressed in the words of Pope John Paul II on science, philosophy, and theology in common quest for understanding, the author develops what he calls a Christian cosmology—the integration of science and divine revelation that reflects a dynamic worldview. He suggests that the horizon defined by specialization in science tends to limit more general awareness of reality. He observes the professed ambivalence of atheists concerning their personal experience of love. He notes that the reductionist claims of materialists in major areas of science have not been proved. He argues for teleology in quantum mechanics as well as biological evolution. The problems of evil, original sin, and evolution are discussed in the biblical context of cosmic powers, with the current crisis on Earth described as a ferocious guerilla war of these cosmic powers, which we know from revelation heaven has already won.[14] Addressing both believers and nonbelievers, the author offers insight into problems that may disturb the faith of the former or impede the latter's search for God. He presents a living universe, a vision of meaning and hope.

Since the story involves a number of intellectual disciplines, readers are advised to skip over any material they find too technical and to read on to follow the thread of the narrative. There has been some minor editing, and an update on the ID movement has been added at the end of chapter 10. Otherwise, the text and references have been left unchanged.

For those interested in further discussion, the Foundation is releasing, as the second volume, the full text of the original manuscript, seen here as an expanded edition of Volume 1.[15] Its more detailed look at the scientific issues with insights from philosophy and theology illuminates the richness of the conceptual development. The table of contents and a synopsis of this Volume 2 are included at the end of the present Volume 1, and its bibliography has become the reference list of Volume 1.

Three manuscripts representing the author's earlier work are being published as Volumes 3 to 5 of the Series. Volume 3 describes the present crisis and the need for a modern cosmology, introducing new concepts of physics and philosophy.[16] In Volume 4, a philosophical interpretation of quantum theory developed by the author leads to a synthesis of Aristotelian with Whiteheadian concepts in a new cosmology compatible with Christian revelation.[17] Volume 5 seeks to integrate this cosmology into a wider theological synthesis—a Thomistic process theology.[18] Consisting of two parts, the latter is concerned with being and its trinitarian structure, and with the pathology of being, which is evil. The first part takes up the doctrines of the Trinity, Creation, Christology, Redemption, and the Eucharist. The second considers the Christian answer to the problem of evil, including original sin and eschatology.

The work of Richard Pendergast is offered in a Series of five volumes, with its main ideas already published in the peer-reviewed literature. The Series is complemented by Volume 6, a reprint in three languages (English, German, and Spanish) of the author's essay on the Eucharist discussed above.[19]

As the fledgling Foundation grows and matures, plans call for the awarding of research grants to investigators who will carry on its mission. For what we are calling the Pendergast Project, this means continued study of the writings of the Jesuit scholar, with integration of emerging developments in science, for an ongoing synthesis that provides a coherent view of the universe.

It gives me joy to believe that the hope concerning his work, expressed to me by Richard Pendergast over thirty years ago, may in the end be realized.

Valerie Miké
President, The Ethics of Evidence Foundation
March 24, 2020

Acknowledgment. I had the opportunity to review Richard Pendergast's work with Bishop Attila Miklósházy, SJ, professor emeritus of systematic theology at the Toronto School of Theology, and we discussed related theological issues. He read this manuscript, as well as the essay "The Mass on the World," and advised me to proceed with publication of the Pendergast material. Bishop Miklósházy died on December 28, 2018.

References

1. Richard J. Pendergast, *Cosmos* (New York: Fordham University Press, 1973).

2. Zachary Hayes, *What Are They Saying about Creation?* (New York: Paulist Press, 1980), 45–46.

3. Valerie Miké, "The Ethics of Evidence: A Call for Synthesis," in *Encyclopedia of Science, Technology, and Ethics*, ed. Carl Mitcham, 4 vols. (Detroit: Macmillan Reference USA, 2005), 1:lii–lx.

4. Robert Spaemann, *Über Gott und Welt: Eine Autobiographie in Gesprächen* (Stuttgart: Klett-Cotta, 2012), 280.

5. Richard J. Pendergast, "The Mass on the World," *Heythrop Journal* 49.2 (March 2008): 269–82.

6. Richard J. Pendergast, "A Thomistic Process Theory of the Trinity," *Science et Esprit* 42.1 (1990): 35–59.

7. Richard J. Pendergast, "A Process Theory of Creation," *Science et Esprit* 43.2 (1991): 135–60.

8. Richard J. Pendergast, "A Process Christology," *Science et Esprit* 64.1 (1992): 45–66.

9. Richard J. Pendergast, "Evil, Original Sin, and Evolution," *Heythrop Journal* 50.5 (September 2009): 833–45.

10. Richard J. Pendergast, "Quantum Mechanics and Teleology," *Heythrop Journal* 52.2 (March 2011): 271–78.

11. Pope Benedict XVI [Joseph Ratzinger], *In the Beginning: A Catholic Understanding of the Story of Creation and the Fall*, trans. Boniface Ramsey, Ressourcement (Grand Rapids: Eerdmans, 1995). English translation of *Im Anfang schuf Gott: Vier Münchener Fastenpredigten über Schöpfung und Fall*, 3rd ed. (Einsiedeln: Johannes Verlag, 2014).

12. Pierre Teilhard de Chardin, *The Divine Milieu*, Harper Perennial Modern Classics (1960; New York: Harper, 2001).

13. Pope John Paul II, Address to Pontifical Academy of Sciences, October 22, 1996, see http://inters.org/John-Paul-II-Academy-Sciences-October-1996.

14. See ref. 9 above.

15. Richard J. Pendergast, *The Cosmic Hierarchy: The Universe and Its Many Irreducible Levels* (unpublished manuscript, 2007). Volume 2 of Series.

16. Richard J. Pendergast, *A Vision for Our Times: In the Sadness of the Modern World* (unpublished manuscript, 1988). Volume 3 of Series.

17. Richard J. Pendergast, *The Living Universe: An Organic Theory of Mind and Matter* (unpublished manuscript, 1990). Volume 4 of Series.

18. Richard J. Pendergast, *Creation, Evil, and the Trinity: A Christian Process Theology* (unpublished manuscript, 1990). Volume 5 of Series.

19. See ref. 5 above.

A Comment about Language

When these works were written, inclusive language with regard to gender was already a major concern of our culture, and the author attended to it as he thought appropriate. Reading the texts again after all this time, I continue to feel comfortable with his language, and specifically his use of the male personal pronoun with reference to God and to the human person in philosophical discourse. In the latter case, keeping the concept of "man" singular with the proper personal pronoun seems the most direct way to convey the arguments. As for reference to God, readers will know that the author means the ultimate, transcendent reality, for whom use of the male personal pronoun has been the tradition in the English language. I am keenly aware of this linguistic issue, as my native tongue, Hungarian, does not distinguish personal pronouns by gender. Given the clarity and simplicity of presentation, there was no compelling reason to change the author's original style.

Preface

In 1973, I published a book titled *Cosmos*, and during the next thirty years or so I gave a great deal of time to thinking about the problems I discovered then. The present book is the fruit of my reflections. In it I discuss cosmology from a point of view shaped by theology, philosophy, and science, one that is motivated by the desire to integrate these fields as coherently as possible. Our age needs a comprehensive vision to guide it. The core of that vision is the good news proclaimed to us two thousand years ago by Jesus Christ. But we also need to see how that divine revelation is related to the scientific understanding of the world that the human race has gained in the past few hundred years.

Nevertheless, neither it nor any merely human explanation of the world is able to compel the human mind. Certainty comes only through faith, which depends on divine grace. In this book, I do not attempt a full account of divine faith and how it comes to human beings. Merely reading it will not of itself make one a Christian, but I hope that a Christian will be convinced that what I say here seems to be correct, and a non-Christian will at least recognize that it is reasonable.

As discussed further in chapter 1, there are three fundamental kinds of truths. The first kind is supernatural truths that can be known with certainty only by faith. In contrast, the second kind can be known by our own natural powers without supernatural grace. The third kind is mixed truths that, in the abstract, human beings are capable of discovering for themselves but in the present sinful order of the world are not actually able to discern, at least not with clarity and certainty. In his mercy, God has revealed to us some truths of this third kind.[1] Having discovered them with the help of faith, one can understand them rationally and may perhaps find oneself saying, how slow I was not to see it before.[2]

Most of the propositions I present in this essay belong to the second or third kind of knowledge. Nevertheless, I also discuss some of the first kind—that is, truths of faith that could never be known were they not given to us by divine revelation. They are dealt with mainly in the final chapters of the book. I speak of them because I think that, without them, neither this book, nor any book, could present a plausible account of all we know about reality. Though Christian revelation does not compel the intellect alone, it provides us with a way of looking at our experience that makes an act of faith in God and his love for us eminently reasonable. This book is intended to provide both believers and nonbelievers with a coherent view of the universe, one that will help dissolve intellectual problems that disturb the faith of the former and impede the latter's search for God. The class of people who have not yet found God but are consciously or unconsciously seeking him may be larger than one might think. Among them are many scientists and philosophers who expressly reject the concept of a personal God yet are at the same time earnestly seeking the truth. My hope is that the view presented here will both challenge and aid them in their search.

This manuscript is divided into a preface, four parts, and an appendix. Part One has three chapters. Chapter 1 is introductory; it discusses the present scene and words of Pope John Paul II on science, philosophy, and theology, leading up to the need for the development of a Christian cosmology. Chapters 2 and 3 deal with some important issues about the higher levels of what I call the cosmic hierarchy, including the questions of whether artificial intelligence is possible, whether the human mind can simply be reduced to the brain, and the nature of human consciousness.

Part Two includes the next four chapters, which deal with the lower levels of the natural hierarchy that pertain to physics, particularly John Cramer's interpretation of quantum mechanics (QM).

Part Three has three chapters that discuss in general the nature of various theories, mainly about biological evolution. This third part leads to Part Four, which has two chapters. In chapter 11, I point out the difference between a "chronicle," which consists of facts that seem to be correct, and a more ambitious theory that relates not only basic facts but also theorizes about the mechanisms that supposedly account for them. In this chapter, I present my own (Christian) theory of evolution. Finally, in chapter 12 I theorize rather briefly about the future of mankind as I conceive of it.

In my view, evolution is a progressive, step-by-step actualization of the successive levels of "the cosmic hierarchy." Rather than a mindless wandering through the space constituted by the possible configurations of inanimate matter, it is progress in terms of ontological value. Evolution, which the biologist Richard Dawkins (1986) calls *The Blind Watchmaker*, is not blind at all. The nature of the interfaces between different levels of the hierarchy, in this case the ones that biology deals with, is crucial. In particular, the relationship of the level of human intelligence to the sensate and vital levels below it is very important for understanding the moral and religious aspects of our human existence.

Darwin himself was very much influenced by his personal experience of evil in the world and the temptation it presents to Christian faith (Keynes 2001). But, unfortunately, he seems never to have believed, as Christian tradition clearly suggests, that the conflict between good and evil in our world is due to the war between "cosmic powers," that is, the angels and demons of which the Bible speaks.

In the final chapter 12, I speculate briefly on the future of the human race in the light of Christian belief in Jesus Christ and his mission. The divine revelation that St. Paul called the "mystery hidden for ages in God" has now in our age found its proper setting. That setting is our modern scientific discovery of the vast universe around us. This scientific view enables us at least to guess at the vastness of God's plan for the whole of his Creation.

In the appendix, I discuss rather briefly some philosophical concepts that may help clarify the point of view in terms of which my ideas are expressed. To me these ideas are important, and for those who may be interested, I have included them in an appendix.

It is evident that to deal with all the ideas presented in this book requires insights from several intellectual disciplines, especially science, philosophy, and theology. Each discipline has its own proper domain and contributes something to the integrated sum of human knowledge. Moreover, they all have "boundary conditions" by which they are related to one another. None of these disciplines can lord it over the others. They all need to negotiate the boundary conditions between them.[3] This is certainly true of philosophy and theology, but today it is especially true of science. In conjunction with technology, its pragmatic success has led many modern people to overrate its undoubtedly genuine importance. For some it has even become what Paul Tillich called their "ultimate concern," a kind of false god that wants to replace the real one.

Specialists in science, philosophy, or theology can suppose and sometimes have supposed that their favorite way of thinking is the only valid one. Galileo's judges were sure that their theological point of view settled the case. Today some of Galileo's heirs are quite convinced that their scientific point of view is all that is needed to understand the beautiful and vast material universe they study. In my opinion they have no more reason for their confidence than did Galileo's judges. Each intellectual discipline tries from its own perspective to be careful in its reasoning, but they are all fallible products of fallible human beings. Recognition of that fact is grounds for a certain skepticism about science and other intellectual specialties. Above all, none of them can be right when it contradicts divine revelation.[4]

Personally, I have loved science from an early age. I recognize its proper place as one of the major accomplishments of modern Man. Yet I have also come to recognize that it is but one among many valuable intellectual disciplines. Science must learn to adjust its "boundary conditions" with its peers lest it inflate itself beyond its reasonable limits. As Pope John Paul II wrote in 1988:

> Science can purify religion from error and superstition; religion can purify science from idolatry and false absolutes. Each can draw the other into a wider world, a world in which both can flourish. (John Paul II 1988, p. m13)

Acknowledgments

My gratitude is due to many friends who have helped me with this book in different ways over the years. Among them are many of my superiors in the Society of Jesus who gave me time to pursue it. I also wish to thank George Coyne, William Stoeger, and Andrew Whitman of the Vatican Observatory, and the late W. Norris Clarke, who read an earlier version of the entire work and gave me useful suggestions. I thank the staff of the Walsh Library at Fordham University, particularly Jan Kelsey, Gail Hitt, Charlotte Labbe, Christine Campbell, Alicia Casstello, and Helena Cunniffe for the excellent help they gave me so generously. I am grateful to Richard Timone, SJ, who read the entire manuscript very carefully and gave me much moral support. Finally, I am most grateful to my friend Valerie Miké, with whom I discussed many of the problems, especially the role of probability theory in evolution. Furthermore, her brother John has been very helpful especially with regard to information about my computer as well as legal matters.

June 16, 2012

Notes

1. On the use of the third-person masculine singular for God, see "A Comment about Language" on p. xxv above.

2. One is reminded of a similar remark made by Huxley when he first heard of Darwin's theory. (We think it might have been Thomas Huxley.—ed.)

3. In physics, the term "boundary conditions" is used frequently. Often a physical system is subject to a differential equation that contains quantities called boundary conditions. These quantities often determine the development of the system.

4. I am, of course, distinguishing between divine revelation and the human science of theology. For me, divine revelation is a presupposition of theology, and theologians sometimes discover that they have misunderstood the revelation they are trying to explain in our human language.

PART ONE

Some Basic Concepts

1 • The Call for a Christian Cosmology
2 • Theories of Matter: The Cosmic Hierarchy
3 • Various Attempts to Explain Away Human Consciousness

CHAPTER 1

The Call for a Christian Cosmology

> ... for the world, which seems
> To lie before us like a land of dreams,
> So various, so beautiful, so new,
> Hath really neither joy, nor love, nor light,
> Nor certitude, nor peace, nor help for pain.

Matthew Arnold's poem "Dover Beach" expresses a recurring theme of twentieth-century thought and literature: the faith milieu, which once lent enchantment to the world, has departed, and now modern men and women find themselves isolated, alone, and without faith in a hostile and alien world.

Obviously, the poet does not speak for everyone. The majority, among Americans at least, continue to believe in God, and some of them pray seriously and consistently enough to experience hope, love, and joy, and to receive help in times of suffering. But there are also many who do not or cannot believe, and some of them react to their situation with the kind of sadness and pessimism depicted by Arnold. The general milieu tends to erode faith and put a damper on hope and joy. At the beginning of the sixteenth century, our ancestral home, the Earth, was a stable and fixed place at the center of the universe. The crystalline spheres, in which the stars were fixed, revolved around us. Beyond them lay the heavenly realm, which was the home of God. But within two or three centuries Western culture has changed radically, and now humanity finds itself on a small and apparently insignificant planet circling around an ordinary star on the outskirts of an average galaxy in an enormous universe.

Thus, there were many questions that sixteenth-century people could not answer but that we can, at least up to a point. What are the stars and why do they shine? Why is the grass green? Whence come the winds and the tides? What are fire and lightning? Why do people get sick? What is the meaning of the similarities and differences between living beings? What is life? And so on. But there were also many questions that the medievals could answer and that many moderns cannot—ones that are ultimately far more important: Where do I come from and where am I going? What are my nature and destiny? How did the world come into being and why? What may I hope for? What should I do?

One of the important driving forces behind this cultural change was the rise of science and scientific technology. Science has transformed our view of some aspects of reality and given us satisfying answers to many questions. At the same time it has, to some degree at least, resulted in confusion about our nature and destiny, about morality and goals. In conjunction with technology, it threatens our destruction and gives us only limited advice about how to save ourselves. Partly as a result of modern technical productivity there has been a shift in interest from happiness after death to happiness before death, from spiritual goods to material goods, from salvation by God to human progress. As one ponders the contrast between the medieval and the modern world, one wonders who are the wiser and who the happier? Our society as a whole has no definite answer to these questions, partly because the answer depends upon the values we espouse, and as a group we are confused about values.

My own view of what has happened can be expressed in terms of an insight of Michael Polanyi. He points out that "we usually cannot tell how we recognize a face we know" (1967, 4). The particulars of a face are known only tacitly or implicitly in attending to the face as a whole. If one begins to attend explicitly to the shape of the nose, or the position of the eyes, and so on, one loses the vision of the face. Similarly, a golfer who begins focusing on the position of his elbow or the movement of his hips may lose his feel for the golf swing as a whole. Once Western people knew the detailed structure of nature only very imperfectly, but for them its various features coalesced in a comprehensive vision of reality. Today we understand the particular structures of nature much better, but many of us are unable to integrate them into an overall gestalt. Nobel laureate physicist Steven Weinberg expresses this modern predicament when he writes, "the more the universe seems comprehensible, the more it also seems pointless" (1993, 154).

Our philosophical and religious confusion is a serious problem for everyone, even for those who reject any kind of religious faith or metaphysical view of reality as a whole. The Nobel biologist Jacques Monod made no bones about his conviction that the world is governed by chance and necessity rather than divine providence. Nevertheless, he expressed serious concern about the effects of this conviction on society:

> There is no doubt at all, it cannot be doubted that what we might call superstitions or untenable religious myths, or philosophies, have a function. They have a social function, that is to say, establishing a basic system of values upon which society can be organized so that their value in this coherence of societies cannot be doubted. Really the fundamental question is whether we can do without that kind of ideology, and yet have one that will allow society to function; this is uncertain. I think that Karl Popper's great friend, Professor Hegel, said somewhere that religion is the basis of ethics and that ethics is the basis of the state and therefore we must have religion, and here you are! (Monod 1974, 374)

What is to be done? We cannot return to the age of scientific innocence. Rather, like the golfer who once had a natural swing and has now grown inhibited as a result of trying to improve it, we must strive for a higher kind of integration. The achievements of science must be integrated into a comprehensive vision that will give meaning and significance to science as well as to all the other aspects of human life. The Aristotelian-Thomistic cosmology of the medieval period died hard because in spite of its deficiencies it supplied a worldview that united secular experience with the transcendent. It may not be possible to get everything into such a neat package again. Indeed, even if it were possible it might not be desirable, for science and religion are distinct enterprises with their own distinctive principles and procedures. The experience of the past four centuries shows that it is unwise to make these two disciplines too dependent on one another lest they be contaminated by one another's errors. But neither would it be wise to divide them into two distinct universes of discourse. I believe that these distinct entities can be united to form an articulated whole whose parts are in harmony. Perhaps their unity cannot be as stable and permanent as they themselves, but it might perhaps be beautiful and useful for our own times. I feel sure that we can approach this ideal of integration much more closely than we do at present.

John Paul II on Science, Philosophy, and Theology

The term "humanism" is often used to signify an anthropocentric point of view in which mere human beings are at the center. For those who accept that kind of humanism, the rest of the universe, and even God (if God exists), is understood and valued in terms of its importance to mankind. In his book *Crossing the Threshold of Hope* (1994a), Pope John Paul II spoke about human dignity in a different way. For the Pope, humanity as such is not the center. Our great dignity comes from our relationship to God as he reveals himself in the incarnate Logos, Jesus Christ. The Pope was therefore a "humanist," but a Christian humanist centered on Jesus Christ rather than on merely human creatures. For him, the rights and the dignity of mankind come from God in Christ, and he is sure that without our relationship to God we would possess little or no real dignity or rights at all.

John Paul confessed that he never had a special predilection for science but has rather been fascinated by humanity. He recalls that, after the Communists seized power in Poland, one might have expected that the cultural struggle would center around the philosophy of science and of nature in general. But in fact it soon became a struggle over the nature, dignity, and morality of human beings (John Paul II 1994a, 199). Nevertheless, the Pope admired science's magnificent accomplishments and recognized not only its humanistic importance but also its strictly intellectual and technological value. This view was expressed in the message he sent to the study group that assembled at Castel Gandolfo near Rome on September 21–26, 1987, to commemorate the three hundredth anniversary of the publication of Newton's *Philosophiae naturalis principia mathematica* (*The Mathematical Principles of Natural Philosophy*). Near the beginning of that message he stated that the theme of the conference (expressed in the title of its proceedings, *Physics, Philosophy, and Theology: A Common Quest for Understanding*) "is assuredly a crucial one for the contemporary world," and for this reason he wished to address some of the issues involved (John Paul II 1988, 1995, p. m1).

He begins with an overview of the world situation: Our world is fragmented and disjointed, filled with warring factions. Yet at the same time there is a growing awareness of the need for unity and reconciliation. The Church has entered into this movement for unity and is striving to foster it. One aspect of this striving is concerned with the "definite, though still fragile and provisional, movement" toward a better relationship between science and religion (p. m4). "It is crucial that this common search based on critical openness and interchange should not only continue but also grow and deepen in its quality and scope" (pp. m4–m5). The impact that both religion and science have "on the course of civilization and on the world itself, cannot be overestimated, and there is so much that each can offer the other" (p. m5).

From the viewpoint of the Church, "the unity we perceive in creation on the basis of our faith in Jesus Christ as Lord of the universe, and the correlative unity for which we strive in our human communities, seems to be reflected and even reinforced in what contemporary science is revealing to us. . . . Contemporary physics furnishes a striking example" in its quest for a final unifying theory of matter (p. m6). The life sciences exhibit a similar movement with the new understanding achieved by molecular biology of the unity of life on this planet.

The unity the Pope seeks to encourage "is not identity" (p. m8). Religion and science each have their own proper integrity, which would be compromised by any attempt to reduce one to the other. The unprecedented opportunity we have today is for a common interactive relationship in which each discipline retains its integrity and yet is radically open to the discoveries and insights of the other.

> But why is critical openness and mutual interchange a value for both of us? Unity involves the drive of the human mind towards understanding and the desire of the human spirit for love. When human beings seek to understand the multiplicities that surround them, when they seek to make sense of experience, they do so by bringing many factors into a common vision. Understanding is achieved when many data are unified by a common structure. The one illuminates the many; it makes sense of the whole. Simple multiplicity is chaos; an insight, a single model, can give that chaos structure and draw it into intelligibility. We move towards unity as we move towards meaning in our lives. Unity is also the consequence of love. If love is genuine, it moves not towards the assimilation of the other but towards union with the other. Human community begins in desire when that union has not been achieved, and it is completed in joy when those who have been apart are now united. (p. m9)
>
> Theology has been defined as an effort of faith to achieve understanding as *fides quaerens intellectum* [faith seeking understanding]. As such, it must be in vital interchange today with science just as it always has been with philosophy and other forms of learning. Theology will have to call on the findings of science to one degree or another as it pursues its primary concern for the human person, the reaches of freedom, the possibilities of Christian community, the nature of belief and the intelligibility of nature and history. The vitality and significance of theology for humanity will in a profound way be reflected in its ability to incorporate these findings. (p. m10)

This point must be carefully qualified. Theology does not judge, nor is it judged by, the validity of properly scientific findings. But it should take them seriously and see what resources they afford for the performance of its own proper task. "Theologians might well ask, with respect to contemporary science, philosophy and the other areas of human knowing, if they have accomplished this extraordinarily difficult process [of integrating science into their thought] as well as did these medieval masters" (p. m11).

Pursuing such questions "would entail that some theologians, at least, should be sufficiently well-versed in the sciences to make authentic and creative use of the resources that the best-established theories may offer them." Such expertise would prevent both "uncritical and overhasty use" of science "for apologetic purposes," as well as neglect of really relevant ideas. In this process believers who are active scientists (and even in some cases both scientists and theologians) "could serve as a key resource."

> The matter is urgent. Contemporary developments in science challenge theology far more deeply than did the introduction of Aristotle into Western Europe in the thirteenth century. Yet these developments also offer to theology a potentially important resource. Just as Aristotelian philosophy, through the ministry of such great scholars as St Thomas Aquinas, ultimately came to shape some of the most profound expressions of theological doctrine, so can we not hope that the sciences of today, along with all forms of human knowing, may invigorate and inform those parts of the theological enterprise that bear on the relation of nature, humanity and God? (p. m12)

Ten years later, in September 1998, John Paul issued an encyclical entitled *Faith and Reason* (in Latin, *Fides et Ratio* [FR]), which is concerned about matters closely related to those discussed in his message of 1988. *Faith and Reason* begins with a vivid metaphor: "Faith and reason are like two wings on which the human spirit rises to the contemplation of truth; and God has placed in the human heart a desire to know the truth—in a word, to know himself—so that, by knowing and loving God, men and women may also come to the fullness of truth about themselves (cf. Ex. 33:18; Ps 27:8–9; 63:2–3; Jn. 14:8; 1 Jn. 3:2)" (§1).

Faith and Reason relies upon the documents *Dei Filius* of the First Vatican Council and *Dei Verbum* of the Second Vatican Council. Both Councils insisted upon the radical distinction between revealed truth and the truth that the human mind can attain by its own natural efforts. Yet they also insisted that truth is one and that both revealed truth and natural truth cannot contradict one another. Rather, when properly understood, they confirm and harmonize with one another. Thus, as I did in the preface, one can distinguish three kinds of truths: (1) truths whose intrinsic intelligibility surpasses the scope of human reason and can be known only by divine revelation, (2) truths that can be grasped by human reason through its own efforts and so do not need to be divinely revealed in order for us to know them, and (3) truths that ideally could be attained by human reason but that, in the present sinful order of things, cannot actually be known, at least widely, clearly, and with certainty, without the help of revelation.

Human beings can easily deny or misunderstand natural truths—and even more easily divine ones. But it seems that it is in dealing with the third kind of truth that error becomes most acute. There the Church (or, perhaps better, churchmen) has made some bad mistakes and has sometimes been reluctant to admit them—as, for example, in the case of Galileo or with regard to the eternal salvation of Jews, Muslims, and other non-Christians. Whether they are scientists, philosophers, or theologians, all human beings are prone to error in this area. Specialized groups often need one another's help to untie the knots that arise. Speaking to bishops and other Christians, the Pope reminds them that "even in the philosophical thinking of those who helped drive faith and reason further apart there are found at times precious and seminal insights which, if pursued and developed with mind and heart rightly tuned, can lead to the discovery of truth's way" (FR §48).

Christian Cosmology

In medieval times, the vision of reality held by educated people was identified largely with Christian theology and philosophy. Now this vision has expanded greatly. As a result, educated Christians aspire to an understanding that spans not only current Christian theology and philosophy but also modern science, including not only the physical sciences but also psychology, anthropology, sociology, and so forth. What should such a modern vision of the world be called? Let us call it "Christian cosmology." It involves adjusting the "boundary conditions" between the relatively distinct disciplines of theology, philosophy, and science in such a way as to permit them to form a single integrated yet also articulated body of knowledge, a "one" that includes "many." Such a kind of knowledge is speculative and therefore inevitably fragile. It has to pay close attention to seemingly well-established results of Christian theology, philosophy, and science, yet it cannot afford to be controlled by them. For none of the latter are themselves divine revelation but are rather the results of limited human judgments. Christian cosmology knows that there is but one truth, and therefore it also knows that ideal theology, philosophy, and science cannot contradict one another. If they seem to do so, it is because at least one of them is mistaken.

At least occasionally, serious problems have resulted from boundary disputes between Christian theology and science. To some extent such disputes are inevitable, due simply to the fact that human knowledge and human methodologies are limited and imperfect. But sometimes they are the result of intellectual imperialism on the part of either scientists or theologians or both. In the days of Galileo, the theologians had social power, and some of them made bad mistakes by using it wrongly. Today the scientists may have more of it, and some of them are in turn making bad mistakes by using it wrongly. The great theories of modern science (namely, quantum mechanics, relativity, and biological evolution) are to some extent in disagreement with Christian philosophy and theology, as well as with one another. With regard to differences between quantum mechanics and relativity, on the one hand, and Christian theology, on the other, disagreements are not very acrimonious. Indeed, they are sometimes hardly noticeable—partly, I believe, due to the fact that relatively few theologians are very interested in cosmology and most modern theologians are not ready to disagree with science on what seems to be the latter's own home ground. Furthermore, physicists themselves generally admit that there is something wrong with quantum mechanics and/or relativity, and they want to change one or both of them in order to arrive at a more adequate, synthetic theory.

But with regard to the theory of biological evolution, the situation is different. To put it bluntly, I think that some evolutionary biologists are not only attacking religious dogmas precious to billions of human beings but, in doing so, are even misinterpreting science itself. I wish they would desist, or at least that other scientists would call them to task. But I see little likelihood of that happening soon. I will return to this matter below.

The Faith of Scientists

The truth about the objective relationship between science and religion is one thing; the attitude of living scientists toward religion is another. In the September 1999 issue of *Scientific American*, Edward J. Larson and Larry Witham reported the results of a survey that they conducted in 1996 and 1998. They followed in the steps of psychologist James H. Leuba, who in 1914 and again in 1933 asked American biological and physical scientists what their views were regarding "'the two central beliefs of the Christian religion'; a God influenced by worship, and an after life" (Larson and Witham 1999, 89).

Leuba's survey had two parts in both 1914 and 1933. The first part addressed the two questions to a random sample of scientists listed in *American Men and Women of Science*; the second part addressed a group of scientists designated by the same reference work as eminent in their field. As to scientists in general, in 1914 Leuba found that 40 percent said they believed in a personal God, and 50 percent said they believed in personal immortality. But the percentages he obtained from his "greater" scientists were lower; fewer than a third expressed belief in a personal God and a slightly larger percentage in immortality. When he repeated his survey in 1933 Leuba found that scientists in general answered his questions in about the same way. However, his sample of eminent scientists showed higher levels of doubt. More than 80 percent of the eminent scientists said no to both questions.

In 1996 and 1998, Larson and Witham repeated the same questions to scientists of the same two categories. Scientists in general were selected from *American Men and Women of Science*; "eminent scientists" were members of the biological and physical sections of the (American) National Academy of Sciences (NAS). About 40 percent of the general group said yes to both questions. On the whole, the percentages for this group had not changed very much since 1914. However, the percentage of the eminent scientists who said yes was much lower.

> Disbelief among NAS members responding to [the] survey exceeded 90 percent.... NAS biologists are the most skeptical, with 95 percent ... evincing atheism and agnosticism. Mathematicians in the NAS are more accepting: one in every six of them expressing belief in a personal God. (Larson and Witham 1999, 90)

With regard to the past century in the United States, Larson and Witham comment:

> [W]hat stands out is an image of American natural science that has not fundamentally changed since 1914. Measured by religious belief, professional science is like a pyramid, or a three-tiered ziggurat. At the top is acute disbelief. Scientists in the middle are significantly less believing (by more than half) than citizens in general. The wide and heavy base is more firmly sunken into religious America—evidence suggests that there is more personal religion among physicians, engineers and members of other technological occupations that involve applied science. (Larson and Witham 1999, 90)

These conclusions of Larson and Witham regarding the religious faith of American scientists cohere with the common opinion that in the West supernatural faith has been declining among intellectuals ever since the rise of modern science and technology some three hundred years ago. The reasons for this phenomenon are complex. There are many factors, but one of them is the specialization that has become very common in modern culture, especially among scientists. Specialization makes people sensitive to some aspects of reality, but it can also render them oblivious to others.[1] The problem can be expressed in terms of the metaphor of "horizon."

> Literally, a horizon is a maximum field of vision from a determinate standpoint. In a generalized sense, a horizon is specified by two poles, one objective and the other subjective, with each pole conditioning the other. (Lonergan 1968, 211)

Thus the objective pole of a scientific horizon is specified in terms of the facts, data, theories, problems, and so on, of the science in question, and its subjective pole by the skills, inclinations, experience, aspirations, and the like, that are characteristic of the scientists who are in the particular field. One can take it for granted that eminent physical and biological scientists are highly intelligent, and so their personal horizons include more than just science. But I conjecture that, for these scientists as a group, not only their scientific but even their personal, intellectual, and spiritual horizons tend to be specialized. Objectively, they are persons who are sensitive to and pay more attention to certain kinds of things, especially things that are either scientific or can somehow be related to science. They invest their time and energy accordingly. Subjectively, they have corresponding interests, habits, and ingrained opinions. In other words, they have intellectual and spiritual horizons of a certain sort. I suppose that this is quite obvious to most members of groups like the National Academy of Sciences, at least to the extent that they think about it. However, in living their lives, they, like other human beings, find it difficult to make due allowance for their particular prejudices.

There is a great contrast between my own religious horizon and the one suggested by the data collected by Larson and Witham. One early occasion on which this came home to me in a vivid way was a conversation I had when, as a young priest, I joined the faculty of St. Peter's College in Jersey City. On one occasion I began talking to another faculty member who was somewhat younger than I—a chemist or biologist I believe—married, likable, and philosophically inclined. I soon found out that he didn't believe in God, and, since he knew I was a priest, he was somewhat apologetic about that. We talked and at one point I asked him how he related his intellectual viewpoint to his evident love for his wife and family. The main thing I can remember now is that he admitted quite frankly that he had no way of doing so.

Years later I was reminded of that conversation when I read James Gleick's biography, *Genius*, of Richard Feynman. I always admired Feynman, who grew up in the New York area as I did and was not many years older than myself. As Gleick recounts it, soon after getting his Ph.D. at

Princeton Feynman married the sweetheart of his teenage years, Arline Greenbaum. The unusual circumstance of their marriage was that they had discovered a few years earlier that she had tuberculosis but had decided to marry anyway. In a few years more she was dead. More than a year after her death Feynman wrote her a remarkable letter that was found in his papers after his own death. It is worth reading:

> D'Arline,
>
> I adore you, sweetheart.
> I know how much you like to hear that—but I don't only write it because you like it—I write it because it makes me warm all over inside to write it to you.
>
> It is such a terrible long time since I last wrote to you—almost two years but I know you'll excuse me because you understand how I am, stubborn and realistic; & I thought there was no sense to writing.
>
> But now I know my darling wife that it is right to do what I have delayed in doing, and that I have done so much in the past. I want to tell you I love you. I want to love you. I always will love you.
>
> I find it hard to understand in my mind what it means to love you after you are dead—but I still want to comfort and take care of you—and I want you to love me and care for me. I want to have problems to discuss with you—I want to do little projects with you. I never thought until just now that we can do that together. What should we do. We started to learn to make clothes together—or learn Chinese—or getting a movie projector. Can't I do something now. No. I am alone without you and you were the "idea-woman" and general instigator of all our wild adventures.
>
> When you were sick you worried because you could not give me something that you wanted to & thought I needed. You needn't have worried. Just as I told you then there was no real need because I loved you in so many ways so much. And now it is clearly even more true—you can give me nothing now yet I love you so that you stand in my way of loving anyone else—but I want you to stand there. You, dead, are so much better than anyone else alive.
>
> I know you will assure me that I am foolish & that you want me to have full happiness & don't want to be in my way. I'll bet you are

surprised that I don't even have a girl friend (except you, sweetheart) after two years. But you can't help it, darling, nor can I—I don't understand it, for I have met many girls & very nice ones and I don't want to remain alone—but in two or three meetings they all seem ashes. You only are left to me. You are real.

My darling wife, I do adore you.
I love my wife. My wife is dead.

Rich

P.S. Please excuse my not mailing this—but I don't know your new address. (Gleick 1992, 121–22)

A remarkable letter indeed. Feynman was not only very intelligent but also highly sensitive. But he did not know at the time, nor apparently was he ever able to discover, the truth another brilliant thinker, Pascal, had expressed long ago: "The heart has its reasons of which reason knows nothing" (Pascal 1996, 423).

> This, the most famous of Pascal's sayings, is also the one most frequently misunderstood. It is not sentimentalism or irrationalism. Pascal does not oppose the heart to reason and demean reason by exalting the heart. In the contrary, he says the heart has its reasons. The heart does not only feel, it sees. The heart has an eye in it. (Kreeft 1993, 231–32)

The "heart" referred to here is not, of course, the bodily organ, nor is it merely the faculty of affectivity. It is the core of the person in which both intelligence and affectivity are rooted. The quotation above does not attempt to explain the nature of the knowledge of the heart. For now it suffices to affirm its reality. Feynman's heart was trying to tell him something very important, something that he desperately needed to know. It was trying to tell him that the wife he loved was still real and that through love he was in contact with her. Her new address was "with God" but, as Feynman said, he did not know it. Like many scientists, he was locked into a horizon that permitted important scientific truths to manifest themselves to him but which made far more important spiritual ones inaccessible. Let us call the ideology associated with this horizon "scientism." Scientism draws a great deal of its persuasiveness from a collective hubris that inclines its victims to scientific imperialism and to the delusory belief that science is the most important kind of human knowledge.

Another striking demonstration of the power of scientism can be found in Alexis Carrel's memoir *The Voyage to Lourdes*, with its introduction by Stanley Jaki. Carrel (1873–1944) was a French physician and scientist who worked at the Rockefeller Institute in New York and received the Nobel Prize for medicine in 1912. He was baptized as a Catholic but lost his Catholic faith during his medical studies. However, he did not become an outright atheist. Convinced that "it is a huge scientific error to deny facts before examining them," he was intrigued by the reports he had heard about the shrine to the Virgin Mary at Lourdes in France. In 1902, he went there as the attending physician of an official pilgrimage of the sick. His attention was soon drawn to an extremely sick patient, Marie-Louise Bailly, who was on the point of dying from tubercular peritonitis. As it happened, he was with her at Lourdes when she regained perfect health in the course of a few hours. Stunned, he found himself saying the moving prayer to the Virgin with which he concluded his memoir (1994, 94).

However, this striking event was not the end of Carrel's spiritual pilgrimage. As Jaki describes it in his introduction to the book, Carrel found himself in a divided state of mind somewhat like the one Feynman expressed in his letter to his wife. It was to take Carrel some thirty-five or forty years to resolve his confusion. His yearning for the spiritual peace he had once possessed as a boy, and his love for the Virgin, struggled against his Kantian philosophy and his early twentieth-century scientific outlook.

One milestone in his journey was his encounter in 1937 with Dom Alexis Presse, the abbot of a French Trappist monastery. Dom Alexis told him that "love was the only way of really grasping God," an assurance that made a great impression on Carrel (1994, 35). By 1942, he was able to affirm in his diary that he believed "in the existence of God, the immortality of the soul, in Revelation and in all that the Catholic Church teaches, in its admirable doctrine of sacrifice which is its very core" (ibid.). Carrel died in 1944 after receiving the last sacraments of the Church. A few days earlier he had told a visitor, "When one approaches one's own death, one grasps the nothingness of all things. I have gained fame. The world speaks of me and of my works, yet I am a mere child before God, and a poor child at that" (1994, 35–36).

Both Feynman and Carrel struggled with the problem of reconciling the powerful personal experience of love with the powerful personal experience of science. From my point of view, Carrel's life was successful. I do not know about Feynman's. My hope, however, is that his early experience of genuine human love prevented him from ever really separating himself from Love itself. Moreover, Feynman was tremendously impressed by the wonder and mystery of the universe. There is certainly a relationship between the mystery of the world and the mystery of God.

Be that as it may, the struggles of Feynman and Carrel demonstrate how difficult it is to overcome the scientism endemic to our times. One reason for its power is modern specialization. It is difficult for outsiders to understand the highly technical concepts of scientists. It is just as difficult for outsiders to understand the thinking of philosophers or theologians. Highly intelligent and successful people in one or other of those fields often find themselves novices with regard to the others. Because this age is dominated by science and technology, the high priests of science are especially vulnerable to the hubris to which all human beings are prone, and as a result, from my point of view, some become intellectual imperialists. In the days of Galileo, the prestige attached to their specialty led some theologians to commit folly. Today some scientists and philosophers of science are following in their footsteps.

Note

1. There is an amusing parable about "The Blind Men and the Elephant," which is attributed to John Godfrey Saxe (1806–1887). Each of the blind men described the beast in accord with the part of it he happened to feel and then, like true academics, disputed about it at great length.

CHAPTER 2

Theories of Matter: The Cosmic Hierarchy

Atomism was first proposed in the fifth century B.C. by the Greek philosophers Leucippus and Democritus. They held that all material beings are either indestructible elementary entities (atoms, from the Greek *atomos*), or else accidental and mechanical systems constructed out of such atoms. Thus, from its very beginning philosophical atomism was reductionistic. Everything was understood in terms of the atoms and the more complicated entities that are, supposedly, constructed out of them.

But how could this theory account for the seemingly more valuable properties of living things, especially human ones, which can be observed quite readily? Because it seemed impossible for atomism to account for this, it was eclipsed by other philosophies. Aristotle understood the essential nature of material entities in terms of two fundamental metaphysical principles, prime matter (Greek *hylē*) and form (Greek *morphē*). Prime matter was the ultimate principle of potentiality. Of itself it possessed no actual qualities or properties whatever. In contrast, substantial form was the principle of definiteness and actuality. Neither principle could exist of itself. They come into existence together as united co-principles of real substances. This explanation of substance is called *hylomorphism*.

But how did it come about that matter and form are united? They have no reason in themselves to account for this. Aristotle believed that the two must be united by the action of an existing efficient cause. But then a further question arises: Why does the efficient cause act? According to Aristotle, it is always moved to act by a final cause, a goal or telos that attracts the efficient cause to act. Thus, four fundamental kinds of causes—efficient, final, material, and formal—were required in order to explain real material being. For the sake of some final cause, or end, an agent acted efficaciously to unite matter and form and thus bring into being a real effect.

In the medieval era, Aquinas and others accepted the Aristotelian schema, and before the rise of modern science it was, in the West, the more common way of understanding material beings. However, in the medieval world the Aristotelian-Thomistic schema was rivaled by a somewhat different one of Bonaventure and the Augustinian-Franciscan school to which he belonged. Bonaventure and his school were influenced by Augustinian Neoplatonism as well as by Aristotelianism.

The Augustinian-Franciscan and Aristotelian-Thomistic schools agreed that material beings are composed of both prime matter and substantial form. But they disagreed about whether an entity can have more than one substantial form. According to the Thomists, a substantial entity can have only one. That one form defines its essence. A second substantial form would cause it to have two different essences at once, which was, they believed, impossible. However, the Franciscan school thought that substantial forms of differing ontological value are ordered to one another. Prime matter and one or more substantial forms were required in order to produce inanimate entities. An additional, higher, vital form was required to make something alive; another sentient form to make it sentient; and a final, rational form to make it human. Each higher form presupposed and further actualized the lower ones.

The Thomists defended their position against the argument of the Franciscans that higher forms obviously presuppose lower ones by claiming that, even though an existing entity can have only one substantial form, its efficacy is such that it functions like an ordered set of forms. In the case of a human being, his substantial form (i.e., his human soul) functions not only as rational but also as inanimate, animate, and sentient. The "virtual" forms comprised within the one, unique, substantial form were thought to possess the power to do just what an ordered set of subordinate substantial forms did in the Franciscan system.

In the medieval context, it was hard to choose between these two views. Does a human entity possess one substantial form comprising several "virtual" ones, or does it possess one ultimate substantial form and several subordinate but still substantial ones? It seems that the question was never settled definitively.

Modern Holism

Modern science has changed the horizon within which one views the nature of material things. Ancient and medieval thinkers were unable to perceive or to analyze clearly their microscopic parts. As a result, they did not realize fully how much the properties of the whole depend upon them, nor how complicated and complex these parts really are. But with the help of better technology, modern science has succeeded in observing and describing in minute detail many of the properties and operations of the parts. Moreover, it is possible to predict, at least in an approximate way, how the parts contribute to the properties and operations of the higher wholes. It has become clear that the parts possess their own characteristic properties and behavior whether or not they are part of a larger system. Whether an electron is in an atom or in a vacuum, it appears to be substantially the same. Likewise, whether an atom is part of a molecule or in a vacuum, it still appears to be substantially the same thing. Rather than thinking of complex entities as being composed of metaphysical principles, it seems more plausible, as well as more useful, to understand them as systems consisting of smaller subsystems. In the modern period, the systems point of view has proven to be fruitful both scientifically and technologically (Nichols 1996, 303–18; Koestler 1969).

Like the ancient atomists, many modern thinkers believe that all complicated systems are always mere accidental unities. Physicists are still unable to predict precisely the behavior of a system made of a dozen smaller components. But many assume that it is only the complications of the system that are the obstacle to understanding. Indeed, in spite of the fact that there are billions of neurons in the human brain, reductionists still cling to their guns. Many think that the properties of the brain are completely determined by its microscopic components and the way they interact with one another. But, according to the holists, it is not only the components of a system and their interactions that account for the properties of the whole. In addition, there are higher properties of the whole itself that must be considered. The components and their interactions are mere conditions for the coming of a new and higher entity. The brain gives rise to a mind that makes use of the brain as a necessary but insufficient condition. The components of the brain still cannot account for the remarkable properties of the human mind—especially, as we shall see, the property we call consciousness.

The majority of ancient and medieval philosophers were quite right in thinking that atomistic reductionists were overlooking the obvious. Aside from ancient and medieval atomism and hylomorphism, there is still another alternative, namely, *holism*.[1] It seems to holists that the world consists of a vast number of different kinds of entities that exist on different irreducible levels that are hierarchically organized. Lower entities and their interactions still do not account for all the properties of higher-level entities. The higher-level entities transcend those of the lower levels. Lower entities and their interactions are conditions for higher-level ones, but the lower ones do not explain completely the properties of the higher ones. In particular, the ability of a human being to understand and love cannot be understood entirely by the operations of his brain and other bodily organs.

I refer to the set of various irreducible levels in the universe as the "cosmic hierarchy." The medieval scholastics distinguished between inanimate, living, sentient, and rational entities. I believe that besides these four irreducible levels there are at least two others. One is the lowest level, which consists of a multitude of elementary entities, or events, that are as simple as possible and so cannot be divided at all, either spatially or temporally. Another additional level is the highest one, which consists of one unique entity, the Logos. The Logos unifies and unites within himself the rest of the entire universe. Besides these six levels there may be many others.

As we have already seen, each new and higher level adds a new characteristic or emergent property that the lower levels do not possess. The brain of Man is a material condition for the spiritual operations of what we call his soul. The human soul is an emergent element that lower organisms do not possess. In other words, higher entities cannot be explained completely in terms of their parts and the interactions between them. When its parts are assembled in the right way, they allow the emergence of the higher-level entity, whose operations the lower ones condition but do not cause completely. In the beginning, higher entities are mere potentialities inherent in the nature of the universe. They become actual only after the realities of the lower levels become actual.

As one descends the levels of the cosmic hierarchy, the size of each of the entities involved becomes smaller and smaller. At the same time, they also seem to become simpler and simpler. My conjecture, then, is that this simplification continues till one finally arrives at the elementary entities, or events, that are as simple as possible and cannot be divided any further. The only actions of these elementary entities are the connections they make with one another and also with the higher entities on the higher levels of the hierarchy.

How small are these elementary entities? They must be very small indeed. There are hints in modern physics that they are as small as, or even smaller than, objects on the Planck scale![2] In any event, it seems that all complex material entities depend on simple and tiny entities that are ontologically jejune and incapable of love or knowledge.

Before quantum mechanics, many supposed that all physical processes are governed by necessity. Einstein believed this and often remarked that God does not play dice with the universe. But in the light of quantum mechanics it seems that he may do so after all. Many scientists now believe that there is a fundamental, random element in the behavior of nature that makes it impossible to predict exactly how things will turn out.[3] They are convinced that the world is a somewhat wobbly, unreliable machine that is governed by both chance and necessity. Occam's razor seems to support this conclusion. One should not introduce extra unnecessary conceptual factors into one's thinking. But for a Christian holist there are other considerations. He asks, how can an irrational factor be fundamental to the world when its sole Creator is rational? It seems that elementary events must be affected by downward causality from the highest level, that is, from the Logos. For, unlike the other entities in the universe, he is not in the beginning a mere potential but rather the "firstborn of all creation" (Col. 1:15–17).

Mayr versus Weinberg

In his book *Dreams of a Final Theory*, the physicist Steven Weinberg talks about a debate between himself and the evolutionary biologist Ernst Mayr. At one point Mayr wrote that an article by Weinberg was "a horrible example of the way physicists think" and referred to him as "an uncompromising reductionist." Weinberg replied in an article in the journal *Nature*: "I am not an uncompromising reductionist; I am a compromising reductionist" (1992, 53).

What did he mean? I take it he meant that he is a reductionist with respect to the ontology of nature but agrees with Mayr that physics is not superior to biology and will not supplant or assimilate it. Nevertheless, Weinberg insists that, in a certain sense, physics, and especially particle physics, is more "fundamental" than biology, as well as other sciences. If I understand him correctly, he believes that the way things are on the lowest level of nature determines completely what happens on the higher levels (allowing, of course, for quantum uncertainty). I think Weinberg admits that the way things work out on the higher levels is just as interesting as the foundational processes that are the object of physics. Indeed, in many ways they may be more interesting. Nor can physicists explain the characteristics of living entities or predict how they will behave. In order to do so biologists have had to discover new concepts unknown to physics, and doubtless they will continue to do so in the future. I think Weinberg would also agree that the intellectual brilliance exhibited by biologists in their work is just as estimable as that shown by physicists in theirs. I doubt that he would quarrel with Mayr's claim that Darwin was the most influential scientist since Newton (Mayr 2000, 78–83). He probably does not want particle physicists to hog either the money or the prestige that society allots to scientists as a group. Although he is a reductionist with regard to ontology, he may be quite willing to compromise when it comes to the epistemology and methodology, as well as the economics of science.

However, these concessions were not enough for Mayr. Indeed, though Mayr is certainly not a holist, holists too believe that, in a structured system, new properties emerge at higher levels of integration that could not have been predicted even from complete knowledge of the lower-level components. Mayr, as I understand him, wanted physical and chemical processes to give rise to life, but he did not want life itself to be *merely* a physico-chemical process.

But how was he to reconcile these two stipulations? He had trouble doing so because he, like Weinberg, was an atheistic materialist and could not accept the possibility that there is an already existing, creative, spiritual cause, or causes, that can organize the lower entities into something that is essentially higher than themselves. Yet in spite of that he pointed out many specific differences between living and nonliving entities that suggested the two kinds are essentially different (Mayr 1997, 22–23). Such are self-replication, metabolism, growth and differentiation by means of a genetic program, homeostasis, perception of and response to stimuli from the environment, and above all, in the case of higher organisms, consciousness of self.

In the debate between Mayr and Weinberg I certainly prefer Mayr's position. Nevertheless, he was unable to pin down philosophically the essential difference between living and nonliving entities. One reason for this is that he did not believe in essences, and so his explanations were confusing not only to Weinberg and other ontological reductionists but also to theistic-minded historians of scientific ideas like John C. Greene (1999).

St. Augustine tells us in his *Confessions* that for many years he could not understand the concept of a spiritual substance. When I first read this statement many years ago, I wondered how such a remarkably intelligent person was unable to understand what seemed to me such a comparatively easy concept. Now I suspect that perhaps his problem was his lack of another concept that is by no means easy to grasp, namely, the notion of the act of existing, *esse*. A person who does not recognize the act of existing is liable to think that for an essence to be real is for it to be embodied in matter. This is an error, albeit a natural one. However, "real" is not equivalent to "embodied" but rather something more. Certain essences have to be embodied first in matter and then can be actuated by *esse* in order to exist. (See the appendix below.) But there are others that are perfectly self-consistent and intelligible even though they are not material, and so to exist they need only *esse*. The union of a lower form with matter is still on the level of essence, and as such it does not yet exist. A form–matter compound still needs to be actuated by *esse* to become real.

Whatever way it was that the young Augustine reasoned, the way I attributed to him seems to be the way modern materialists do. Without the notion of the act of existing (or the related notion of the divine act of Creation) they cannot easily imagine what people mean when they speak of spiritual substances and spiritual persons. They are, of course, familiar with abstract concepts that are immaterial in a certain sense. Concepts are not spread out in distinct parts and so they are, in a way, immaterial. However, concepts are accidents that exist in intelligent substances, rather than things that exist in themselves. Immaterial substances would be quite different. What would cause them and what would they do? How could they interact with us who are material? Materialists like Richard Dawkins suppose that in human experience one interacts only with other material beings. If a person has never met an immaterial being and does not believe the testimony of people who have, then what evidence in favor of their existence would be acceptable? Materialists think that their own experience qualifies them to judge that of others. For them, the "physical" has to be "material." Since they think human souls, angels, and God himself cannot be physical, they believe that these entities have to be ghosts or fearful illusions.

In contrast, for the Aristotelian-Thomistic tradition "physical" is a broader term than "material." To be material means, among other things, to be spread out in distinct parts. There is nothing contradictory in the concept of a substance that exists but is not composed of distinct material parts. To be embodied, one needs to be material. To be real, one needs only *to be*. The expectations of many scientists, including both Weinberg and Mayr, rest upon presuppositions that are by no means evidently true. They confuse embodiment with being. They hope that the kind of scientific methods scientists employ so well with regard to material beings provide the best means for attaining deeper truths. A workman likes his own tools and admires the sort of things he can make with them. That is all right as far as it goes, but unfortunately many not only love science but also exaggerate its importance. The intellectual imperialism that Mayr rightly recognized in some physicists also affects many biologists—including Mayr himself!

THE EMERGENCE OF CONSCIOUSNESS

Reductionists encounter severe problems when they try, either experimentally or intellectually, to synthesize living beings out of inanimate components, or to analyze living beings completely in terms of their inanimate parts. Mayr escapes those problems. He does not reject analysis. But he also insists on the importance of the organism as a whole. Some of the higher properties of living organisms evaporate when the properties are subjected to analysis. This does not prove that higher properties were not there before the analysis but rather that they were there in partial dependence upon conditions that are destroyed by analysis.

Many of the biological capacities that Mayr lists above can be described and understood only in terms of concepts that physics and chemistry know nothing about. But of course some people will ask, Is it possible that in the future physicists and biologists will find a way to bridge the gap between their sciences? After all, even though for a long time no one was able to explain the amazing properties of superfluids and superconductors in terms of quantum mechanical principles, now it has been done. Some hope that eventually the even wider gap between biological phenomena and physical principles will be bridged. But Mayr for one did not think this is possible. He was convinced that the "characteristics of living organisms distinguish them *categorically* [my emphasis] from inanimate systems" (Mayr 1997, 23).

The emergence of higher properties manifests itself most clearly in the phenomenon of human consciousness. Human acts of knowledge and of appetency are both *conscious* and *intentional*.[4] They have both an initial and a final term, the initial term being the subject, the final term the object. In knowing the world objectively, or thematically, the person also is aware of himself subjectively, or unthematically, as the one who is performing the act. This tacit, peripheral, implicit knowledge of oneself as subject and agent is a necessary condition of one's express, focal, explicit knowledge of the world. Conscious knowledge necessarily includes subjective awareness of oneself as the subject to whom and within whom the world is manifesting itself objectively. The subject from whom and within whom acts of knowledge and appetency emanate is aware of himself as *one*. His awareness of his own unity as the one who knows and responds affectively to the world is the primitive experience by which he understands the meaning of the ontological unity and irreducibility of higher entities.

The person is not only subjectively aware of himself but he also knows himself objectively as part of the world. He creates an objective image of himself as he creates an objective image of the world that includes himself. But objective knowledge of oneself emanates from the intelligent subject who already possesses in a tacit and subjective way what he expresses objectively. Subjective and immediate awareness of oneself makes possible an objective image of oneself. Subjective awareness of self as one agent makes it clear that reductionism is an inadequate philosophy. Reductionists have an insoluble "binding problem" in explaining how a person who possesses many disparate faculties can possibly feel himself to be one existing agent. The act of existing is the act of one existent, not a cooperative venture of many. Every time a person says "I," he falsifies reductionism.

However, reductionists avoid reflecting upon human consciousness or else try to handle it in inadequate and unconvincing ways. One such way is to regard it as a "problem" or a mystery—as indeed it is—but to overlook the fact that, even though no one understands it fully, it is nevertheless evidence that falsifies reductionism. Another is to create a reductionistic theory of consciousness that fits their presuppositions, one that invariably turns out to be inadequate. In either case they distract themselves and others by pointing out and exaggerating the problems of holism. But it must be admitted that holism does not explain consciousness completely.

Beings within Beings

I regard reductionism, hylomorphism, and holism as the three principal ways of understanding the ultimate structure of the world. Of the three, reductionism seems to me the worst. In ancient and medieval times hylomorphism was a plausible theory, but in modern times our scientific knowledge of matter makes it difficult to accept. I believe that modern holism is considerably more plausible than either of its rivals. Pondering this problem, one might perhaps be inclined at first to think that none of the three major rivals is adequate, and that no one has yet found a good way of explaining the structure of material being. However, further consideration leads me to the conclusion that holism is the correct solution.

Let us begin by considering Michael Polanyi's explanation of the different levels in human language production. The human performance of verbal communication

> includes five levels; namely the production (1) of voice, (2) of words, (3) of sentences, (4) of style, and (5) of literary composition. Each of these levels is subject to its own laws, as prescribed (1) by phonetics, (2) by lexicography, (3) by grammar, (4) by stylistics, and (5) by literary criticism. These levels form a hierarchy of comprehensive entities, for the principles of each level operate under the control of the next level. The voice you produce is shaped into words by a vocabulary; a given vocabulary is shaped into sentences in accordance with grammar; and the sentences can be made to fit into a style, which in its turn is made to convey the ideas of a literary composition. Thus each level is subject

to dual control; first, by the laws that apply to its elements in themselves and, second, by the laws that control the comprehensive entity formed by them. (Polanyi 1967, 35–36)

Much of what Polanyi says about the activity of speech production can be said analogously about the act of existing. The lower-level elements of language have a certain autonomous character of their own even though they function differently depending on the higher-level contexts in which they are found. Analogously, the act of existing of entities on a given level of nature is substantially the same whether they exist independently or are included in a more comprehensive entity. From the viewpoint of the lower entity, its existence within a higher entity is accidental. But from the viewpoint of the higher level, the accidents that adapt the lower entities to existence within higher ones are of great importance, for they allow the lower-level entities to contribute to the more valuable existence of the higher one. As in Polanyi's analogy with speech production, entities lower in the cosmic hierarchy are, in spite of their partial autonomy, incorporated into the existence of higher entities.

Of course Polanyi's analogy illustrates and suggests, but it does not prove. One can think of the cosmic hierarchy in the light of an analysis of speech production, but one must judge on the basis of evidence whether or not the same pattern really applies to both. However, reductionists tend to restrict their search for evidence to the lower-level entities that are the objects of physics, chemistry, and the chemical aspects of biology. They think that the methods of those sciences give us the paradigm for valid thought. Hence they often neglect subjective experience—even their own—and do not admit that careful reflection about human relationships and about faith, hope, love, joy, beauty, morality, and so forth enable us to find objective truth about reality. The most valuable and important truths have to do with human beings rather than electrons. Truths about human consciousness and human conscious activity are more important and more evident than the truth about the operations of electrons.

Part of my explanation involves the nature of accidents. If a substance on a given ontological level is part of a substance on a higher level, the two substances must somehow be adapted to one another. In order for that to happen, the lower-level substance must have accidents that adapt it to the higher-level one. Thus, for the human body, and especially the human brain, to be adapted to the needs of the human person, there must be not only accidents that perfect the animal body and brain as such, but also accidents that adapt them to the higher needs of the rational person that includes and integrates them. One can say that the first kind of accidents is natural, whereas the second is "more-than-natural" with respect to the lower nature in which it inheres.

The relationship of higher realities to lower ones can be expressed in terms of the originally Hegelian word "sublation."

> What sublates goes beyond what is sublated, introduces something new and distinct, puts everything on a new basis, yet so far from interfering with the sublated or destroying it, on the contrary needs it, includes it, preserves all its proper features and properties, and carries them forward to a fuller realization within a richer context.[5]

Sublation integrates lower-level entities into a single higher entity. This process can be repeated time and time again. Elementary events are sublated into elementary particles like quarks and electrons, the particles into atoms, atoms into molecules, and so on. Even though we cannot be sure about how many levels there are, I believe that there are at least six or more, and hence there are at least five or more steps or interfaces between the various levels.[6] These interfaces can be considered synchronically, in terms of their spatial organization, or diachronically, in terms of their temporal evolution. Both their structural, synchronic aspect and their evolutionary, diachronic aspect must be considered for full understanding. To understand the diachronic aspects it will be necessary to discuss the nature of time, as I will in Part Two, and in the process of evolution as I will in Part Three. For now it will be sufficient to say that at each evolutionary step a higher unity sublates previously existing lower-level entities into a higher kind of being.

Amalgamating several of the steps in the evolutionary process into one, we can say that a human person and the subordinate entities that make it up exist in different ways. Of itself a neuron of the brain cannot know or love on the human level. But when lower entities become part of a human person they become capable of participating in such higher activities. For that to happen they have to be adapted by intrinsic accidents that transcend their own basic natures.

For Christians, a good example of sublation is the transformation of a human person that results when he acquires personal relationships with Jesus Christ and his Holy Spirit. This transformation involves the "supernatural" accident called "sanctifying grace," which Christian theologians have discussed for many centuries. Sanctifying grace adapts human nature to divine realities that transcend not only the human level of the cosmic hierarchy but the created world entirely. Therefore the phrase "more-than-natural" can apply to accidents that adapt a substance to a higher level within the natural hierarchy, or to ones that adapt a substance to a reality that completely transcends the material universe. Let us say, then, that sometimes such accidents are "relatively supernatural," and sometimes they are "absolutely supernatural."

In Karl Rahner's theology, created grace is a reflection or echo within a believer's humanity of the uncreated gift of the Holy Spirit who has been given to him by the Father and the Son.[7] The believer's personal relationship with the Spirit modifies his ontological reality, not in an "essential" way but in an "accidental" way. In receiving the Spirit, he remains himself and has the same human nature as before. Nevertheless, he is also changed in a radical way. He has been "divinized" and become a son or daughter of God, and a member of the body of Christ. The reflection within his humanity of the supernatural relationships he has with Jesus and the Spirit is the absolutely supernatural accident called created grace. The person who possesses it has a kind of "second nature" which is more valuable than his or her first nature, even though the first nature continues to be a necessary prerequisite for having the second. As Christians believe, the Holy Spirit inspired St. Paul when he compared the believer's relationship to Christ to the relationship of the members of the human body to the human person who possesses them.[8] The knowledge conveyed by his inspired words is far from being the full understanding we desire; nevertheless it gives us some genuine understanding. Our experience of having a body with many parts gives us some idea of the relationship between Christ and the Church.

Relatively supernatural accidents are analogous to the absolutely supernatural grace that elevates a human person, especially his soul, to participation in the higher existence of Christ. It is not, of course, their sublating accidents alone that enable the neurons of the brain and nervous system to operate in a way higher than the activities proper to one-celled entities. Just as supernatural grace is the consequence of the action of the Holy Spirit himself, so the relatively supernatural accidents of human neurons are due to the influence of the human person. That influence is downward rather than upward. Neurons contribute to and make possible the relatively supernatural action of the human person. Using Aristotelian concepts, one can say that the soul is formal with respect to the brain, while the brain and its operations are material with respect to the soul.

It is evident from what I have said that the term "accidental" covers an enormous range of meanings. From the viewpoint of human nature, our membership in the higher unity of the whole body of Christ is "merely" accidental. Yet from the viewpoint of the higher level on which the whole Christ exists, the supernatural life that its members share is their true life, the life for which they were created and in terms of which they have eternal significance. The relationship of a human member of the body of Christ to Christ himself is not merely emotional, conceptual, or psychological. It is "super-substantial" and "super-physical." The Christian has his own existence and freedom, yet he is also governed by Christ. This seems to be like what Polanyi has called "marginal" control (Polanyi 1967, chap. 2).

The believer's awareness of this state of being is usually tacit and subjective rather than objective. If asked why he believes so firmly in the love and action of God in his life, he often says that he believes it by faith and may be unable to say anything more definite. Nevertheless, when a person is "converted" he often says that his world has changed, or that he has been "born again." Everything remains the same, and yet it is also somehow different and is experienced as such. The basic reason for this difference is his new existence as a member of Christ. As such, he has a different horizon within which all his experience transpires. At times the Holy Spirit may stir up his faith in such a manner that he becomes conscious of his membership in Christ more intensely than usual. This occurs not only to canonized saints but also to many ordinary people. For besides the vivid and powerful mysticism of the saints, there is also the "everyday mysticism" of ordinary fervent Christians. This experience is much more common than most reductionists and even some Christians suppose. It makes clear to those who have it that, besides the level on which human beings exist by nature, there is also a supernatural level. In his letter to the Galatians, Paul tells us that "it is no longer I who live, but it is Christ who lives in me" (Gal. 2:20). Many ordinary but fervent Christians can recognize their own experience as a faint echo of the more intense experience of specially chosen people like Paul, Augustine, Teresa of Avila, and other saints.[9]

Conclusion

Perhaps the theological analogy I have just discussed may not persuade non-Christians. However, one does not have to be a believing Christian to accept the reality of the hierarchic relationship between a person and his brain. Both higher entities like human beings and lower ones like neurons and neural networks are real existents. The latter are necessary for the normal life and activity of the former, yet at the same time the experience of human consciousness and freedom shows that the person governs and makes use of the neurons and other components of the brain. The overall relationship is sometimes referred to as the mind–brain or soul–body relationship. In Aristotelian terms, the mind or soul is formal with respect to the brain or body, which is material with respect to the soul. My thesis is that the entire cosmic hierarchy is governed by that kind of relationship. There are at least six or more irreducible levels in the hierarchy and five or more interfaces between adjacent levels. We have direct experience of the interface of the rational level with the sentient level, and through it with the levels below. I understand the other interfaces by analogy with the rational/sentient interface, and in a different way with the cosmic/rational interface. At each interface a higher entity sublates one or more lower ones.

I generalize the concepts of soul and body and say that at each interface a soul sublates a body, which exists on the ontological level immediately below that of the soul. The various instances of that relationship are different from one another, but nevertheless they are also analogously similar. These analogies are needed for us to understand that the universe is one and its overall structure is intelligible and consistent. Reductionists are partially blind to important values like unity, goodness, truth, and beauty. They neglect the kind of evidence that led most ancient and medieval philosophers to reject atomism, especially evidence about living beings, and particularly about human beings.

Notes

1. As I explain below, holism is similar in one way to the thought of the medieval Franciscan school. But it is different inasmuch as it claims that the entities of each level are real beings, not substantial forms.

2. The Planck scale is on the order of 10^{-35} m. See Penrose 1989, 348.

3. In the past few decades physicists have also realized that, even aside from quantum mechanics, the temporal behavior of most natural systems is so responsive to extremely small variations in their initial conditions as to result in radically different consequences. As someone has said, today the fluttering of a butterfly's wings somewhere in the tropics can produce a tornado next week up here in the United States. The study of such phenomena is often referred to as chaos theory. However, to the extent that chaotic phenomena are classical, they are determinate, even though we are unable to predict their behavior.

4. For the meaning of "intentional" in this context, see the appendix below.

5. Lonergan, *Method in Theology*, 241. As Lonergan points out, he and Rahner understand sublation in a different manner than Hegel did.

6. Do the angels constitute another ontological level higher than that of Man? In some way they do. And yet Jesus and his mother are greater than they. Most human beings may not be equal to angels in every respect, but

nevertheless human souls have a dignity and independence that make them equal to the angels rather than being subordinate to them.

7. For a convenient summary of Rahner's views on grace, see Dych, *Karl Rahner*, chap. 3; also McCool, *A Rahner Reader*, chap. 9 and the bibliography, pp. 367–68.

8. In two classic books, *The Whole Christ* (1938) and *The Theology of the Mystical Body* (1951), Emile Mersch has discussed the theology of the Pauline doctrine.

9. Christian faith is a gift of God that is offered to at least some individuals in this life. If they choose to accept it, their testimony will enable others to receive the same gift. I also am inclined to think that before or at the time of their death everyone will have an opportunity to accept or reject faith in Christ and thus to determine their eternal destiny. For a good theological explanation of Catholic doctrine about faith, see Dulles, *The Assurance of Things Hoped For*.

CHAPTER 3

Various Attempts to Explain Away Human Consciousness

Artificial Intelligence

In the previous chapter I discussed the cosmic hierarchy and argued that the properties of higher levels cannot be reduced to those of lower ones. This thesis applies especially to human beings as well as to lower entities. In this chapter I discuss two important problems. The first is the relationship between human intelligence and the so-called artificial intelligence (AI) of computers; the second is human consciousness, especially in relation to the human brain and nervous system that support it. In other words, the former expresses belief that computers are useful tools that can help humans in activities of various sorts, especially intellectual ones. Other people also believe that computers will help us understand the true nature of human minds, and even the nature of intelligence in general (*Routledge* 1988, Artificial Intelligence). There can be no objection to the first aim, namely, to build useful tools that help human beings accomplish various tasks. This effort has already attained many useful results. But the value of the second aim is at best ambiguous. From my point of view the obvious objection is that human beings are substantial unities, beings that perform individual acts of existing, whereas machines are not. Machines lack the kind of ontological unity that human persons possess, and which is necessary in order to perform intellectual acts. They are mere accidental systems made of inanimate entities that produce some effects that resemble some of the effects human beings produce. A human being can pull a sled; a team of dogs can pull a sled; a tractor can pull a sled. They all produce the same result in essentially different ways. Likewise, a human being can play chess and a computer can play chess, but they do it quite differently. A human being does it intelligently, but the computer does it unconsciously under the control of a program that was designed by a human being.

A few years ago a powerful computer programmed in a sophisticated way (the combination was named Deep Blue) outplayed the world chess champion Garry Kasparov. Deep Blue is intelligent in the sense that it reflects in an accidental way the intelligence of the human beings who created it. But neither the program, nor the computer it controls, nor the two of them together are conscious or possess substantial unity. They are only accidentally one rather than being an intelligent substantial unity that performs its own act of existing. For many years some scientists believed that the question about how well computers can play chess is closely related to the question of whether they are intelligent in the proper sense of the word. In relation to that belief it is interesting to read the following remarks coming from IBM, the corporation that created Deep Blue.

> Does Deep Blue use artificial intelligence? The short answer is No. Earlier computer designs that tried to mimic human thinking haven't been very good at it. No formula exists for intuition. So Deep Blue's designers have gone "back to the future." Deep Blue relies more on computational power and a simpler search and evaluation function. The long answer is No. "Artificial Intelligence" is more successful in science fiction than it is here on earth, and you don't have to be Isaac Asimov to know why it's hard to design a machine to mimic a process we don't understand very well to begin with. How we think is a question without an answer. Deep Blue could never be a Hal-2000 (the prescient, renegade computer in Stanley Kubrick's *2001*) if it tried. Nor would it occur to Deep Blue to "try." Its strengths are the strengths of a machine. It has more chess information to work with than any other computer, and all but a few chess masters. It never forgets or gets distracted. And it's orders of magnitude better at processing the informa-

tion at hand than anything yet devised for the purpose. "There is no psychology at work" in Deep Blue, says IBM research scientist Murray Campbell. Nor does Deep Blue "learn" its opponent as it plays. Instead, it operates much like a turbo-charged "expert system," drawing on vast resources of stored information (for example a database of opening games played by grandmasters over the last 100 years) and then calculating the most appropriate response to an opponent's move. Deep Blue is stunningly effective at solving chess problems, but it is less "intelligent" than the stupidest person. It doesn't think, it reacts. And that's where Garry Kasparov sees his advantage. Deep Blue applies brute force aplenty, but the "intelligence" is the old-fashioned kind. Think about the 100 years of grandmaster games. Kasparov isn't playing a computer, he's playing the ghosts of grandmasters past. That Deep Blue can organize such a storehouse of knowledge—and apply it on the fly to the ever-changing complexities on the chessboard—is what makes this particular heap of silicon an arrow pointing to the future. (Floridi 1999, 153–54)

This quotation reflects the informed opinion of many computer scientists that, after forty or fifty years of work and the expenditure of great amounts of money, the research program that tried to create genuine human-type intelligence has failed (Dreyfus 1992; Floridi 1999, 4). This failure should have been anticipated from the beginning, for the obvious reason that machines do not possess substantial unity and substantial unity is one of the essential presuppositions for genuine intelligence.

Consider a very simple machine, namely, a lever such as one might use to move a boulder. A lever consists of a rod and a rock. The rock is placed near the boulder and the rod is laid on top of the rock with one end under the boulder. Then one pushes on the other end of the rod and the boulder moves. The lever is not a substance but only an accidental system consisting of a rod and a rock. One builds computers in essentially the same way. One takes semiconductors and other inanimate objects, fits them together in accord with some intelligent design, and then uses the resulting accidental system to do things one could not do without it. The people who design and make the system are intelligent, whereas the computer is not even stupid. It doesn't think at all. Rather, it is forced to perform a nonintellectual operation in conformity with a human concept.

Some may object to my comparison between a lever and a computer. Obviously the latter is a far more complex tool than the former, and designing it is a far more clever feat than using a bar to move a boulder. Nevertheless, both complex tools and simple tools are merely tools. Relating two inanimate things by means of interactions proper to their individual natures does not change the essential nature of either one, nor does the system made of the two transcend the ontological level of its components. The same is true of a system comprising any number of inanimate things. It is true that with a lever one can do something one cannot do with either a bar or a rock by itself. And certainly one can do more with a computer than one can do with one transistor. But what is possible to computers is already immanent in the nature of its components. Likewise, an organization like IBM or a nation like the United States can do more than any of the individual human beings belonging to them. But rather than having a superhuman nature, complex human groups can only actualize possibilities already immanent in human nature. Complex accidental systems remain on the same ontological level as their parts. The system comprises many individuals, each of which realizes its nature in a particular way. But the nature and action of each individual specimen remain within the bounds set by its nature. Together they may realize rather fully the possibilities of the natures of the individuals, but they do not pass beyond the bounds of the conjunction of entities of the species to which they belong. The human race realizes the possibilities of human nature more fully than any one human being does. Nevertheless, their joint action remains merely human. Similarly, the set of entities that make up a computer realizes more fully the possibilities of the various kinds of things in the computer. But all the components are inanimate. Their joint action remains just as essentially mindless as the computer's components.

It is true, of course, that the joint action of the components of a computer is intelligent in an accidental way. This is to say that, like any artifact, the computer and its action reflect intelligent design. The scheme in the mind of an intelligent designer is imposed upon the components of the computer, just as the thought of an intelligent writer is imposed upon the letters of the alphabet he uses. But the letters do not think. Programmers can instruct a computer to search through its so-called memory bank to see if it contains a given sequence of symbols, and then to do one thing if it does contain it and another if it does not. But such mechanical procedures are nothing like intelligent human action. The ultimate reason why computers and computer programs cannot perform intelligent acts is that there is no person there to do it. They are only accidental systems, not existing, substantial, intelligent beings.

One no longer hears very often the sort of enthusiastic, naïve predictions that were often made forty or fifty years ago to the effect that computers would soon outstrip human beings in a wide range of intellectual tasks.[1] Painful experience has humbled those in AI, and so they now speak in a much more measured way. Nevertheless, some of them still miss the philosophical point I made above, that computers are not substantial entities but merely accidental ones. Hence they continue to hope that, if one makes a computer system complex enough, at some point it will become intelligent in the proper sense of the term.

Why do they persist in this belief? Perhaps they are persuaded that nature builds human beings by simply fitting atoms and molecules into the proper complex pattern. If nature can do it, then why can't we? Reductionists labor under the false assumption that human beings are only complex structures made of elementary particles. In other words, they believe that by adding enough intellectual zeros one eventually gets a positive number.

Recall that, for Aristotle and the scholastics, material substances are composed of prime matter and substantial form. The form of a living being was often called its "soul" and its organized matter its "body." The soul was "embodied" in matter and matter was "informed" by the soul. Although, as I believe, Aristotelian hylomorphism is inadequate as an account of the nature of material entities, the terms "form" and "matter," "body" and "soul" are still useful. I claim that on any level of the cosmic hierarchy, except the lowest and the highest, a substantial holon (or integron) is the soul of a body consisting of a set of lower-level holons. The dominant holon, or soul, sublates and organizes the body.

The Limits of Neuroscience

Neuroscientists are well aware of how much more there is to learn about the human brain, as well as some related aspects of the human mind. Nevertheless, it appears that some of them are falling into the same kind of trap that caught early workers in AI. Hubert Dreyfus once compared the latter to a man who climbs a tree and then announces to the world that he has taken the first step in going to the moon. It seems that now some neuroscientists are repeating the same error.

A human being is a close union of soul and body, and so he can do things that are proper to his brain alone, things that are proper to both his brain and his mind, and things that are proper to his mind alone. The soul possesses emergent properties that are unknown on the lower levels. These emergent properties can be understood only by reflecting upon the nature of the soul itself. If one ignores the emergent properties of the soul, one can easily suppose that an entity comprising soul and body is merely an accidental system on the level of the body. This enables one to misinterpret the nature of the emergent properties of the soul and suppose that one's false concept of them represents their true nature. Reductionists misinterpret the nature of genuine intelligence, conceptualize its operation as a mechanistic process, and suppose that the way they think the intellectual faculty works is the way it really works. They draw a false analogy and identify the clickety-click-click of a machine with intelligent thinking. A human body, and especially a human brain, bears the impression of the human soul that informs it. Up to a point the impression is like the higher entity that causes it. Michelangelo (who, of course, knew better) is said to have exclaimed to the statue of Moses he had made, "Speak, Moses!" However, a statue of Moses is not Moses.

The all-too-common kind of mistake I have been describing is illustrated by the theory of consciousness proposed in 1999 by a well-known neuroscientist, Antonio Damasio, in his book *The Feeling of What Happens* (1999a).[2] There he outlined the "problem of consciousness" as he understood it and went on to propose a theory about its nature. His theory is rooted in his experience as a neuroscientist and physician, but it is an extrapolation that reaches beyond science into the domain of philosophy. As a layman with regard to neuroscience, I found the scientific aspects of the book interesting. Furthermore, it is beautifully written, and its author comes across as an intelligent and cultured man. But he is also a materialist, and his inadequate philosophical-theological perspective limits severely his ability to deal with human consciousness.

In Damasio's theory, the structure of consciousness has three levels: (1) a state of *emotion*, (2) a state of *feeling*, and (3) a state of *conscious feeling*.[3] Of themselves Damasio's emotions are neither mental nor conscious. They arise when some object or event, external or internal, affects the organism. The immediate response to the original object is a neural pattern in various specific regions of the brain. For example, if one unexpectedly encounters "Aunt Maggie," whom one loves and whom one has not seen for some time, the external senses produce neural patterns of her in sensory centers of the brain (1999a, 68–69). Having been thus activated, and even before one has recognized Aunt Maggie, these sensory centers have already dispatched signals all over the brain and produced additional neural patterns. They in turn trigger still other essentially similar patterns in centers that are interested in Aunt Maggie. The resultant excitation constitutes a complex emotion that is not yet mental or conscious. It is not yet an image in one's mind but is merely an objective, neural pattern in one's brain. Damasio's emotions are propensities to internal and/or external actions that, under certain conditions, immediately take place. However, in many circumstances action is inhibited until further processing occurs.

Damasio's emotions do not feel themselves. It is only in the second stage of processing that they are "felt" and become mental images. But in Damasio's terminology, his "feeling" is not of itself conscious in spite of the fact that, unlike the emotions it feels, it is an image in the mind. He tells us that an organism may represent in neural and mental patterns the state that we conscious creatures call a feeling, without ever knowing that the feeling is taking place.... For example, we often realize quite suddenly, in a given situation, that we feel anxious or uncomfortable, pleased or relaxed, and it is apparent that the particular state of feeling we know then has not begun on the moment of knowing but rather sometime before. Neither the feeling state nor the emotion that led to it have been "in consciousness," and yet they have been unfolding as biological processes. (1999a, 36)

It seems that Damasio has recognized the difference in a human being between what I have called his vital, sensate, and spiritual components. He has also distinguished the problem of how to explain the relationship between the vital and the sensate components from the even more difficult problem of how to explain the relationship between the sensate and the rational components. His focus is on the latter problem, perhaps because he feels that the first one will soon be handled by current scientific methods. He thinks that the movie-in-the-brain, which neuroscience is now investigating, will soon be seen to be also a movie-in-the-mind. He admits that at present there is a certain explanatory gap between the two movies, but he expects it to disappear under the persistent scrutiny of science.

Damasio recognizes the difference between the kind of patterns that come into the brain and the mental patterns that appear in the sensate mind of an animal. One of the differences between the two has to do with the "qualia," the qualitative colors, sounds, tactile impressions, and so on, that make up the mental images that animals, including ourselves, experience. The movie-in-the-mind is expressed in terms of qualitatively different colors, sounds, and so on, whereas the movie-in-the-brain is in terms of physical things like electromagnetic and acoustic frequencies. How does one get from one to the other? We do it all the time but we don't know how. Clearly, there is a great difference between merely neural patterns and mental images on the sensate level. The input to the senses is neural patterns—let us say electromagnetic waves of a certain frequency. Its output is mental images, say green and blue patches. Many philosophers are quite convinced that the nature of the senses that transform neural patterns into mental images is a serious problem. Why Damasio thinks it will soon be understood is quite puzzling. He ought to solve this problem first and then go on to the more difficult problem of moving the sensate images to the level of rationality. However, he does not, and instead goes immediately to the harder problem.

His explanation of how feeling becomes conscious is summed up in the following passage:

> [T]he brain uses structures designed to map both the organism and external objects to create a fresh, second-order representation. This representation indicates that the organism, as mapped in the brain, is involved in interacting with an object, also mapped in the brain. . . .
>
> Such newly minted knowledge adds important information to the evolving mental process. Specifically, it presents within the mental process the information that the organism is the owner of the mental process. It volunteers an answer to a question never posed: To whom is this happening? The sense of a self in the act of knowing is thus created, and that forms the basis for the first-person perspective that characterizes the conscious mind. . . . [Thus] the sense of self in the act of knowing emerges within the movie. Self-awareness is actually part of the movie and thus creates, within the same frame, the "seen" and the "seer," the "thought" and the "thinker." There is no separate spectator for the movie-in-the-brain. (Damasio 1999b, 117; see also 1999a, 189–92)

In this explanation Damasio simply tells us that somehow or other the movie-in-the-brain turns into the movie-in-the-mind and that somehow or other the sense of self emerges within the movie. He starts with many neural patterns located in many different parts of the brain and explains how they get unified successively in a sequence of more and more inclusive neural patterns. Finally, the process concludes in a single neural pattern. All this reminds me of how many distinct electronic patterns are united in a single visible-audible pattern by a TV set. Such a process is easy for electronic engineers to understand. But of course engineers seldom believe that TV monitors become conscious. The TV viewer supplies the consciousness. In the case of a human being, how does consciousness get into the picture? Damasio says it does but never really explains how. Evidently he does not recognize the tacit understanding that gives rise to explicit knowledge. The subject already knows tacitly the answer to the "question never posed." He knows tacitly that he himself is the one who owns the mental process going on within his brain.

A *homunculus* is defined as a "little person in the brain who 'sees' an inner television screen, 'hears' an inner voice, 'reads' the topographic maps, weighs reasons, decides on actions, and so forth" (Churchland 1986, 406). Damasio deprecates the homunculus and tries to explain why it is unnecessary. He insists that "there is no separate spectator for the movie in the brain." However, without a homunculus, or something like it, what would one have? There would be a first set of maps in the brain that has captured the information coming from various individual senses, internal or external; then a second set that partially unifies what is in the first set; a third set that further unifies what is in the second set; and so on, till one comes to a final map that unifies all the information in the brain and then—let us assume for the sake of argument—also uses this unified information to regulate the entire system that Damasio calls the organism. But this final map is still objective. He has not yet explained how an organism can be a subject. The organism would have become a successful robot that would have no consciousness and no sense of self. There is no one there to interpret the final map or to freely decide what to do.

In her book *Neurophilosophy*, Patricia Churchland insists that there are no homunculi in our heads.

> There are just neurons and their connections. When a person sees, it is because neurons, individually blind and individually stupid neurons, are collectively orchestrated in the appropriate manner. So much seems obvious, and even a brief immersion in the neurosciences should proof one against the seductiveness of homuncular hypotheses. Surprisingly, however, homunculi, or at least the odor of homunculi, drift into one's thinking about brain function with embarrassing frequency. (1986, 406)

As she says, it is indeed difficult for a human being, even a reductionistic philosopher like herself, to keep thinking about consciousness and still remain free of "contamination" by homunculi, or at least from something like homunculi. She is right in thinking that there is no little homunculus in the brain, but in fact there is a higher-order entity, a soul or spirit, that is present to the brain and the whole human body, sublating it into its own reality. She is intuitively aware of the action of her own soul and is mistakenly interpreting it as the odor of a homunculus.

It is difficult to ignore the influence of the soul, even though that influence can easily be misinterpreted. When any intelligent person sees, hears, reads, weighs reasons, decides on actions, and so forth, he knows what he is doing and that he is a substantial, existing, conscious, subjective agent, not a merely accidental system of entities. His existence and his intelligent acts are on a higher ontological level than any of the subordinate entities within him. It is the person himself who sees, hears, feels, and so on, and, most of all, sublates those subordinate entities and their activities. He is the one who does the orchestrating Churchland speaks of. He is an ontologically higher entity who is sublating his body, and especially his brain and its operations, into his own reality. The role of the soul in conscious understanding and other immaterial operations cannot be avoided. It is not to be found on the level of the brain or any merely material entity. Of itself, it is not in space, although it is in space in virtue of its influence upon the lower entities that are in space.

In Damasio's final explanation of consciousness he tries to explain how entirely objective patterns are interpreted. But interpretation is a subjective act by which a person gives meaning to an objective representation. Damasio has missed the fact that consciousness is a property more of a subject than of an object. The objective concepts, which I am conscious of, are illuminated by a light that comes from my subjective self.

The Nature of Consciousness

What is consciousness? It is a certain qualitative property of an intelligent subject who is acting. The subject is known tacitly and unthematically because, by the nature of the act, he is always focusing on its object. The symbols that emanate from him express objectively and explicitly the tacit being-knowledge present within him. The consciousness connected with it is more subjective than objective. The objective signs and mental words are indeed conscious, but somewhat in the way that visual objects are luminous because they reflect the light in which they are bathed. The light of consciousness comes more from the inner than the outer side of being. That is why machines are not conscious no matter how complex or powerful their activities may be. They have no substantial unity, no interior from which the light of consciousness can emanate. As complex accidental unities they have no act of existing from which acts of knowing can come. The light of consciousness emanates from personal intellectual acts. There is no person in the machine to perform the acts of knowing from which shines the light of consciousness.

Scientists and engineers have learned to generate, transmit, amplify, manipulate, and display marvelous complex electro-chemical-mechanical patterns of various sorts. Stimulated by this technological development, many AI people think of computers as resembling artificial brains, and some neuroscientists are attempting to understand in a similar way the patterns that they find in human brains.

I see Damasio's theory of consciousness as influenced by this scientific-technological development. He seems to think of human thought and human consciousness by analogy with electro-chemical-mechanical patterns. However, the great deficiency of applying that way of thinking to human beings is that it leaves out the subjective element. As we have seen, consciousness is essentially a qualitative property of the act of knowing. That act belongs to a subject who is a substance, one who exercises an act of existing. The patterns produced by computers or TV sets are the cooperative accomplishment of many different substances. There is no single "I," no substantial unity that exercises one unified act of existing or one unified act of thinking. There is no one there to say "I exist" or "I think" or "I see." Television sets detect, amplify, manipulate, and finally display intricate forms. A TV set possesses the picture that the viewer can see on the screen, but the TV set itself knows nothing about it. It does not know what it is doing because there is no one in it to know. To know there would have to be a conscious subject that sublates the rest of the material system.

Damasio's theory, and similar theories, remind me of an often-reprinted cartoon. As I recall, it shows two Einstein-like professors looking at a chalk board that displays complex mathematical equations that terminate in QED (*quod erat demonstrandum*). But in the middle of the equations is an arrow to which is attached the statement "Here a miracle occurs." One professor is saying to the other, "I think you should explain that step a little more." What makes that cartoon funny has to do with the contrast between complicated ingenious scientific reasoning and some mysterious qualitative element in the situation that makes the professor's labored reasoning relatively unimportant. Presumably his mathematics are ingenious and technically correct and so he is very happy about it. But as far as the main point goes, it does no good whatever. He, however, is not willing to face the fact, and as a result he is funny.

As far as the traditional object of neuroscience—namely, explaining in a precise scientific way the operations of the brain and nervous system—is concerned, the work of neuroscientists is important and valuable. But as far as explaining the operations of the rational human mind that makes use of the brain is concerned, neuroscience becomes a boundary condition for the work of philosophers and theologians. As a negative check on what the latter say, neuroscience is important at times, but it certainly is not the main thing. But early in "How the Brain Creates the Mind," Damasio tells us that for some neuroscientists "the classic mind-body problem—has become almost a residual problem" (1999b, 112). Believing that is a bad mistake. He ends up by trying to advance his impossible project of deriving the mind from the operations of the brain by inserting into the middle of his neuroscientific arguments an explanation that makes little sense, much as the professor in the cartoon does.

Why did he do that? Perhaps it is for the same reason that Galileo's judges felt sure they could judge the Copernican theory, why physical cosmologists are now trying to show how the world is eternal, and why evolutionary biologists are trying to show how evolution can be explained without teleology. Intellectuals are often prone to intellectual hubris, and the great success of modern science has made scientists especially vulnerable to it. As Damasio says, today some of them are feeling the "vertiginous feeling that no problem can resist the assault of science if only the theory is right and the techniques are powerful enough" (1999b, 112).

Further Discussion of Consciousness

In recent years, progress in neuroscience has occasioned a great deal of philosophical discussion of consciousness. John R. Searle has reviewed a portion of this discussion in his book *The Mystery of Consciousness*, published in 1997, two years before that of Damasio. I single out Searle's book because it contains clear, sensible criticism of a number of ideas about consciousness that I believe to be wrong, and also because he himself holds or exemplifies other erroneous theses that I wish to criticize. I begin with his criticism of others.

The molecular biologist Francis Crick (1994), the neuroscientist Gerald Edelman (1989; 1992), and the mathematical physicist Roger Penrose (1994) have written books that are similar in a certain way.[4] They all purport to discuss consciousness, but in fact they speak more about the physical prerequisites for consciousness. What these eminent scientists tell us about the physical basis of consciousness is frequently interesting and perhaps valuable, but there are many serious objections about their philosophical comments on the nature of consciousness itself.

Searle's general conclusion about these books is that their authors are on the right track but that much more is needed in order to explain consciousness (Searle 1997, 196). He believes they are on the right track because he too is convinced that consciousness is caused entirely by physical processes in the brain, but he is also convinced that there is a huge explanatory gap between our present understanding of those third-person physical processes and the first-person conscious states that everyone experiences. He agrees that Crick is right in thinking that the first step in closing the gap is to discover in more detail the neural correlates of consciousness. But Searle goes on to say, "neural correlations are not going to be enough. Once we know two things are correlated, we still have not explained the correlation. Think of lightning and thunder, for example—a perfect correlation but not an explanation until we have a theory."

We are not even certain that the mechanisms that supposedly produce consciousness are, as many suppose, at the level of the neurons. Perhaps the fundamental units of explanation are groups of neurons, as Edelman suggests, or units even smaller than neurons, as Penrose suggests (Searle 1997, 198). Thus, according to Searle, we still have a long way to go. Of course, Damasio's book came out two years after Searle's and may be designed to help bridge the explanatory gap that Searle complained about. But, as I have claimed, while it may possibly contain good suggestions about the neural correlates of consciousness, it is no help at all in explaining consciousness itself.

The next book Searle discusses is Daniel Dennett's *Consciousness Explained* (1991). To put it mildly, Searle does not agree with it—nor do I. He thinks, rightly, that Dennett solves the problem of consciousness by denying the evident data. Dennett seems to believe that what most people assume to be real is actually an illusion, and he is trying to dispel it. But he does not pay attention to the fact that after reading his book most human beings still have the illusion, and that if they really didn't they might well be locked up. Why does Dennett hold the remarkable position he does? According to Searle, he is "in the tradition of behaviorism—the idea that behavior and dispositions to behavior are somehow constitutive of mental states—and verificationism—the idea that the only things which exist are those whose presence can be verified by scientific means" (1997, 97).

Perhaps Dennett believes that, because consciousness itself is not intrinsically objective and so cannot be studied like an object, it cannot therefore be a datum for science. And it seems that, for him, only scientific knowledge, or thought based upon it, is true knowledge. Searle also seems to believe that only science, and thought based upon it, is true knowledge. But he is certain that science can study anything that is real, whether or not it exists in the first-person mode or in the third-person mode. He believes that consciousness is subjective, but he also thinks that scientists can study it objectively and come to true conclusions about it (Searle 1997, 12–14). From my point of view, Searle easily gets the better of the exchange between him and Dennett, yet at the same time he himself is relying on false premises.

Finally, Searle devotes a long chapter, with its appendix, to the views of another philosopher, David Chalmers. Searle's conclusion (1997, 176) is that "for all its ingenuity I am afraid his book is really no help in the project of understanding how the brain causes consciousness." On the back page of Searle's book another philosopher, Colin McGinn, writes, Searle's "vigorous common sense and bracing clearheadedness are a welcome addition to the literature. ... [His] talent for exposing error and confusion is here displayed to considerable effect." But Chalmers's work (1996) is more like Searle's than the latter is willing to admit.[5] Both are ultimately materialists. Searle wants to avoid both dualism and the traditional sharp distinction between physical and mental attributes. He claims that conscious attributes are biological ones like digestion, even though they are unusual in being first-person ones. In contrast, Chalmers "bites the bullet" (a favorite phrase of his) by adopting a certain kind of "property" dualism, that is, by claiming that there are two essentially different kinds of attributes, even though both belong to material substances.

Searle (1997, 135–43) begins his criticism of Chalmers's position by locating it in relation to contemporary mainstream English-speaking philosophy of mind. He classifies Chalmers's position as a species of *nonreductive functionalism*. In the early twentieth century, *behaviorists* tried to explain conscious states in terms of behavior and dispositions regarding behavior. That approach didn't work as it stood. Then *physicalists* modified behaviorism by recognizing mental states but arguing that they are simply identical with physical states. But that didn't work either. Now *functionalists* claim that "mental states are physical states all right, but they are defined as 'mental' not because of their physical constitution but because of their causal relations" (Searle 1997, 139). Clocks and carburetors are material but what makes them clocks or carburetors is their functional organization, which enables them to work in different ways. Similarly, according to functionalists, mental states are physical states organized in a certain way. As adherents of strong AI claimed some fifty years ago, on the day when the electronic states of a computer are organized in the correct way, the machine will be ipso facto intelligent. (We are still waiting.)

Chalmers is a functionalist up to a point because he claims that all behavior, including intelligent behavior, can be explained in terms of the functional organization of neurons or other physical elements. However, he also claims that subjective, first-person mental states cannot be explained in that way. They are, he insists, irreducible to physical states. To Searle it seems impossible to reconcile Chalmers's thoroughgoing functionalism in the realm of behavior with his claim that our subjective experience cannot be reduced to physical states. Suppose that I hit my thumb with a hammer, feel pain, and cry "Ouch!" Behaviorists teach that the physical damage done to my thumb by the hammer causes a certain physical state of the brain which in turn causes the behavioral act of crying "Ouch!" For them, "pain" is essentially the person's behavior and related dispositions, which in this case include crying "Ouch!" and the physical damage that causes it. Both the physical states of my thumb and brain, and the behavior that they cause, are thoroughly objective and third-person in character.

In contrast, my experience is that the objective event of my hitting my thumb causes me to have an unpleasant subjective feeling called "pain" and that this subjective feeling motivates me to cry "Ouch!" My subjective, first-person feeling, which most people would call "pain," is the central factor in explaining what happens. The behaviorist explanation takes no account of this subjective feeling but explains everything in terms of objective, third-person states. The behaviorists' "pain" is not the same as the subjective pain I feel and on account of which I act.

For Chalmers, the behaviorist-functionalist account is complete and adequate to explain the objective train of events. The subjective mental feelings of pain and the desire to escape it are causally independent of what happens in the objective world. The objective event of my crying

"Ouch!" is insufficiently connected with my subjective desire to cry "Ouch!" on account of my painful feeling. Although Chalmers produces ingenious arguments to back up his position, Searle is right in judging that it is impossible to reconcile his concept of what happens objectively with his concept of human beings' subjective experience.

Nevertheless, as Searle wrote (1997, 143), Chalmers's book "has been getting much attention [in 1997], and has been a subject of debate at conferences of philosophers and cognitive scientists." Searle thinks that this is a symptom of "a certain desperation in cognitive studies today" (1997, 145). In such a situation many people are ready to accept a solution that "seems to combine functionalism, which people want on ideological grounds, with an acknowledgement of the existence and irreducibility of consciousness, which many people in cognitive studies are—at last—prepared to admit" (ibid.).

It seems to me that Searle too feels the same desperation, but his response is different. He hunkers down and claims that consciousness is a natural biological phenomenon that must be explained in fundamentally the same way that other biological phenomena like metabolism, growth, and reproduction have been explained. But, unlike many others, he faces obvious facts and admits that it hasn't been done yet. He puts his faith in science and eschews solutions like that of Chalmers, which he considers absurd, believing that, when biological science has explained in more detail how the brain works, then it will become clear how consciousness emerges from its processes.

To summarize, I believe Searle is right in saying that Chalmers's position has at least three unacceptable consequences: (1) He places an enormous chasm between behavior and behavioral dispositions, on the one hand, and conscious experiences, on the other. As a result Chalmers has to assume a kind of "preestablished harmony" between the two which is reminiscent of Leibniz (Copleston 1985, 4:308). But because he cannot, like Leibniz, rely on God, he is forced to produce an ingenious but enormously complex theory to keep them in step. (2) For Chalmers, consciousness becomes "explanatorily irrelevant to anything physical that happens in the world" (Searle 1997, 168). (3) Furthermore, even a person's "own claims about [his] own consciousness are not explained by consciousness. If you say 'I am in pain,' when you are in pain, it cannot be because you are in pain that you said it" (ibid.).

Ultimately both Chalmers and Searle are defeated by the same false presupposition, namely, reductionism. This position entails an incorrect understanding of the nature of science, as well as the relationships between science and philosophy. To those who want science to be the most important kind of knowledge, to accept the limitations of science seems like a comedown. However, hubris is no reason for not facing the truth that the world is richer, more intelligible, and more beautiful than reductionists believe.

As Paul Tillich has written, a mature person always has an "ultimate concern" that, whether he realizes it or not, is theological in character (1961, 1:11–15). He may not call it God, but in a certain sense it is his private personal god. Scientism is one of the major faiths of the modern era, and for its adherents science itself, or one of its theories (often evolution), is god. The life and struggles of Alexis Carrel that I referred to above express in a vivid way how hard it is for a true believer in science to convert and demote his former god to the status of a creature. The central drama of such a person's life resembles the struggle of the people of Israel to choose between Yahweh and one or another of the Baals.

Conclusion

Reductionists must explain how a complex system, consisting of nothing more than a set of interacting elementary entities, can be conscious. How can such a system perform conscious, intentional activities like understanding, love, and the perception of transcendental values like unity, goodness, truth, and beauty? Such an accidental system cannot do so. Reductionism overlooks the essential questions or else provides elaborate but inconsistent answers. It distracts from its dismal failure about essential questions by shedding light on interesting but subordinate ones.

Ever since the time of Galileo, Western culture has been impressed by the success of reductionistic science in dealing with the lower levels of the hierarchy of being. It has seemed plausible to many to suppose that when more fully developed it will also be capable of handling higher realities. But just because a student is able to solve simple problems, it is by no means certain that he will be able to solve more difficult ones. Some years ago it was common to speak of modern man as having come of age. But I think it would be better to compare him to a conceited adolescent. The modest understanding of consciousness that we can glean from philosophy and theology does not satisfy reductionists, who naively suppose that they can do better by means of their own familiar methods. They begin with enthusiasm, like the man who climbed a tree and announced that he has made the first step in getting to the moon. At the present time some neuroscientists, and philosophers interested in neuroscience, seem to have that sort of misguided enthusiasm. They suppose that science is about to explain everything. They need to slow down and reflect on important truths that can be gotten by quite different methods. Then they might see that, in spite of their intelligence and scientific knowledge, they have missed the whole point about consciousness. The main reason is that they are confined to a materialistic horizon into which consciousness can never fit. That is pretty much the same thing that happened to early workers in AI.

Let me conclude this chapter by asking the following question: In defining and explaining consciousness in the way I did here, have holists succeeded in "solving" the so-called problem of consciousness? Certainly not. Consciousness is a mysterious qualitative property of our own actuated being that we experience and partially understand, but which we cannot understand fully in this life. In order to understand it fully we will have to understand our own essence directly and clearly, and we will never do that here on Earth. In this life we understand essences only through the actions that flow from them. Thus, we understand them only mediately, in their actions rather than in themselves. Such understanding is true up to a point, but it is not complete or clear and distinct. According to Thomistic theology, we will understand essences fully only when in heaven we see the divine essence from which finite essences are derived. For reductionists, the problem of consciousness is the problem of how to reduce consciousness to the operations of a subhuman mechanical system. We can understand such systems and their operations, and so reductionists think that therefore we should be able to understand consciousness in the same way. They are puzzled because they are finding it impossible to do so.

NOTES

1. For examples of such now-embarrassing statements, see Dreyfus 1992.

2. Also in a brief précis of the book entitled "How the Brain Creates the Mind" (1999b) that appeared in *Scientific American*, December 1999, 112–17.

3. For what follows, see Damasio 1999a, chaps. 2 and 9, and also pp. 317–23. The same stages have also been noticed earlier by Thomists but labeled somewhat differently. For them, Damasio's emotion is the "bodily resonance" and his feeling is their "emotion." Furthermore, these stages also seem analogous to the three levels of the cosmic hierarchy—living, sentient, and rational—that are used to classify different species.

4. Crick, *The Astonishing Hypothesis* (1994); Edelman, *The Remembered Present* (1989), and *Bright Air, Brilliant Fire* (1992); Penrose, *Shadows of the Mind* (1994).

5. Chalmers recognizes this. See his *The Conscious Mind*, 370n2.

PART TWO

Quantum Mechanics

4 • Past Interpretations of Quantum Mechanics
5 • Entanglement
6 • The Nature of Time
7 • A New Interpretation of Quantum Mechanics

CHAPTER 4

Past Interpretations of Quantum Mechanics

In chapters 2 and 3 I discussed the existence and character of the cosmic hierarchy, and paid special attention to its human level. Now, in chapters 4 through 7, I concentrate on the lower levels of the hierarchy, the ones that are the proper subject matter of physics. In particular, I shall begin by discussing several important interpretations of quantum mechanics (QM).

Quantum mechanics is a branch of physics that began with attempts to understand the behavior of atoms and the atomic particles that make up those atoms. Max Planck, Albert Einstein, Niels Bohr, Louis de Broglie, and others laid down its foundation. But in 1925–26 Werner Heisenberg and Erwin Schrödinger discovered two seemingly different versions of QM itself. The two versions were later found to be essentially the same, yet QM still remains rather baffling. Perhaps it can be described as an algorithm, a mathematical procedure that, after the better part of a century, is still seeking an interpretation that will make it a completely satisfying, full-bloomed theory. This algorithm combines two distinct procedures: the "unitary" one called U, and the "state reduction" one called R. U is continuous and deterministic; R is discontinuous and probabilistic. In the first phase, a quantum system is guided by U, and during that phase it seems to be like a wave function or wave packet. Yet, when the wave packet reaches some macroscopic detector, R comes into play and abruptly transforms it into a particle. What is the nature of this mysterious "collapse of the wave packet"? There are a number of explanations.

The Copenhagen Interpretation

The "Copenhagen interpretation" of quantum mechanics can be defined historically in terms of the ideas of a group of physicists associated with Copenhagen and Göttingen. They included Bohr, Heisenberg, Wolfgang Pauli, Max Born, and Ernst Pascual Jordan. What exactly did these men hold? John Cramer, following the historians Max Jammer and Michael Audi, lists five of their basic assumptions (Cramer 1986, 649–50):

1. *Heisenberg's uncertainty principle.* Immediately after the publication of Heisenberg's original papers on QM, it seemed possible that, although both pairs of "conjugate variables" like position and momentum had precise values, for some reason nature was systematically concealing them from prying investigators. It was thought by some that even though the technology available at the time did not permit one to know the details of the microworld, one had to be content—at least for the time being—to know only its statistics. However, at the end of his paper Heisenberg stated his belief that both such precise underlying quantities are unknowable in principle and are even meaningless. It seems that the passage of time has confirmed the truth of his conjecture (Jammer 1966, 330).

2. *Born's statistical interpretation of the meaning of the wave function.* The wave function is a certain likelihood that the entity under consideration is here, and another likelihood that it is there, rather than a certainty that it is in any definite place.

3. *The complementarity principle of Bohr.* This principle is a rather slippery one. It has to do with the relationship between the particles and waves that QM deals with. It implies that the nature and significance of experimental data depend not only upon what is measured but also upon the measuring apparatus and the relationship between the two.

4. *Identification of the wave function with knowledge of the system.* This interpretation of the wave function explains how it can collapse

abruptly, in much the way that our provisional knowledge of the probable winner of a horse race changes abruptly at the close of the race. Of course, critics of the Copenhagen interpretation demand, *Whose knowledge?* and *What knowledge?* Unfortunately it is sometimes hard to tell.

5. *A certain positivism and empiricism.* Because of this, one focuses on observables and refuses intellectual significance to questions about ontological truth. However, later Heisenberg and others softened this stark positivism.

How do these five elements of the Copenhagen interpretation fit together? Henry P. Stapp has given us a synthetic view of Bohr's ideas that was approved by Heisenberg, as well as by another one of Bohr's close collaborators, Léon Rosenfeld (Stapp 1993, chap. 3). According to Stapp, the Copenhagen interpretation is a pragmatic one akin to the pragmatic philosophy of William James. Stapp discusses the latter's ideas and then shows from Bohr's writings that Bohr agreed with them. It is possible that Bohr came to know James's ideas through the Danish philosopher Harald Høffding, who was a friend both of Bohr's father and of James, and whose lectures Bohr attended as a student. According to James T. Cushing, "Bohr explicitly acknowledged the influence of Høffding's philosophy on his own formulation of complementarity" (Cushing 1994, 97). In any event, Bohr later expressed his enthusiastic approval of James's philosophical view.

Stapp's exposition of Bohr's view begins with the essential elements of quantum mechanics from the point of view of actual practice in the field of atomic physics. The experimental physicist writes down wave functions that express the way he prepares a quantum system and measures its properties. Are these wave functions direct expressions of the nature of actual quantum objects? According to the Copenhagen interpretation, they express probabilities rather than actualities. That is why they can change so abruptly when measurements are made.

Next Stapp outlines the pragmatism of James. The latter distinguished between "(1) private concepts, (2) sense objects, and (3) hypersensible realities" (Stapp 1993, 60). *Private concepts* are "ideas"—that is, mental realities—that are features of a person's experience. They are something like Kantian phenomena. *Hypersensible realities* are real things existing outside the mind. They resemble Kantian noumena that transcend human consciousness. James believed that there is a real objective world beyond our human consciousness but he did not think we can know it directly or precisely. Real objects outside our minds are very different from ideas, and he saw little reason for thinking that they resemble our ideas, except inasmuch as they cause the ideas in a general way. To "know" is to "agree." We "know" by means of "ideas," and ideas agree only with other ideas, not with external objects. *Sense objects* belong to the realm of experience, but they are nonetheless common and public. Supposedly, the sense objects of one person are like those of others, and so they are the basis of a common social reality and the pragmatic definition of truth.

According to Stapp,

> [T]he logical essence of the Copenhagen interpretation is summed up in the following two assertions:
> 1. The quantum-theoretical formalism is to be interpreted *pragmatically*.
> 2. Quantum theory provides for a *complete* scientific account of atomic phenomena. (Stapp 1993, 61; italics original)

Like James, Bohr believed in the existence of the external world. But also, like James, he believed our direct experience is of ideas, not external reality. As to the question of whether or not randomness is a characteristic of nature, or of our thinking about nature, Bohr seems to have limited himself to simply asserting that individual experimental events are unique and our laws about them are statistical. Apparently he believed that answering the question in more detail would require going beyond the evidence.

As to the completeness of quantum mechanics, if one accepted the classical point of view, as Einstein did, one might perhaps judge that QM is not complete. But from Bohr's pragmatic point of view "no theoretical construction can yield experimentally verifiable predictions about atomic phenomena that cannot be extracted from a quantum theoretical description" (Stapp 1993, 66). Thus, one cannot, as Einstein wished, get beyond ideas and probabilities to know "the really real."

Hidden Variables

For many years the Copenhagen interpretation of quantum mechanics remained the commonly accepted one. Yet Einstein, Schrödinger, de Broglie, and others regarded it right along with suspicion. They admitted that, practically speaking, quantum mechanics was the best theory available at the time. But it was not at all the kind of realistic theory they were looking for. Indeed, very early both de Broglie and Einstein had espoused different versions of the so-called *hidden variable interpretation*. According to this view, the quantities of quantum mechanics are statistical averages over the precise values proper to an underlying theory that ought to be found in the future. In somewhat the same way, the quantities of classical thermodynamics are now thought to be averages over the precise quantities governing the molecules of which gases consist. For example, temperature is believed to be a measure of the average energy of many gas molecules.

De Broglie first proposed his "theory of the double solution" in an article shortly before the fifth Solvay conference of 1927 and presented it again at the conference itself (Jammer 1966, 292–93, 357). At the same conference Einstein attacked the Copenhagen interpretation head-on. But in spite of their prestige both failed to persuade the majority. Perhaps this was because the "Copenhagers," Bohr, Heisenberg, Pauli, and Born, presented a united front, while their opposition, Einstein, de Broglie, and Schrödinger, were divided in their opinions. As James T. Cushing claims, the triumph of the Copenhagen interpretation may very well have been due to historical contingency. Suppose that, as seems possible, Einstein's early doubts had resulted in his formulating a Bell-type theorem around 1930. Then the community of physicists might have made a very different choice (Cushing 1994, esp. chap. 10). But that was not to be.

As I have claimed, many physicists are ultimately realists who want more than empirically adequate theories. But finding an empirically adequate theory is so difficult that sometimes they have little time or energy left for philosophical speculation. In the circumstances, the Copenhagen interpretation seemed plausible enough, so most accepted it, for the time being at least.

In 1932, the alleged proof of John von Neumann that hidden variable interpretations are impossible confirmed the community of physicists in their acceptance of the Copenhagen viewpoint. However, in 1952 David Bohm published a counterexample to von Neumann's theorem, an alternative—albeit augmented—theory of quantum mechanics that produces very nearly the same observational results as the orthodox one.[1] It can do so because it entails effects, or at least correlations, at a distance. Before Bell's theorem was published in 1964 such correlations were regarded as impossible, but, as we have seen, since then a number of experiments have provided evidence in favor of their reality. Nevertheless, to many physicists, Bohm's theory appears more cumbersome than orthodox quantum mechanics. As a result Occam's razor is thought to favor QM (Stapp 1993, 84–85). Even some opponents of the Copenhagen interpretation are not satisfied with present-day hidden-variable theories in spite of the fact that they regard them as valuable demonstrations of the possibility of nonlocal theories other than QM.

The fifth conference of the Solvay Institute, at which Bohr and Einstein debated the merits between the Copenhagen and hidden variable interpretations, occurred in October 1927. This event is often regarded as having established the Copenhagen interpretation as the quasi-official doctrine of the physics community.

Many-Worlds

The baffling nature of quantum mechanics invites language that almost suggests there are two distinct realms in nature, the microscopic realm inhabited by basic quantum processes that are governed by Schrödinger's equation and the macroscopic realm governed by classical entities and processes. The mysterious "collapse of the wave packet" brings about the transition between the two realms. But what causes the collapse of the wave packet? Schrödinger's equation does not demand it. What, then, is its existential status? Is it real or just a mathematical device? For Bohr and others, it seemed to be simply a feature of the mathematics of probability that is required by our ignorance. Today, to others it now seems something that may not be understood at present but whose existence is imposed upon us by the facts. For the latter, to deny the existence of the collapse of the wave packet would be like sawing off the limb of the logical tree on which we are sitting.

But in 1965 Arno Penzias and Robert Wilson discovered the low-temperature microwave background which fills the whole universe and which appears to be a feeble echo of the Big Bang in which the universe originated some 13.7 billion years ago. This discovery aroused great interest in the field of cosmology, and since then intense effort has been made to apply quantum theory to the universe as a whole. Since the universe comprises all finite beings, there cannot be any natural cause outside it that would make the wave function of the universe collapse.[2] Therefore, the explanation that the wave function of a system under observation collapses because of the influence of the experimental apparatus being used and the environment with which it is connected cannot apply in the case of the universe. But if the wave function of the universe as a whole does not collapse, how can a wave function of part of it collapse?

The conclusion drawn by Hugh Everett in 1957 is that the collapse of the wave packet does not occur at all.[3] According to his "many-worlds" interpretation of quantum mechanics, at each moment when nature seems to choose between several possible outcomes, no choice is really made. Instead the world splits into many parallel worlds. It duplicates itself so that rather than just one possibility being realized, all possible outcomes are realized, but each in a different branch-world. If there are N possible outcomes, the result is N distinct parallel worlds, none of which is aware of or influenced by (at least to any appreciable extent) the others. The world is like a tree. At many points each branch splits into many branches, which in turn branch again, and again, and again, and so on. If I apply this to myself, I am invited to believe that I exist in many parallel worlds in each of which I am living out a different possibility. If I try to choose between two contrary courses of action, instead I do both, but in two different worlds in each of which there is a me unaware of the me doing the opposite in the other world.

As John Polkinghorne remarks, this "is enough to make poor William of Occam turn in his grave."[4] Nevertheless, for empiricists this bizarre theory is no more or less true than any other theory, and its logical coherence is attractive. Moreover, even though in its literal form it appears absurd to realists, it does suggest related but less implausible possibilities that I will discuss below.

Consciousness

The difference between the quantum and classical realms entails what has been called the "infamous boundary" between the two.[5] In the classical realm, physical systems exist in just one of many mutually exclusive possible states. A system might be capable of existing in either state A or state B, but classically it cannot be in both at the same time. However, in the quantum realm it may be in both. The theory suggests that an entity located at a definite point will in due time diffuse under the guidance of Schrödinger's equation in such a way as to be located at many different points at the same time—its presence at each being qualified, of course, by its probability amplitude. It may be both here and there—as, for example, in the two-slit experiment, where it goes, at least in a certain qualified sense, through both slits. More generally, a system may be in different possible states at the same time. The unitary development governed by Schrödinger's equation entails a "quantum and." But the collapse of the wave packet turns the "quantum and" into a "classical or." It compels the system to cross the infamous boundary that separates the quantum and the classical realms. How does it do that, and when?

Take the *when* question first. In 1935, Schrödinger dramatized the problem by recounting the story of an unfortunate cat. Supposedly the cat is enclosed by a fiendish scientist in a box that completely isolates its contents from the world. Also in the box are a radioactive atom, which has a 50 percent probability of decaying in an hour, a vial of poison gas, and a triggering device that will release the gas that will kill the cat if the atom decays. According to quantum mechanics, the state of the radioactive atom is "entangled" with that of the triggering device, the state of the triggering device with that of the poison gas, the state of the gas with that of the cat. As a result, after an hour, just before the box is about to be opened, not only would the wave function of the radioactive atom be a superposition of two equal probabilities, but the wave function of the cat would be too. If its wave function truly represents the physical state of the cat, then the cat would be in a nonclassical superposition of two states, namely, the state of being dead and the state of being alive, with 50 percent probability for each state.

The implausibility of this concept seems to reduce to absurdity the possibility of interpreting the wave function in a realistic way. That is why, according to the fourth axiom of the Copenhagen interpretation, the wave function expresses directly not the real physical situation but our imperfect knowledge of it. But, of course, what are we then to make of the real state of the cat? The Copenhagen interpretation won't tell us and insists that no one can. This is not a very satisfying answer to scientists, most of whom took up their profession in order to find out the truth about the world.

But perhaps the collapse of the wave packet occurs before the cat gets into such a metaphysically wretched condition. Eugene Wigner, who believed that quantum mechanics is, or at least ought to be, objective and ontological rather than subjective and epistemic, apparently decided to make things worse in order then to make them better. He modified Schrödinger's story by introducing into it a second scientist. In Penrose's version (1989, 290–93), this colleague is clad in a space suit and sits inside the box during the experiment. Thus, he is able to observe whether or not the gas is released and the cat killed, so that from his point of view it is always either alive or dead. But now quantum mechanics is giving two different answers, one to the original experimenter and another to his collaborator. The collaborator knows whether the cat is dead or alive but the experimenter does not. Moreover, from the point of view of the latter, his friend is entangled with the cat in the same superposition as the radioactive atom. He both knows the cat to be dead and also knows him to be alive. It seems that the supposedly objective character of science is being fragmented into a chaos of contradictory philosophical opinions.

Some of those who believe in the objective character of quantum mechanics respond to this story by saying that things obviously cannot go that far. The collapse of the wave packet must occur on the inanimate level. But when? Does it happen when the radioactive atom interacts with the triggering device, or when the device interacts with the vial of poison gas, or when the gas interacts with the cat? Where is the infamous boundary between quantum and classical? The theory does not tell us.

Wigner himself thought that perhaps, someway or other, consciousness brings about the collapse of the wave function. After all, conscious entities know that they are alive, and so they have to be part of the classical world. Therefore the cat itself might cause the collapse of the wave function. If cats are not conscious, or sufficiently conscious, the observer inside the box might do it. In any event, the outside scientist knows there is a definite situation inside even though he does not know what it is.

If one accepts the consciousness interpretation of quantum mechanics, the question arises, How can conscious entities induce the collapse of the wave function of an inanimate system? Wigner could suggest only that consciousness modifies the situation in a way that would be reflected in Schrödinger's equation, possibly by the addition to it of a nonlinear term. But still, how would consciousness produce a physical effect? We are back to something like Descartes's problem about how the soul can influence the body.

Note that in the consciousness interpretation inanimate entities that exist below the level of consciousness would inhabit the quantum world habitually. For the superpositions that inevitably arise with regard to elementary particles would have to spread almost instantaneously to the larger systems composed of them. The final result would be that, as Einstein once observed, the moon would be in a definite place only when someone looked at it (Pais 1979, 907). Who would do the looking? With regard to our moon, it might have been one of our early ancestors. But what about all the stars and galaxies that have been observed only in the past century? It would seem that, in this hypothesis, astronomers have a much greater role in the universe than we usually suppose! As one reflects upon the consciousness interpretation as well as the fourth axiom of the Copenhagen interpretation, both of them appear to be a morass of metaphysical and epistemic problems that would be well avoided if at all possible. It seems that the only obvious way of cutting through that morass would be to accept constructive empiricism. But to do so would be to accept the opinion that Cardinal Bellarmine once suggested to Galileo, namely, to accept science as an intellectual game in which one aims to save the appearances. I respect and revere Robert Bellarmine as a saint, but, like most realists interested in science, I do not want to accept his scientific and epistemological opinions.

Spontaneous Localization and the Role of Gravity

The consciousness interpretation pushes the notorious boundary between the quantum and classical worlds upward toward the higher ontological levels. Other interpretations push it downward toward the level of the elementary particles. Advocates of both types recognize that of itself the unitary process of Schrödinger's equation cannot explain how the system passes the frontier between the quantum and classical worlds. It does not account for the collapse of the wave packet. If the collapse is on a higher level, consciousness might cause it; but if it is on a lower level, what might its cause be? It is said that the interaction between the system under measurement and the measurement apparatus forces the system to conform to the latter's classical nature. But if quantum mechanics is the basic theory that explains the physical constitution of the whole universe, this explanation is inadequate. There is no apparatus outside the universe to cause the collapse.

In 1985, Gian Carlo Ghirardi, Alberto Rimini, and Tulio Weber (GRW) suggested a modification of Schrödinger's equation that preserves its usual results but adds to them spontaneous random collapses of the wave function of the system. Such a collapse would immediately cause the wave function to become well localized around a random point of spacetime. Such collapses would prevent embarrassing macroscopic superpositions like the one illustrated by the fate of Schrödinger's cat. On the classical level, everything would look as it should, and thus empirical adequacy would be restored (Goldstein 1998 [April], 38).

But what might cause such sudden, seemingly random collapses of the wave function? As Penrose has observed, the scheme of Ghirardi, Rimini, and Weber is ingenious but very ad hoc. He proposes that the required modification of Schrödinger's equation is due to the influence of gravity upon the system in question (Penrose 1994, 335–47). Presumably there is some intelligible law that governs the way gravity produces these collapses.

Surely it is highly desirable to unify quantum mechanics with gravitational theory, and doing so may provide answers to many puzzling questions. So it is not unreasonable to hope that among those answered questions might be the true nature of the collapse. However, while this suggestion is an attractive extension of the scheme of Ghirardi, Rimini, and Weber, it is not an established theory. As Penrose himself believes, it is almost certainly the case that something new is needed to explain the experimental data that current relativity and quantum theory cannot explain. The new "something" probably entails some insight more radical than a slight modification of present theory. The question of the true nature of the collapse still remains.

The Propensity Interpretation

There are still two more interpretations of quantum mechanics that I want to consider. They do not seem to be popular among physicists—primarily, I suspect, because they are more philosophical than the others and do not seem to offer any empirical or mathematical advantages. Nevertheless, they suggest ideas I deem important with regard to interpretation. The first one, the propensity interpretation, can be traced as far back as Heisenberg and has been developed by Henry P. Stapp (1993).

The early Heisenberg was something of a positivist, but as he got older he, like Einstein, became more metaphysical. It seems that in his early days he agreed with Bohr that the formulae of quantum mechanics are merely "rules of calculation for the deduction of expectations about observations obtained under well-defined experimental conditions specified by classical physical concepts" (Bohr 1963). But later he came to understand the quantum mechanical wave function as a representation of quasi-Aristotelian potentialities that are objectively real in some sense even though they are not fully actual (Heisenberg 1962, 41, 53, 180, 185).

Stapp (1993) has combined Heisenberg's notion of potentiality with concepts derived from the philosophy of Alfred North Whitehead. The mind–body problem is at the focus of his interest. In classical physics, ideas and things are radically different, and it is difficult to see how they can interact at all. However, for Stapp, as for Heisenberg, the potentialities of quantum physics are propensities (Stapp 1993, 118; Heisenberg 1962, 53; Popper and Eccles 1977). They are not just abstract ideas but are also inclinations to become the fully actual things they already adumbrate. Stapp's central hypothesis is that the collapse of the wave packet is a creative decision, an event that makes fully real just one of the propensities inherent in the physical situation. Thus he points out a way of introducing choice, meaning, and value into the world (Stapp 1993, chap. 8). Of course, he does not claim that QM *proves* that the world has meaning and value. However, he shows that a world subject to the rules of quantum mechanics is open to them.

THE TRANSACTIONAL INTERPRETATION

The basic idea behind the transactional interpretation comes from a reformulation of classical electromagnetic wave theory developed by John A. Wheeler and Richard P. Feynman in the 1940s (1945, 157; 1949, 425).[6] Their approach did not seem to succeed in dealing with the problems they originally had in mind. However, as Cramer and others have shown, it can be used to explain quantum mechanics (Cramer 1986, 647–87).

Many of QM's basic equations have two sets of wave solutions. One set describes waves that travel in space in the way that we are familiar with. One can say that these waves go in the direction of time, that is, from earlier to later times. They are often referred to as "retarded solutions" because they are first generated and then, after traveling for some time, produce their effects, just as one would expect. However, the other set of solutions are so-called advanced solutions that travel opposite to the direction of time, that is, from the present into the past. Such a wave is absorbed before being emitted. In other words, their effects occur before the events that cause them.

It might seem that if an event were to do such a thing it might produce seemingly impossible effects, like altering the causes that produced it. What if a time traveler were to bring about the untimely death of his own parents? Therefore physicists normally assume that only the retarded solutions of the wave equation make sense, and discard the advanced solutions. Nevertheless, in theoretical physics, equations sometimes turn out to mean something different from, and perhaps more than, what their discoverers originally supposed. So John Cramer decided to regard the waves traveling backward in time as significant, and by using them he succeeded in constructing his "transactional model" of quantum mechanics.

Looking at what happens from a godlike point of view that transcends time, one sees the following: At time t_1 an event e_1 sends a wave (call it Φ) toward the future. Φ represents the efficient influence of event e_1 upon the future event e_2. Then, at a later time, t_2, the formerly future event, e_2, absorbs the wave Φ and responds by returning a wave Φ^* back into its past to the original event e_1 at time t_1. The combination of the two waves, Φ and Φ^*, traveling in opposite directions in time, is mathematically equivalent to a single wave, Ψ, traveling forward in time just as in the usual picture.

Thus, Cramer's model takes account of both present events and future events. I am, of course, assuming that, for Cramer, there are many possible future events that could form a real relationship with e_1, and which one of them actually does so depends upon the sort of stochastic decision long familiar in QM. Likewise, there are many present events that could form a real relationship with a particular e_2, and which one does so depends upon the same kind of decision.

From my point of view, Cramer's interpretation cannot be entirely correct. Like many physicists, he looks upon past, present, and future from a geometric point of view. From that viewpoint all three exist in the same way, and he looks down upon past, present, and future in somewhat the way classical theologians think God looks at the world from his eternity. Adopting that viewpoint, Cramer has produced a scenario that is coherent mathematically and empirically, but that is inconsistent with ordinary human experience of time. However, below I show that his interpretation can be reinterpreted within my own horizon. I believe that in a reinterpreted form it makes good theological, philosophical, and scientific sense.

Notes

1. Bohm's theory is deterministic and it denies many of the Copenhagen axioms. See Cushing, *Quantum Mechanics*, chaps. 4, 5.

2. From the theological point of view, which I accept in general, God as creator is the infinite cause of the universe who empowers all finite causes. As such, he would not normally act directly in order to collapse the wave function of the universe. Rather, he would cause the universe itself to do whatever is necessary.

3. In what follows I am using the language of Polkinghorne 1984, 67–68.

4. Polkinghorne, *The Quantum World*, 68. The logical rule known as Occam's razor states that entities are not to be multiplied without necessity.

5. This phrase may have come originally from Bell, *Speakable and Unspeakable in Quantum Mechanics*, 35, and has been used as the title of the book *The Infamous Boundary*, by David Wick (1995).

6. See also comments by Mr. X (= Feynman) in Gold, *The Nature of Time*.

CHAPTER 5

Entanglement

Quantum mechanics (QM) is a marvelous algorithm that has been put together on the basis of skillful experimentation and brilliant mathematical intuition. It has been remarkably successful for nearly a century in predicting the nature and behavior of complex molecules, atoms, and the even smaller subatomic particles (like quarks and gluons) that make up atoms. But the interpretations being given to it seem to be inadequate. Many of the important founders, including Einstein, de Broglie, and Schrödinger, were convinced almost from the beginning that some important insight was missing. In this chapter I will attempt to clarify the nature of QM in a theological and philosophical way.

ENTANGLEMENT AND SIMULTANEITY

Already in 1926 Erwin Schrödinger, one of the co-discoverers of quantum mechanics, recognized the quantum phenomenon now known as "entanglement." And in 1935 he remarked that entanglement is not "*one* but rather *the* characteristic trait of quantum mechanics."[1] According to Amir Aczel, "the most perplexing phenomenon in the bizarre world of the quantum is the effect called *entanglement*. Two particles that may be very far apart, even millions or billions of miles apart, are mysteriously linked together. Whatever happens to one of them immediately causes a change in the other one" (2001, xi).

In his book *Entanglement*, Aczel traces its history. Significant episodes were: (a) the publication in 1935 of a famous paper by Albert Einstein, Boris Podolsky, and Nathan Rosen that featured the so-called EPR thought experiment; (b) a simpler and clearer version of essentially the same experiment, now often known as the EPRB experiment, that was published by David Bohm in 1952; (c) John Stewart Bell's remarkable theorem of 1964; and (d) the experimental and theoretical work of John Clauser, Michael Horne, Abner Shimony, Richard Holt, Stuart Freedman, Edward S. Fry, M. G. Thompson, and others in the 1970s, which terminated in the early 1980s with the decisive experiments of Alain Aspect and his colleagues in Paris.

According to Ian Hacking (1983), a theoretical concept becomes an accepted reality when it is applied in practical ways and is taken for granted in ordinary practice. In other words, its reality is perceived when it becomes part of the habitual understanding that guides and interprets the usual life of the community. At present, the concept of entanglement seems to have attained that status.

THE EPR THOUGHT EXPERIMENT

Besides inventing relativity theory, Einstein helped lay down the foundations of quantum mechanics. Yet he never fully accepted the full-blown theory. He was convinced that "the essentially statistical character of contemporary quantum theory is solely to be ascribed to the fact that this (theory) operates with an incomplete description of physical systems."[2]

One can compare QM with thermodynamics. The macroscopic variables proper to thermodynamics, such as volume, pressure, and temperature, are not the most fundamental and irreducible ones. According to the statistical mechanics that Einstein employed so masterfully, they are statistical averages over the underlying variables of Newtonian mechanics. What we perceive as a continuous gas is really a swarm of individual molecules. The average kinetic energy of the many gas molecules appears on the macroscopic scale as the temperature of the gas, and the macroscopic pressure of the gas turns out to be the average effect of many impacts made by the microscopic molecules that make it up. Einstein suspected that in like manner there are "hidden variables" that characterize deeper structures as yet unknown to physicists, and that in quantum mechanics we are dealing with statistical averages of those variables. Therefore in the late 1920s,

> [Einstein] set to work to try to demolish the accepted version of quantum mechanics. The point to which his assault was directed was the distasteful uncertainty principle. He sought to show by ingenious argument that it must be false because he could find thought experiments that circumvented it. The late 1920s resounded to a ding-dong battle between Einstein and Bohr on this issue. The one would propose clever trick after clever trick to beat the Heisenberg relation, whilst the other would show with equal persistence that further thought revealed a flaw in each successive suggestion. In the end the immovable object vanquished the irresistible force. The uncertainty principle survived unscathed.... Nevertheless [Einstein] remained highly skeptical of quantum theory. (Polkinghorne 1985, 54–55)

So in 1935 Einstein and two young collaborators, Boris Podolsky and Nathan Rosen, proposed a thought experiment that they believed showed the implausibility of quantum mechanics as an ultimate account of the nature of physical reality. (Their thought experiment is often referred to as the EPR experiment, and the three authors themselves are often referred to by the same acronym.) EPR were convinced that in order to be plausible a complete physical theory must be both *realistic* and *local*. "Realistic" means, roughly, that the world exists and possesses definite properties whether or not any human being or sentient animal is around to observe them. A tree falling all by itself in the middle of the forest still makes a noise. Assuming that general point of view is true, EPR defined carefully what they meant by physical reality: "If, without in any way disturbing a system, we can predict with certainty (i.e. with probability equal to unity) the value of a physical quantity, then there exists an element of physical reality corresponding to this physical quantity."[3] With Max Jammer, let us call this the *reality criterion*. In addition to the reality criterion, EPR also stated a *completeness criterion*: "Every element of the physical reality must have a counterpart in the physical theory" (ibid.).

Thus, in 1935 Einstein was willing to admit that QM gives correct statistical statements about the world, but he was not willing to admit that it gives us the full story. He was still convinced that it leaves out details about the hidden variables he thought lay behind QM. These hidden variables would, he believed, appear in the future theory he desired, one that would describe all the important elements of reality. With regard to Einstein's realism, it is also important to note that his view of the world was deterministic. Even though he did not say so explicitly in the EPR article, for him realism was associated with determinism. This was the view of most physicists in the classical era during which Einstein formed his basic understanding of the world.

"Locality" implies that "action at a distance" is impossible. If two systems are not in direct contact with one another, then they can affect one another only mediately, that is, through some intermediate entity or entities. It takes time for one system to act directly on a medium and then for the medium to relay the influence of the first system to the second. According to Einstein's theory of relativity, this cannot happen any faster than the speed of light. Therefore, if two events are too far apart for a signal traveling at the speed of light to go from the first one to the second before the second is already over, then the first event cannot influence the second one in any way. In such cases one says that the two events are "spacelike separated."

Assuming the validity of both locality and relativity theory, EPR proceeded to propose their thought experiment. According to the basic laws of well-accepted physics, the two identical particles have equal and opposite velocities and are now located equal distances away from the motionless source, one of them to its left and the other to its right. However, in QM one still cannot know exactly where either of the particles is situated. In order to do so one must measure the position of one of them (say L). In that case one could also know the position of R even without measuring it. Furthermore, even though one has not actually measured the momentum of L, one still could have done so. This means that, in virtue of EPR's principles of reality and completeness, R really has a definite momentum.

This line of reasoning contradicts the usual Copenhagen interpretation of QM according to which the position and momentum of a particle do not have simultaneous reality. Therefore, EPR concluded, in spite of the fact that QM cannot know them simultaneously, a complete future theory would be able to do so. Supposedly, the present theory, QM, is an incomplete theory that does not give us complete information about either R or L (Einstein et al. 1935, 780; B. Greene 2004, 101).

For Einstein and his collaborators, to be a fundamental theory quantum mechanics had to be at once realistic and local. Bohr probably agreed with Einstein that quantum mechanics is and should be local. But by no means did he agree with Einstein's deterministic realism or the incompleteness of QM. Many commentators have been baffled in their efforts to grasp clearly the nature of Bohr's philosophy. Einstein confessed that, in spite of considerable effort, he never managed to do so. Nor did Bell. But according to Henry Stapp, in spite of his obscure style Bohr was probably a straightforward pragmatist very much akin to the American psychologist and philosopher William James.

At any rate, for the better part of the past century the Copenhagen interpretation of quantum mechanics propounded by Bohr, Heisenberg, and others has proven to be very useful scientifically. Nevertheless it seemed to Einstein, Schrödinger, de Broglie, Bohm, Bell, and other outstanding physicists inclined to realism, that in the final analysis it does not make philosophical sense. According to Polkinghorne, in the face of the EPR argument of 1935,

> Bohr as usual was imperturbable. The Copenhagen school had made a special point of emphasizing that one ought never to think of quantum mechanical systems without also annexing to them the array of classical measuring instruments with which it was proposed to make the observations. It was, in their view, a package deal. Change the observations you were going to make and you had a new situation, even if the system to be observed remained the same. This was their way of making the celebrated assertion that quantum mechanics does not allow a separation between observer and the system observed. (Polkinghorne 1985, 71)

For Bohr, an experimenter who has chosen to measure one of two conjugate variables could not legitimately take account of what would have happened if he had chosen to measure the other. That view of things may seem purely arbitrary to a scientific realist like Einstein, but for Bohr QM seems to have been ultimately a set of pragmatic rules that govern correct thinking about the microworld. For him, that thinking is obviously right because it provides a coherent set of procedures that yield empirically adequate results. Empirical adequacy decides about the nature of reality, rather than one's intuitive beliefs.

> This reply illustrates the strengths and weaknesses of the rather positivist approach of Bohr and his friends, with their emphasis on classical measuring apparatus. It enabled them to shrug off EPR, but at the cost, one might think, of refusing to face the issue. There is a way of proceeding in conceptual matters whose method is to define away any inconvenient difficulty. All the really tricky questions are declared meaningless, despite the fact that they are sufficiently well comprehended to give rise to perplexity. On the EPR paradox it seemed that the Copenhagen school had achieved just such a Pyrrhic victory. (Polkinghorne 1985, 72)

Bohm's Improved Experiment

The EPR thought experiment of 1935 had exhibited a paradox its authors believed to be at the heart of quantum mechanics. Nevertheless, on the whole, physicists paid little attention to it. I suppose that their focus was on the remarkable new discoveries about nature they were making by means of QM. Even if it might be defective in some way or other, they thought it was a good enough practical means to enable them to make further progress. Let someone else worry about its theoretical foundations.

However, there were others besides Einstein and Bohr who were fascinated by questions about its foundations. One was David Bohm, who in 1951 simplified and improved the original EPR experiment. His modified version is sometimes called the EPRB experiment. In a later essay, he and his colleague Yakir Aharonov considered not the position and momentum of two elementary particles like electrons or protons, but their "spin" (Bohm and Aharonov 1957, 1070–76).

The spin of an elementary particle like an electron is in some ways like the spin of a baseball. Like a baseball, an electron spins around an axis through its center of gravity. However, unlike a baseball, an electron is always spinning at the same rate, so its spin seems to be one of its fundamental properties. Even though its magnitude is known, the direction in which the spin is oriented is often unknown. When it is measured, the spin lines up or down in the spatial direction along which it is being measured. As a result, the measurement can tell us the spin's present orientation, not what it was before the measurement.

In their 1957 essay, Bohm and Aharonov pointed out,

> [I]n order to find out whether the EPR particles behaved in the way Einstein and his colleagues found objectionable, one would have to use a delayed-choice mechanism. That is, an experimenter would have to choose which spin direction to measure in the experiment only after the particles are in flight.[4]

Einstein had assumed that in the beginning of an EPR experiment two particles, say L and R, would interact and thus become entangled and acquire certain correlations with one another. When they separated far enough from one another they would become spacelike separated, and so a change in the state of one would no longer be capable of affecting the other. Therefore, L would not be able to inform R what had happened to it before the experiment was over. The measurement of L in some random direction would disrupt the original correlation between the two, and the results of the two measurements would no longer show the same sort of correlation as existed between them in the beginning—unless there was some faster-than-light connection between them.

Let me summarize the EPRB experiment that John Bell had in mind when he developed his famous theorem in 1964. It consisted of a long sequence of repeated, independent trials. The reason for the repetition is that the behavior of individual electrons exhibits a stochastic element, and as a result seeing what one of them does on a given occasion may not tell us much about the average behavior of electrons in general. Just as one has to experience human behavior repeatedly in order to acquire wisdom about it, so physicists must get statistical data about how electrons behave on average, as well as how much they are likely to vary from the average on particular occasions.

In each trial a suitable source emits two electrons that are "entangled" with one another in such a way as to constitute a single quantum system whose total spin is zero. Both spins are oriented in the plane perpendicular to the x-axis along which they are traveling, and are opposite to one another in that plane (i.e., the y/z plane). The two electrons (call them L and R) travel away from the source in opposite directions, L in the −x direction, and R in the +x direction. They are not scattered or otherwise interfered with before both arrive at experimental areas on the left and right respectively. When the electrons arrive in the experimental areas, the device on the left sets itself to measure the spin in a random way along either axis θ_1 or axis θ_2. Similarly, the right-hand detector sets itself to measure in a random way along either ψ_1 or ψ_2. The two switching devices are independent of one another so that there is no correlation between the axis of measurement on the left and the one on the right. Moreover, the measurements are not made before L and R have separated far enough apart to make it (seemingly) impossible for information about what happens on one side to reach the other side before both measurements have already been completed. In other words, the two measurement events are spacelike separated. Only a faster-than-light (superluminal) signal, which relativity theory says is impossible, would make possible cooperative behavior between what happens on the left and what happens on the right.

Bell's Theorem

John Bell discovered his remarkable theorem in 1964. As Amir Aczel tells us, it "presents a *theorem of alternatives*: either local hidden variables are right, or quantum mechanics is right, but not both. And if quantum mechanics is the correct description of the micro-world, then nonlocality is an important feature of this world" (Aczel 2001, 145).

It was now up to experimental physicists to determine whether or not the rather subtle predictions of QM about this matter could be verified experimentally. During the 1970s and early 1980s they accomplished the task. The work of a number of people culminated in the experiment performed by Alain Aspect and colleagues in Paris in 1982. Their experiment showed that something about the conventional point of view is wrong. What is it? The only likely possibility seems to be that the measurements of L and R are not independent and are influencing one another in spite of the fact that they are spacelike separated. Quantum theory seems to have been saying this in a covert way ever since the beginning, in spite of the fact that this was not recognized clearly before Bell's theorem pointed it out. Entangled spacelike separated particles seem to exert upon one another the kind of instantaneous "spooky" action at a distance that Einstein abhorred.

The experimental evidence obtained by EPRB experiments does not absolutely prove that superluminal signals are transmitted instantaneously, but only that they are transmitted much faster than light. One might suppose perhaps that these signals depend on some sort of medium different from the medium light signals rely on, and that even though they travel much faster than light they are not instantaneous. However, since 1982 the distances involved in EPRB experiments have been extended greatly. To explain the results in one experiment, superluminal signals must have traveled at least ten million times the speed of light (Aczel 2001, 237). It is much more likely that the prima facie interpretation suggested by QM is correct and that entangled particles adjust the correlations between themselves instantaneously.

For almost twenty years after Bell published his theorem, many physicists seemed to have ignored or minimized its importance. However, after the Aspect experiment in the early 1980s, the tide began to change. That experiment was a relatively full embodiment of the EPRB thought experiment, one that plugged most of the loopholes left by earlier work. Physicists feel insecure unless theory is confirmed by experiment, so the work done between 1964 and 1982 is very important, as well as interesting. However, for my mainly philosophical purposes I need report only that the work was done and has been confirmed by further theoretical and experimental work.

I should mention that, even though Bell's theorem was originally obtained by reflection upon quantum spin, experimentalists found it better to make use of photons and their polarization, instead of spinning electrons. The polarization of photons is analogous to the spin of electrons. In the same way that the microscopic spin of electrons can be (partially) understood, so in the same way the microscopic polarization of photons can be understood.

Notes

1. Aczel is quoting Erwin Schrödinger, from the *Proceedings of the Cambridge Philosophical Society* 31 (1935): 555.
2. P. A. Schilpp, ed., *Albert Einstein, Philosopher Scientist* (Evanston, IL: Library of Living Philosophers, 1949), 666; quoted by Bell, *Speakable and Unspeakable in Quantum Mechanics*, 90.
3. Einstein et al., *Physical Review* 47 (1935): 777. There is a distinction between the mathematical models used in physics and the real entities they are meant to represent. For that reason the authors speak of both the mathematical quantities they use and the elements of physical reality.
4. Aczel, *Entanglement*, 127–28, referring to the article of Bohm and Aharonov entitled "Discussion of Experimental Proof for the Paradox of Einstein, Podolsky and Rosen." Bohm and Aharonov also pointed out that not only leptons like electrons but also bosons like photons could be used to study the EPR paradox.

CHAPTER 6

The Nature of Time

Sixteen centuries ago, St. Augustine made a famous remark about time: "What then *is* time? If no one asks me, I know; if I want to explain it to a questioner, I do not know" (*Conf.* 11.14; Augustine 1943). Nevertheless, it seems to me that even though we still do not understand time as well as we would like, we have learned something about it in recent centuries.

For Aristotle, the fundamental motion of the universe was the rotation of the stars around the Earth. To him this motion seemed to be eternal, but for us of the twenty-first century the rotation of the stars is obviously not eternal. It seems that the fundamental motion of the universe is the process of cosmic evolution. At each new moment of time the world develops and becomes more than it was. We who are part of the world participate in and experience this development.[1]

But when I speak of "cosmic evolution," exactly what do I mean? Among other things, I think that the past does not vanish, as many assume. The coming into existence of the physical universe is like the building of a skyscraper one story at a time. The story being built now is being supported by the stories beneath it. As we have seen in Part One, each new moment of the world occurs on several different levels that are hierarchically organized. The lowest level of the hierarchy helps determine the levels above it. The entities on the higher levels rely upon the lower ones, much as a literary composition relies upon the letters and the vocabulary that its author uses. Even though processes on the higher levels are much more important in many ways than those on the lowest one, nevertheless the development on the lowest level partially determines all the higher levels. Our consciousness is focused explicitly upon the novelty of the present moment, but we are still subjectively aware of what we experienced in the past.

Let us symbolize in a quasi-mathematical way what I just said. There was a first moment of time. That first moment has been followed by a very large but finite number of further moments. Let us label them with the positive integers: 1, 2, 3 . . . p. To each such moment, say n, there corresponds a "slice" of the universe, say $S(n)$, that corresponds to it. In the first moment, the universe consisted of $S(1)$; in the second, it consisted of $S(1) \cup S(2)$; in the third it consisted of $S(1) \cup S(2) \cup S(3)$; in the present moment, p, it consists of $S(1) \cup S(2) \cup \ldots \cup S(p)$, and so on into the future. Moment p is the present moment, and all the others, $(n \leq p-1)$, are collectively the past. The term $\cup$ symbolizes a kind of process by which the past is being augmented with a new moment. In one sense, the past always remains what it is and never changes; yet when a new moment is added to it, the former past acquires new relationships to the new moment.

Each moment is a minimum and irreducible unit of time. This unit has no subunits into which it can be divided. Each new slice that is added to the sequence enriches and fulfills what already exists, somewhat as further touches of an art object enrich and fulfill the intentions of the artist. Both past and present exist, but in different ways. The past is what has happened so far and as such cannot change. But the present is a process that is adding novelty and significance to the past.

The past and present are real, while the future is still potential. The future, though still potential, is drawing the past into new existence. It is like a magnet that is attracting the past and helping it become more than it is. Nevertheless, the future is not yet exercising its possible future act of existing. It is a set of propensities, only one sequence of which will come about in the future. The cosmic hierarchy has a highest level on which there is only one entity that sublates all the lower ones. This unique entity, the divine Logos, is the one in whom the future principally resides.[2]

Let me repeat what I just said. We can picture the four-dimensional universe as an enormous skyscraper that is being built story by story. This image illustrates several important characteristics of time. First of all, just as the stories of a skyscraper that are already completed support the one that is now being built, so the past supports the present. Nascent entities and their spatial relationships are being caused now by the entities and relationships of the past, but they are also being drawn by the live possibilities of the future, which are already present in the plans of the architect.[3]

Even though the world was initially created by God out of nothing, and the whole is now being supported by him in existence, finite entities are historical ones that depend not only upon God's primary causality but also upon their historical antecedents.[4] If that were not the case, history would be merely a set of still-life tableaux assembled by God into a pseudo history rather than a real one. In a narrow sense of the term, the present stands in opposition to the past. However, in an inclusive sense, present reality includes both the past and the present novelty that is now augmenting the established past. Sets of new simultaneous elementary events come into full existence one after the other. After these new temporal "slices" of the universe come into existence, they are "everlasting."

There seems to be a conflict between this hypothesis and Einstein's relativity theories. According to the latter there is no such thing as absolute simultaneity. An observer who is moving relative to me will not agree with me about which events are simultaneous. Thus, according to relativity, only entities that move in the same direction at the same speed as I do will agree with me what events are simultaneous. But the work of John Bell in the 1960s and the many experiments that have followed since then appear to demonstrate the fact that so-called entangled particles affect one another instantaneously. It seems that the "now" of one particle is also the "now" of the whole universe. Besides the kind of interactions between particles described by relativity theory, there are also instantaneous correlations between entangled particles. The past is real rather than a mere memory, and the present moment is adding a new element to it. Like a skyscraper that is being built, the universe is always growing and developing.

A common way of understanding time among some physicists supposes that past, present, and future exist in the same way and that it is only our subjective point of view that makes them appear different to us. According to Christopher Isham and John Polkinghorne, "the central thesis of those who support the idea of a block universe is that (i) the notion of a set of spacetime points is meaningful; and (ii) all such points have an equal ontological status. In particular, no fundamental meaning is to be ascribed to the concepts of 'past,' 'present,' and 'future'" (1993, 135–44). One can agree with the supporters of the block universe that the past, present, and future are objective realities. But our conscious experience shows that they are also three different kinds of reality.

As we have seen, the past comprises the finite events that have already come into existence. The past continues to exist as the cause of what is happening now in the present.[5] The present is a boundary zone between past and future in which an immediate future possibility is becoming actual and is being integrated into the past.[6] The future is manifestly different from both past and present. It is not fully real in the same ways that past and present are. This is to say that the things belonging to the future do not exercise their own acts of existing, as do the things of both past and present. Yet the future has its own proper reality as a set of real possibilities, or propensities, that beckon or repel me, some of which will in due course become part of my established past. Evidently these future potentialities exist not in themselves but in other beings that are real right now. As we shall see presently, the principal being in which the future resides is the unique entity that exists on the highest level of the natural hierarchy—namely, the Logos, or Word of God. But present finite agents also bear part of the future within themselves.

Past, present, and future are real, but they all have different modes of being. The future is potential reality, the past is fully established reality, and the present is a dynamic boundary zone between future and past. It is an actual process by which future possibilities are assimilated and integrated into the past. The entire universe is an ordered temporal and historical structure that lives by continually choosing among many future possibilities and assimilating one of them now into its already established reality. The purely geometric block model common in physics does not represent these distinct aspects of time adequately. It tends to minimize the dynamism that gives time its irreversible orientation.

The Discreteness of Time

Some years ago, the eminent physicist John Wheeler compared matter to clouds in the sky. Just as opaque clouds are made out of the same air and water vapor that make up the transparent atmosphere, so the elementary particles we observe are but regions of the vacuum that are in a more energetic state than its regular portions. In his book *The Elegant Universe*, Brian Greene envisions spacetime as a fabric whose threads are the "strings" that some theorists believe are the fundamental elements of matter (1999, 377–78). From this point of view, the elementary particles of current-day physics are spacetime strings that are in a more energetic state than the similar ones constituting empty spacetime itself. In his book *Three Roads to Quantum Gravity* (2000), Lee Smolin discusses a somewhat different approach to the ultimate unity that many contemporary physicists are seeking, namely, "loop quantum theory." String theory suggests connections with well-accepted present-day physics, whereas loop quantum theory proposes a plausible way of bridging the gap between spacetime and the matter and energy it contains. Both Smolin and B. Greene (2003, 71) express the hope that the combined strong points of string theory and loop quantum theory, and perhaps other approaches as well, will lead to the ultimate unified theory they and others are seeking. These theories are quantum theories that involve discrete quantities.

For the ancient atomists, actual matter was made of very small, simple entities equipped with "hooks" that held them together. The entities and their hooks were discrete and individual. Even though modern physics is quite different from ancient speculation, nevertheless the "loops" and "strings" of current theory remind one of them. Physicists have discovered that matter and energy are discrete, and many suspect that even space and time are too.

Heisenberg's uncertainty principle shows that Planck's constant sets a limit to the precision with which one can measure simultaneously "conjugate" physical quantities. Preeminent among such conjugate quantities are length and momentum, time and energy. It is plausible that the reason for these limitations is the existence of minimum units of both space and time. The minimum possible intervals of space and time are often suspected to be the Planck spatial length, $l_p \approx 10^{-33}$ centimeters, and the Planck time interval, $t_p \approx 5 \times 10^{-44}$ seconds (Barrow and Tipler 1986, 292). The fact that both these units are astonishingly small on our everyday spatial and temporal scales would explain why the discreteness of time and space has not yet been detected empirically, and may very well never be detected in a direct way.

To sum up, modern quantum physics has demonstrated that matter and energy come in discrete packets and may be in the process of showing that space and time also consist of discrete quanta. If all the fundamental physical quantities are quanta, then history, which consists of events and their interactions, must also consist of a set of very small quanta.

THE COSMIC TREE

Further insight into the nature of time can be obtained in terms of another image, namely, the image of the *cosmic tree*. The universe is real, but it is also contingent. It did not have to be the way it is, nor indeed did it have to be at all. Actuality presupposes a broader structure of potentialities. This structure of potentialities is like a tree. It has a trunk from which grows a set of oriented branches. From these branches grows another set of branches, from each of which grows still another set of branches, and so on.[7] The trunk represents the universe at the moment of creation. The branches that grow immediately out of the trunk are potential candidates for being the second actual moment of the universe. The next set of branches are candidates for being the third actual moment, and so on. Thus, the cosmic tree contains all the possible histories of the universe. Only one of these histories can become actual, but all of them will always remain in the tree as potentialities, whether they are actualized or not.

Of itself this "cosmic tree" is timeless. Originally, "before the world began," the cosmic tree existed only in the eternal mind of God as the idea of a possible world that would participate in his being if he were to create it.[8] The divine intellect contains an infinite number of such cosmic trees. Some of them are very simple and uninteresting, whereas others are, like ours, very rich and complicated. The divine idea or cosmic tree of this world became the object of God's will when he decided to create it. At that first moment of time, it began to participate in God's being and acquired an act of existing in an initial state that was real, albeit undeveloped.

In the theology of Karl Rahner, the world has a nature that is more than merely "natural," due to the fact that God has decided to interact with it in a personal way, indeed, to enter it himself (Dych 1992, chap. 3). Thus it is, and always has been, a "supernatural" world. It was elevated by "grace" at the very first moment of time. Grace does not cancel or change nature but raises it to a new level that involves the personal participation of God himself. So at the moment of creation the supernatural nature of the world already possessed more than a purely natural endowment. When sin and evil entered the world, creation found itself in a situation that, humanly speaking, seemed to afford no way of escape. Yet at the same time it was given a divine promise of redemption in some mysterious way that no finite mind could grasp before the event. As a result we have to say that the future of the world is mysterious to creatures. It has a set of natural possibilities for the future, but also divine promises of salvation, which at present we cannot understand fully. The fullness of the cosmic tree still exists only in the mind of God. We can know it only in part.

Cosmic history is more than mere potentiality. Therefore, to represent history we must add something to the cosmic tree. I imagine the branches of the tree that already exist as having an intrinsic radiance that represents their act of being, their *esse* (see the appendix below). The radiance of actual existence began to shine first within the trunk of the tree and since then has been climbing upward moment by moment as it has traversed a particular second-moment branch, a particular third-moment branch, and so on. The topmost branch in the luminous path, the branch that is only now beginning to shine, represents the novelty of the present moment. Thus, at each moment actual history includes the past as well as the present. The set of branches that the radiance has never touched and which are no longer accessible to it represents potentialities that can never become actual. Branches not yet illuminated, but which the light can still reach, represent moments of possible futures.

Obviously, the first moment of time is unique, inasmuch as it has no created past. The image of the cosmic tree depicts this fact by representing its trunk as rooted in a ground external to itself. That ground is, of course, the mind and will of God, who alone transcends time and history.

I said above that the many-worlds interpretation of quantum mechanics is unacceptable, but at the same time it is interesting and suggestive. What it suggests is the cosmic tree. Quantum mechanics has two distinct elements, one having to do with potentiality, the other with actuality. The potential aspect is associated with Schrödinger's equation, and the actual one with the collapse of wave packets. However, one must recall that Schrödinger's equation deals only with the natural component of the cosmic tree, that is, events that can only happen naturally, and not with supernatural events like miracles that depend on the direct intervention of God.

Cosmology and Eschatology

The lower levels of the cosmic hierarchy are the ones dealt with by physics, and they are the ones that the higher levels depend upon materially. As we have seen, in a block universe, past, present, and future would have the same ontological status. They would all exist in the same way, and the principal thing distinguishing them would be our human perspective. This view may simplify the problem of time for physicists, but it certainly does not fit well at all with most people's personal experience of real time. I am certain that to discover the full ontological truth about time we must take account of the obvious distinctions between past, present, and future, which most people accept in a general way.

However, the concept of the block universe is correct inasmuch as it asserts that past, present, and future are real in some way. Regarding the future, it would be a mistake to suppose that it does not exist at all. "Before" the world began it already existed in the divine Logos, who knew in eternity all the possibilities inherent in all the worlds he might create. Now it also exists partially in the nature of the actual universe. Though it does not have the full existence proper to entities that exercise their own acts of existing, it includes a set of live future possibilities that somehow attract existing agents.

Let us call my view of time the "cosmological perspective" and contrast it with what I will call the "eschatological perspective." As Zachary Hayes tells us in his book *Visions of a Future*, etymologically speaking the word "eschatology" means "doctrine about the final reality." In the early part of the twentieth century it was understood as the Church's doctrine about "those things which awaited the individual person in death and beyond (death, judgment, purgation, heaven, hell) and that which awaited the whole human race at the end of history (the return of Christ, the general resurrection, and the general judgment" (Hayes 1989, 11). At around 1950 eschatology began to change. Now it is also concerned about the nature of Christian hope and its relation to the secular hopes for human activity in this world.

Both the cosmological and the eschatological perspectives are valid ones from which to understand real ontological time, but they are based on different interests and different insights. What I call the eschatological perspective on time depends not on physics but on divine revelation, on common human experience, and on the philosophical-theological reasoning of people like Augustine, Aquinas, and Rahner. It reflects the role time plays in our human and religious lives more than my cosmological perspective does. However, it takes little account of science. It gives us an understanding of specifically human and spiritual things whose connection with time I have discussed comparatively little, but it does not spell out fundamental characteristics of time that modern science has discovered, or at least hinted at.

The cosmological and eschatological perspectives on time are complementary. Though in this essay I have not discussed the latter to any great extent, I do want to make some brief remarks about it now.[9] One of the basic themes of this essay is that intellectual specialties like science, philosophy, and theology depend to some extent on the boundary conditions between them. All have something to contribute to the full truth their practitioners ultimately seek. Thus, Christian eschatology can contribute fuller meaning to our cosmological understanding of time, and the cosmological perspective can give concreteness to our religious understanding of eschatology.

Wolfhart Pannenberg has been a major contributor to contemporary theological understanding of eschatology. As Hayes tells us, Pannenberg holds that the usual "notion of causality ought to be reversed." Rather than thinking primarily that the present causes the future, we should realize that it is "the magnetic power of the future that draws us beyond our present reality." Pannenberg claims to know this from the apocalyptic consciousness of scripture. As perceived through the eye of apocalyptic, human existence reveals a proleptic structure. By this Pannenberg means that in the human search for meaning, the dynamic of human experience tends to anticipate the future. Put in other terms, the future acts on the present like a magnet drawing the present beyond itself to something basically new (Hayes 1989, 138).

When I first encountered this idea in Pannenberg's writings many years ago, I rejected it as unrealistic. However, I now believe that, even on the lowest level of the cosmic hierarchy, future propensities cooperate with present actualities to determine what will happen in the future. My present cosmological understanding of time supports Pannenberg's belief that the future draws the present toward new possibilities. My reflections on QM, entanglement, and Bell's theorem have led me to believe that modern physics can and should be interpreted in terms of teleology, the cosmic hierarchy, and the cosmic tree.

Pannenberg does not believe that the future is merely our human conjectures about something that does not exist at all. Similarly, in my understanding, it is something that exists even now as a set of live possibilities for the universe, some of which will in due course become fully real. However, even though as a set of live possibilities the future exists now, it does not as yet exercise its own act of existing. In the image of the cosmic tree, the luminous light that represents full actuality has not yet reached any of the branches that represent the future. But those branches do exist as potentialities in the tree. This is true with regard to the whole universe, to each of its irreducible levels, and to its lowest level in particular. The entire tree has been a fundamental element of reality from the very first moment of creation, even though at each moment of history some of its parts are fully real and others only potential. These future possibilities exist as possible goals for present agents, which of themselves would be unable to bring about the future.

Notes

1. To us it seems that even an older person who is losing the ability to use his former powers retains them within his past and adds to them the new experience of senescence.

2. In Part Four I explain this in more detail. The unique highest entity is the divine Logos, who governs the whole universe.

3. I choose the skyscraper image because some of its characteristics illustrate the points I am trying to make. Obviously, it has many other characteristics that must be ignored.

4. There is, of course, one exception, namely, the initial state or first moment of the universe, which has no finite antecedents and depends entirely upon the will of the Creator.

5. For most Christians this is illustrated clearly by the relationship between the Paschal Mystery of Christ and the Mass. It is believed that in some way the two are identical. But if the death and resurrection of the Lord is only a memory rather than an existing reality, it is hard to account for the identity between the two mysteries.

6. If, as I have claimed, the slice of the universe in which novelty is occurring is very small (on the order of the Planck constant), my psychological

experience will not be able to distinguish sharply between it and the immediate past. I experience together both a slice of the universe that came into being just a moment ago and the novel slice that is being added to it right now. It seems evident that the psychological "now" includes both elements.

7. This structure is certainly enormous. It is infinite since it includes an infinite number of possible successive moments of time and there may be an infinite number of alternative branches growing from each branching point. However, the number of branches is countable.

8. I say "before" because the cosmic tree precedes causally the actual existence of the world. Nor are the thoughts of God distinct from the mind of God.

9. See the last chapter of my 1973 book *Cosmos* for some brief comments about Christian hope and the future. For fuller discussion of important aspects of Christian eschatology, see Hayes's book *Visions of a Future*.

CHAPTER 7

A New Interpretation of Quantum Mechanics

More on the Cosmic Hierarchy

Human beings like ourselves are composed of smaller systems, and ultimately of cells. Cells are composed of molecules, molecules of atoms, atoms of so-called elementary particles like quarks and gluons. My hypothesis is that even the latter particles can be reduced to smaller ones. Each type of entity is like a Chinese box that, when opened, reveals several smaller ones within it. My hypothesis is that one can continue reducing entities to smaller ones until the sequence eventually terminates in an ultimate set of indivisibles.

This process affects time as well as space. Basic processes on deeper and deeper levels take place in shorter and shorter intervals of time. One conjectures that the process of dividing matter will finally terminate in a class of entities, or events, that are not only as spatially simple as possible but are also instantaneous. Let us call such indivisibles *vertices*. Vertices live in the present for only an instant and then become part of the established past. They are the ultimate material quanta, and by their relationships to one another they establish the properties of space and time, matter and energy. Collectively they constitute a network that can be studied and characterized mathematically.[1]

Let us assume that interactions between such *vertices* are of two kinds, either synchronic or diachronic types. We can call the synchronic or spatial interactions *s-arcs*; and diachronic or temporal ones, *t-arcs*. S-arcs form a set of vertices into an instantaneous pattern. The t-arcs are oriented toward the future. Vertices that belong to the same moment of time cause vertices in later moments and are caused by earlier vertices. I assume that the strongest influence upon the present comes from the immediate past, and the present will influence most strongly the near future.

If two synchronic vertices are immediately related to one another in a symmetric way, then they are connected by a pair of oppositely oriented s-arcs. But in general, the shortest path from *a* to *b* does not necessarily have the same length as the shortest path from *b* to *a*. Thus, the usual symmetric definition of "distance" applies only on a sufficiently coarse-grained scale. A set of vertices linked together by their s-arcs belongs to the same moment of time. They appear on a large- or coarse-grained scale to be a smooth, continuous manifold. And just as the successive frames of a movie simulate the smooth flow of time, so the succession of discrete moments in the present model simulates the smooth flow of time. Therefore, viewed on a coarse-grained scale, the lowest level of the cosmic hierarchy appears to be a continuous manifold modified by wavelike disturbances, much as the ocean or the atmosphere is modified by water or sound waves. On a fine-grained scale one discovers that ocean waves are due to many discrete entities. I take it that the quantum that waves physicists deal with are similar.

The properties of such waves are statistical in nature. They are the outcome of the independent interactions of an enormous number of underlying spontaneous entities. Vertices and their interactions are on the lowest level, and they are governed by entities on a higher level. Thus, they are potential with respect to higher entities.

Between the lowest level and the level of living organisms there is a broad realm of increasingly complex entities. The least complex of these intermediate entities may be the presently accepted elementary particles, like the quarks and gluons that are described by the standard model of particle physics. The most complex may be systems of organic molecules, things like viruses that are close to the boundary line between nonliving and living entities.

Are entities on higher levels merely accidental systems that can be completely reduced to elementary events? Or are they substantial beings that exist in their own right? As I explained in chapter 2, I believe that at least some of them are substantial entities that exercise their own individual acts of existing.

At the present time there is a dispute between particle and solid-state physicists. Many of the former believe that solid-state systems can be reduced completely to known elementary particles. But some of the solid-state physicists believe that many systems consisting of a dozen or more particles must be explained by principles that are unknown to particle physicists (Anderson 1972, 393; Laughlin and Pines 2000, 28; Laughlin et al. 2000, 32). In this dispute between experts, it would seem that what tips the balance is the context. A human person is able to know and love as one single being. Those acts demonstrate the essential unity of the entity that performs them, the kind of unity that is required in order to perform the act of existing on the human level. An accidental system lacks the unity required in order to perform the act of existing or the acts of knowledge and love that follow from it. By contemplating the unity in diversity of a human person, one comes to appreciate the holistic perspective in which substantial entities assimilate the potentialities resident in the lower entities within them.

Thus, the relationship of complex, nonliving, substantial entities to events of the lowest level is analogous to the relationship of a human person to his body. A person is aware of himself as one who is performing his own unique act of existing. Yet his life and existence depend upon the many lower-level entities that make up his body. I hypothesize that, in similar fashion, a particle like an electron or a photon is an existing being that depends upon the many events that constitute for it a kind of body. In general, the soul/body distinction that applies primarily to the relationship between a human person and his body also obtains in an analogous way to all the interfaces of the cosmic hierarchy. A higher entity is "soul" to the "body" of lower-level entities on which it depends.[2]

The existence and activity of a soul depend upon the body that it governs. The spontaneity of a body is influenced and governed by its soul in such a way that the body obeys the soul in a probabilistic way. At the same time, the body influences the spontaneity of the soul. The soul of a human person acts upon rational and spiritual motives that the body itself knows nothing about. Of themselves human bodies would not go to the moon. Yet at the same time the soul is also influenced by instincts and impulses rooted in the body that, as we often experience, can oppose or even overcome the rational motivation of the soul. Similarly, I hypothesize that the properties of particles like quarks and leptons both depend upon and are also limited by the events that make up their bodies.

Of itself a soul is not in space but is located at the place where its body is, that is, where it interacts directly with the events within it. By informing its body by means of descending synchronic relationships, a soul becomes present in and to its body. Through its own body a material being can influence another material being. Thus, a particle like an electron can influence its own body. Its own body then influences the body of another particle, which then influences the latter's soul. Apparently the soul of one particle can also influence the soul of another particle in a direct way, as may be the case of the instantaneous interactions between entangled particles that I discussed above.

My preceding remarks can be understood better in the light of theological concepts. Theologians are accustomed to defining God's presence in terms of his action. He has no body but he is present where he acts. He is ubiquitous because he acts everywhere, creating and supporting every finite being in existence. Similarly, an angel is thought to be present where it acts.[3] Unlike angels, human beings depend in an essential way upon their bodies. It is their dependence upon their bodies that causes them to be present to them in a more restricted as well as more intimate way than an angel could. But it is still true that, as in the case of God and angels, human souls are present where they act immediately. Immediate action constitutes presence, and the soul is immediately present where it acts immediately—which is to say that the soul is immediately present to its body.

I conjecture that the particles of contemporary physics are complex entities that exist on both the lowest and on the second or higher levels of the cosmic hierarchy. Just as a human being is composed of body and soul but is primarily identified with the soul, so a "fundamental particle" like an electron can be thought of as composed of body and soul but is primarily identified with its "soul." In this hypothesis, the body of an elementary particle is extended in space, whereas its soul as such is not. However, as I have already said, the soul of the particle is located and extended in space in virtue of its relationship to its body.

The body of an entity like an electron is governed not only by laws proper to its body but also by ones proper to its soul. I associate the former processes with Schrödinger's equation, and the latter ones with the collapse of wave packets. In the two-slit experiment, the two slits do not require the entity approaching the slits to choose between them. Therefore it behaves in a wavelike manner and passes through both. However, when the now duplex wave packet approaches a detector, the latter's complex structure induces the soul of the incoming particle to interact with it at one definite point, or at least in one small region of space. Hence, the influence of the soul on its body causes the latter to become localized.

Since wave packets are patterns of vertices, the sudden change from a diffuse configuration to a well-localized one is not as surprising as would be a sudden change in the shape of a body composed of higher-order entities. The living cells of an animal are substances extended in time. For cells to jump instantaneously from place to place would be quite a remarkable change. But elementary events are instantaneous, and so the events belonging to the moment t are not members of the moment $t + 1$. The set of events existing at time t is succeeded at $t + 1$ by a different set. Therefore it is not so surprising that the spatial shape of a body made of vertices can change much more rapidly than the form of a body made of cells.

Not only does the body of an elementary particle change in a different way from the way a human body changes, but also the former can assume patterns that are not like any of the patterns the latter one can assume. This too should not be surprising. I use the terms "body" and "soul" with regard to elementary particles because the relationship of such a body to its soul resembles the relationship of a human body to its human soul, but not because the shape made of elementary particles resembles the shape of the human body.

Because Einstein thought in terms of one level only, phenomena involving higher-level interactions seemed "spooky" to him, just as people who do not believe in human souls find direct spiritual interactions between distant persons spooky. However, given the requisite experience, there is no special difficulty in understanding, in a partial way of course, either purely spiritual interactions between humans or the kind of interactions studied by John Bell.

Bell once remarked:

> While the founding fathers [of QM] agonized over the question
> "particle" *or* "wave"
> de Broglie in 1925 proposed the obvious answer
> "particle" *and* "wave."
> Is it not clear from the smallness of the scintillation on the screen that we have to do with a particle? And is it not clear, from the diffraction and interference patterns, that the motion of the particle is directed by a wave? De Broglie showed in detail how the motion of a particle, passing through just one of two holes in the screen, could be influenced by waves propagating through both holes. And so influenced that the particle does not go where the waves cancel out, but is attracted to where they cooperate. This idea seems to me so natural and simple, to resolve the wave-particle dilemma in such a clear and ordinary way, that it is a great mystery to me that it was so generally ignored. (Bell 1987, 191)

To Bell and some other physicists it seems that waves and particles are different kinds of things, both of which are necessary. Therefore they believe that the interpretation of de Broglie and Bohm is to be preferred to that of Copenhagen. But most physicists think that their view has a certain redundancy that renders it implausible in spite of the fact that it is just as empirically adequate as the conventional one. To me it seems that both parties are partially right and partially wrong. Bell was right in thinking that both waves and particles are necessary. But the waves are on the lower levels of the cosmic hierarchy whereas the "souls" of the particles are on higher levels. Putting them on one and the same level makes them redundant, as many physicists complain, but in reality they are on different levels. Hence both are necessary rather than redundant.

Let us consider how this point of view applies to what happens in EPRB experiments.[4] I assume that in an EPRB experiment the two correlated particles that emanate from the source are distinct entities that exercise their own acts of existing. However, they are entangled with one another and constitute a single accidental system consisting of correlated parts. Both particles have "souls" that exist on the second level of the cosmic hierarchy and "bodies" that exist on the lowest level of the hierarchy. As we have seen, space is a reality that exists on the lowest level of the hierarchy, and so entities on the second or higher levels are not of themselves spatial. As the particles move apart in space, their bodies lose spatial contact with one another and are no longer directly related to one another. But their souls, which are not in space directly, do not lose their immediate second-level relationship to one another. Because their bodies are far apart in space, no signal of the first level can pass from one to the other before the experiment is over. But because the two particles are immediately related to one another on the second or higher levels, they can instantly affect one another on that level. When a measuring device affects the body of a given particle, the shape of that body is instantly affected. This disturbance affects immediately the soul of the particle in question, which instantly affects the soul of the distant particle, and then the latter's own body.

In 1905, Einstein's special theory of relativity convinced physicists that the commonsense understanding of time was incorrect. It seemed that there is no universal "now," no absolute simultaneity that applies to the whole universe. But the work of John Bell and others seems to have shown that entangled particles affect one another instantaneously. It appears that there are different kinds of "interaction" between two spacelike separated particles. One involves the classical interactions that communicate definite information. The other is the more recently discovered quantum correlations.

How to Interpret Quantum Mechanics

We saw earlier that quantum mechanical equations have two very different kinds of solutions. One, the "retarded" solutions, represents quantum waves that are caused by a given event, e_1, and travel, in the way one would expect, into the future where they are absorbed by the future event, e_2. The other, "advanced" solutions, represents quantum waves that are caused by a future event, e_2, and then travel, against the normal flow of time, into the past, where they are absorbed by e_1. Usually the advanced waves are regarded as "unphysical" and are therefore ignored. However, as we have seen, John Cramer found that by making use of both the retarded and the advanced solutions he could interpret QM in a different way than usual. His "transactional" interpretation yields nearly the same mathematical and empirical results as the standard Copenhagen interpretation, and so to some it seems to provide a conceptual model that helps people "to think clearly about what is going on in the quantum world, a tool which is likely to be particularly useful in teaching, and which has considerable value in developing intuitions and insights into otherwise mysterious quantum phenomena" (Gribbin 1995, 234–40).

Yet in spite of its advantages, the transactional interpretation has not been widely accepted, for as it stands it seems to clash with common sense. However, in the light of the understanding of time that I explained in the previous chapter, Cramer's interpretation can be reinterpreted in a way that makes better sense.[5] In my philosophical context, it makes more sense to begin with the future rather than the present. The future always exists, not as actual but as potential, that is, as a set of propensities. The divine idea of our universe (that is, its "cosmic tree") includes all its possible histories. When the world was created these possible histories came to exist as possibilities in the nature of the Logos. At each moment of time, the live possibilities (the ones that have not yet been bypassed by earlier decisions) constitute the future. These live possibilities are propensities that solicit the cooperation of presently existing entities and invite them to act as efficient agents in such a way as to make some of the live possibilities become fully real. As propensities, they exist now, even though they do not exist as full actualities that exercise their own acts of existing. Since they solicit and attract the cooperation of existing entities, they can be called *telic* causes.

The telic causes are something in the mind of the Logos that guides the whole universe. An agent would not act were it not tacitly aware of the fact that there is a future and hopes that its present action will produce an effect worth its effort. For an agent to act there has to be some live future possibility that induces the agent's present activity. The agent is not sure exactly what this live possibility is, but it knows it is there in some way. The agent is tacitly aware that there is a live possibility that will become fully real in the future and will assimilate the activity the agent is planning to exercise.

An agent conceives of such a live possibility in accord with what it hopes for now. It can, of course, be deceived. Agents in general, and human beings in particular, are subject to illusion and are usually enveloped to some extent in a haze of maya. However, they try their best to see through that haze to the reality of a future that already exists in some way or other. Hope is an essential requisite for activity. Real future possibilities cannot exist now in the sense of exercising now their own acts of existing, but they do exist now in the nature of the Logos as well as in the natures of the particular agents that will help bring the future about. It is true that the explicit goal that a finite agent envisions may never come to be because things may not work out the way he wants. Moreover, sometimes one's goal or final cause was never even possible at all, and there had never been a real potentiality for it in the nature of the universe. Nevertheless, illusive hopes could not exist if real future potentialities did not exist. One can mistake the character of the future, but one knows it exists some way or other. Mistakes are not possible unless there is something for us to be mistaken about.

In the theology of Wolfhart Pannenberg, "the future acts on the present like a magnet drawing the present beyond itself to something basically new" (Hayes 1989, 138). Is Pannenberg's claim true? Does he mean that in some way the future exists now and is thus able to attract the present? The Pauline author of the letter to the Colossians quotes a fragment from an early Christian hymn about Jesus Christ:

> He is the image of the invisible God, the firstborn of all creation; for in him all things in heaven and on earth were created, things visible and invisible, whether thrones or dominations or rulers or powers—all things have been created through him and for him. He himself is before all things, and in him all things hold together. (Col 1:15–17)

These verses do not seem to focus on Jesus's eternal and divine status as the second person of the blessed Trinity. Rather, they apparently focus on his status as the person who is the head of the universe. As such, he is the "firstborn of all creation," the one who from the beginning holds all things together. He is the one who unites all finite beings into his own unity. Since he is the firstborn of all creation, these verses do not refer to his later incarnation but rather to what I call his "incosmation." He unifies all other finite beings as his "cosmic body." This "cosmic nature" of the divine Logos is evidently not identical with his human nature, by which he later becomes an individual member of our race.

In Cramer's scheme, at t_1 event e_1 sends an "offer" wave to e_2 at t_2. Event e_2 responds by sending a "confirmation" wave back in time to e_1 at t_1. It is then up to e_1 whether or not to close the deal. If it does, the potential "transaction" between e_1 and e_2 becomes fully actual (Gribbin 1995, 239). But in my modified version of the scheme, the opposite is true. At t_1, event e_2 is still merely a propensity latent in the nature of the divine Logos. When suitable conditions arise, such propensities solicit the efficient action of e_1. As a propensity, e_2 exerts a telic influence upon e_1 and invites it to become an efficient agent. This telic influence of e_2 upon e_1 is represented in QM by the advanced wave that e_2 sends to e_1. As a propensity, e_2 exists in a qualified sense even at the moment t_1, and therefore, in a broad sense of the term, the present includes the possible future and the possible future is in the present, inviting the agent to act.

One sees that there is a certain ambiguity about the meaning of the term "future" that is similar to the ambiguity about the meaning of the "past" that we noted earlier. Just as the past is in one sense distinct from the present but is in another sense a part of the present, so in one sense the future is distinct from the present but is in another sense a part of it. Before the future becomes fully real it is already a set of present propensities that are exercising influence upon the present. At time t_1, when e_1 is affected by the telic influence of the propensity e_2, it is up to e_1 whether or not to complete the transaction that is being offered to it. If it chooses to do so, its potential causal relationship with e_2 becomes fully actual at t_2. In terms of QM one would say that, in response to the advanced wave from e_2, e_1 sends a retarded wave to e_2 and this wave combines with the advanced wave from e_2 to constitute a real causal relationship between e_1 and e_2.

Suppose that e_1 is an event that occurs at t_1 and at a point in space that is the center of a sphere of detectors. Moreover, e_2 occurs at t_2 at some point on that sphere. But just where e_2 will occur cannot be predicted in advance. In my realistic interpretation, e_1 would have been receiving offers from every point on the sphere. How is one to explain the fact that the offer from one particular point was accepted in preference to any of the others? A similar question arises in any interpretation of QM. My answer is that of Stapp, whose interpretation I have discussed already. The event e_1 is spontaneous and capable of choosing.

The ancient atomists discovered something important about the material universe. But they made a mistake in thinking that their atomic hypothesis is the only important principle for understanding matter. In the past two hundred years, determinism seemed to point in the same direction. But in the 1920s quantum mechanics revealed that we do not live in a deterministic world that forbids human freedom. Now, if I am right in interpreting QM properly, it indicates that the world is teleological even on its very lowest level.

Furthermore, as we will see in the next two parts, the higher entities that are involved in Darwin's theory of biological evolution depend upon their physical components. If the activities of the elementary entities within them are oriented toward the future, then the activities of the biological entities involved in Darwinism are also oriented toward the future. They too respond to the live possibilities offered to them by the future. As we shall see in Parts Three and Four, the live possibilities that exist on the biological level help determine what is to happen.

Conclusion

In his book *The Structure of Scientific Revolutions*, Thomas Kuhn wrote that accepted paradigms, which may well be unduly limited, govern the thinking of scientists and philosophers to a considerable extent (Kuhn

1970). Today, many of them are unable to appreciate the unique dignity of Man and the nobility of his destiny. Nor can they see that finite entities are also agents that act for an end. As a result, they are blind to the intrinsic meaning of the world.

The distinguished Viennese psychiatrist Viktor Frankl, a survivor of Nazi concentration camps and the author of the remarkable book *Man's Search for Meaning*, claimed that the most serious psychiatric problem of our age is the perceived lack of meaning in life (Frankl 1959). Many modern people try to fill the void within themselves with food, sex, money, worldly success, prestige, drugs, or even violence. A brilliant intellectual like Steven Weinberg can be partially satisfied by the meaning he attributes to his research. But if the universe has no intrinsic meaning, neither does his research. When he reflects upon the supposed fact that in itself our world has no intrinsic meaning, he experiences "nostalgia" for a world that proclaimed the glory of God (Weinberg 1992, chap. 11, esp. p. 256). But what about the many who are not intellectuals and are not successful or prestigious? They suffer an emptiness that goes beyond nostalgia. Their emptiness, as well as Weinberg's nostalgia, could be dispersed if they could be induced to question the all-too-common delusion that the world and Man's position in it have no intrinsic meaning or special importance.

Notes

1. A branch of modern mathematics that may be helpful in dealing with such systems is known as *graph theory*.

2. Usually Aristotelians use the terms "soul" and "body" for living things only and call their analogates in nonliving entities "substantial form" and "prime matter." However, I emphasize the analogy between the different levels of being and so I often use the terms "soul" and "body" in place of "substantial form" and "prime matter."

3. Angels are commonly thought not to have material bodies in the same way we do, yet they are still connected with the universe in a different way and can act wherever they wish.

4. For EPRB (= Einstein, Podolsky, Rosen, Bohm), see chapter 5 above.

5. In his book *Schrödinger's Kittens and the Search for Reality*, John Gribbin observes that Cramer's "entire argument works just as well if you start with the 'absorber' electron emitting radiation into the past; the transactional interpretation itself says nothing about which direction of time should be preferred, but suggests that this is linked to the boundary conditions of the Universe, which favour an arrow of time pointing away from the Big Bang" (Gribbin 1995, 238n).

PART THREE

Biological Evolution

8 • Modest and Ambitious Darwinism
9 • The Intelligent Design Movement
10 • The Nature of Evolution
   • Excursus: Editor's Update on Intelligent Design

CHAPTER 8

Modest and Ambitious Darwinism

In chapters 4 through 7 I reflected on the lower levels of the cosmic hierarchy. Now in chapters 8 through 10 I consider its intermediate levels, the ones of concern to biologists. In this chapter 8 I distinguish between the facts of "modest" Darwinism, which I accept, and the "ambitious" hypotheses of neo-Darwinism, which I reject. I also explain my reasons for thinking that even theological opponents of neo-Darwinism should accept modest Darwinism, that is, the basic facts about evolution.

Among the major areas of modern science, the theory of biological evolution is perhaps the most disturbing one to the average Christian because it impinges so directly upon Christian philosophy and theology. When I began thinking seriously about it some years ago, I assumed that the majority opinion of biologists about evolutionary theory is correct. But after reflecting about it more, my opinion has changed. One reason is that I have come to realize that the application of probability theory to physical reality involves two elements. One is strictly mathematical. Like mathematics in general, the basic structure of probability theory is sound. However, its application to concrete situations requires careful study, and, like the case of evolution, is complex and vulnerable to error.[1] At least some modern evolutionists are well aware of this fact, but many of them are still unaware of the plausibility of another explanation. They think that theirs is "the only game in town," when it really isn't that at all. The Christian philosophical and theological approach to evolution suggests a rational alternative. If the interpretation of quantum mechanics I developed in Part Two is correct, then the whole evolution of the universe is a teleological one that has aimed at a goal from the very beginning.

Neo-Darwinism

For many years the late Ernst Mayr vigorously defended biology and biologists in the competitive, albeit cooperative, struggle for prestige that often goes on among scientists and academics in general. Prompted perhaps by *Time* magazine's choice of Albert Einstein as the man of the twentieth century, he argued in the July 2000 *Scientific American* (78–83) that the most influential thinker of the past two centuries was not Einstein but Charles Darwin. He may very well be right. As he pointed out, Darwin and Darwinism have influenced in a powerful way not only evolutionary biology but also the philosophy of science and the zeitgeist of our times. However, whether a thinker is influential is a very different question from whether he is right.

According to Mayr, in founding modern evolutionary biology Darwin contributed four important insights:

> The first is the non-constancy of species, or the modern conception of evolution itself. The second is the notion of branching evolution, implying the common descent of all species of living things on earth from a single unique origin. Up until 1859, all evolutionary proposals, such as that of naturalist Jean-Baptiste Lamarck, endorsed a teleological march toward greater perfection that had been in vogue since Aristotle's concept of Scala Naturae, the chain of being. Darwin further noted that evolution must be gradual, with no major breaks or discontinuities. Finally, he reasoned that the mechanism of evolution was natural selection. (Mayr 2000, 80)

The full title of Darwin's most famous book is *On the Origin of Species by Means of Natural Selection or the Preservation of Favored Races in the Struggle for Life*. But even though this title refers to natural selection explicitly, it was discussed only in the first four chapters. In the remaining ten, natural selection is not the central issue. According to Mayr, they "are almost exclusively devoted to documentations for common descent"

(Mayr 1991, 95). Even though he certainly believed in natural selection and argued for it in his first four chapters, Darwin's main arguments were intended to establish not natural selection but rather the occurrence of common descent, which is characterized by variation.

During the sixty or seventy years after the publication of the *Origin*, most biologists accepted Darwinism in the sense of descent with modification and rejected it in the sense of natural selection. They rejected the latter because, at a time when the field of genetics had not yet been developed, it was hard to see how natural selection could be reconciled with the then-current understanding of inheritance. But between 1900 and 1930 genetics developed rapidly and in the 1930s and 1940s it was integrated with Darwinism to produce what is often called "the modern synthesis," or "neo-Darwinism." Besides modern genetics, neo-Darwinism accepts all the four Darwinian insights Mayr mentions above, including of course the mechanism of natural selection. Therefore, nowadays for most biologists "Darwinism" and "neo-Darwinism" usually mean the same thing.

Thus today Darwin's followers understand Darwinism as essentially a theoretical conception based upon four facts, or seeming facts, about living entities, namely, superfecundity, competition, variation with regard to fitness, and heritability. By *superfecundity* I mean that in each generation populations of organisms tend to produce more offspring than the environment can support. As a result, there is *competition* among them for the resources that will enable them to survive and reproduce. Because individuals *vary* with regard to their aptitude or *fitness* for this competition, some succeed more than others and their offspring tend to *inherit* the same qualities.

In Darwin's day most of his scientific opponents would have accepted, in a general way, the four basic properties I listed above. Many of them had little objection to drawing from those facts the plausible conclusion that

> typically, the history of a species will show the modification of that species in the direction of those characteristics which better dispose their bearers to survive and reproduce; properties which dispose their

bearers to survive and reproduce are likely to become more prevalent in successive generations of the species. (Kitcher 1993, 19)

But they did not believe that such adaptation went so far as to result in a new species. In contrast, Darwin argued that natural selection not only results in better adaptation of existing species to the environment but also brings new species into existence.

Today it seems that in most cases the decisive step in the formation of a new species is *geographical* isolation. In time a population of animals thus isolated drifts away genetically from other members of the same species and eventually becomes so different that it cannot reproduce with them even when geographic isolation ends. When this happens it has become a new species.

Nevertheless, it is also thought that sometimes a new species arises without any geographical isolation. Random variation alone can change some members of a population enough for them to become specifically different from their relatives. As Mayr (1991, chap. 3) points out, Darwin had thus introduced a new concept of the biological species. Prior to Darwin, naturalists classified organisms in terms of ideal types or essences. All the members of a reproductively isolated population of plants or animals were regarded as possessing the same essence and differing from one another only accidentally. Since the members of the population were defined by their essence, they would always have to possess its specific characteristics. Moreover, it was thought that the same thing had to be true for all their descendants. But, for Darwin, a biological population was not defined by a metaphysical essence. For him, the difference between two species was much like the difference between two varieties of the same species. In time the impact of random variation and natural selection could cause some of its members to become quite different from their ancestors and render them unable to reproduce with organisms like their ancestors. In that case it is reasonable to say that the historical population has become a new species, or else, if organisms of the original type still survived, to say that a new species has branched from the old.

By means of deliberate, intelligent selection dog breeders have produced a great many different varieties of dogs, but all these different varieties are still dogs. Darwin's critics needed stronger evidence before they would believe natural selection could do more. To persuade them, Darwin made use of what Philip Kitcher calls "Darwinian histories." A Darwinian history is "a narrative which traces the successive modifications of a lineage of organisms from generation to generation in terms of various factors, most notably random mutations and natural selection. The main claim of the *Origin* is that we can understand numerous biological phenomena in terms of the Darwinian histories of the organisms involved" (Kitcher 1993, 20–21).

Darwinian selection is largely a process of elimination. It erases old information about how to construct organisms that are, on average, less able to survive and reproduce. The gene pool of a population is the aggregate of all the genes in the population. It is somewhat like a library that throws out useless books and buys additional copies of good ones. But having a hundred copies of a book does not mean that the library has more information than it had when it possessed only one copy. The same amount of information is embodied in the hundred copies as there was in the original one.[2] Thus, the immediate effect of selection is usually a conservative one, namely, the elimination of unfit organisms from the population.

Nevertheless, the information contained in one original copy is usually far more vulnerable to extinction than that in a hundred copies. If the gene pool of a species has only one copy of a beneficial mutation, random factors may extinguish it. But if the gene pool has a hundred or a thousand copies of the mutation, it is more likely to survive. Thus, selection can allow beneficial variations to flourish and finally to become predominant in the gene pool. Today random variation and natural selection together are regarded as the main mechanism that produces evolution.

But is the combination of random variation and natural selection really sufficient to cause evolution, as neo-Darwinists claim? Will chance and necessity by themselves produce a better genotype before the sun burns out? Darwin thought they would. Most of his contemporaries thought they would not. Today most biologists believe, like Darwin, that they will, but their belief is now being challenged in the light of modern biochemistry and information theory. What is crucial here is not only the more obvious things that happened in the course of evolution but also the deeper things that caused them to happen. Was it caused by random variation and natural selection, or was it caused by random mutation, natural selection, and a further factor that is even more important, namely, teleology? In other words, does evolution have a purpose, and has it actually attained its goal in the human race, at least in a partial way?

Darwinian histories are not mere chronicles. They intend to tell biologists not only what happened but also why. They explain the empirical facts in terms of a theory about the mechanisms that are supposed to have caused the facts. Thus, from the very beginning Darwinism tended to conflate the empirically observed facts of evolution with the purported mechanisms of evolution. Ever since Darwin it has been harder for biologists to keep the two distinct, and in their discussions many of them still assume that accepting the former entails accepting the latter—which, I believe, is a great error.[3]

Holists claim that evolution is the development of the cosmic hierarchy, that is, the successive development of elementary events to complex inanimate entities, to living organisms, to sentient organisms, and finally to rational organisms. But higher organisms of the cosmic hierarchy cannot be reduced to lower ones. The former have properties that are essentially higher than those of the latter. It seems that something more than the lower organisms must have been at work in order to bring about the higher ones. If the greatest actions of human beings are rationality and altruistic love, then the cause that produced Man must have already possessed the properties of rationality and altruistic love. These qualities do not belong to lower organisms in the hierarchy. Indeed, when one thinks about the first origin of rationality and love in the visible universe, one realizes that their cause must be even ontologically higher than human rationality and love.[4] This cause has to be not only rational and loving but must even be able to conceive of, to design, to make, and to love entities like human beings.

A persistent reductionist may argue that I am simply asserting that something on one of the lower levels of the natural hierarchy cannot produce something on a higher level. But, he will insist, why not? His question reflects his unquestioned assumption that everything exists on the one ontological level and that evolution is a meaningless, accidental rearrangement of elementary entities. But in fact the universe is a cosmic hierarchy that includes at least several irreducible levels. Changes on a lower level can be *conditions* necessary for developments on a higher level, but nevertheless lower-level processes cannot *by themselves* cause or produce the processes on a higher one. The reason, as I have already said, is that the properties characteristic of the higher level are qualitatively and ontologically more valuable than the properties of the lower level. More coming from less is equivalent to something coming from nothing. One must simply deny that something can come from nothing, or more from less, as some reductionists insist. To say that is to deny a fundamental principle of reason and science. I am not talking about minor, accidental characteristics, but the difference between rationality and sentience, between sentience and simply being alive, between being alive and being simply brute matter.

Examination of their arguments reveals that often materialists are covertly smuggling in "something" under the guise of what they claim to be "nothing." Thus, many physicists in their popular writings have sometimes asserted that fundamental particles come from nothing and then proceeded to attribute to nothing all sorts of properties that "nothing" cannot have. There are many ways of concealing the fact that favorite theories are much like perpetual motion machines. If one does not believe in the conservation of energy many ingenious perpetual motion machines can be quite convincing.

Even though my principal reasons for rejecting neo-Darwinism are philosophical and theological, there are also scientific reasons. Biological science differs in some ways from physical science. Due to the extreme complexity of living systems, the causes of a biological phenomenon are often complex and obscure. In the 1950s, Francis Crick and James Watson discovered the chemical structure of DNA. Early researchers in molecular biology made marvelous progress by studying problems that could be illumined by biochemical methods. But as Barry Commoner, an ecologist, pointed out in a more recent article, it has turned out that the genome is not as simple as the pioneers of molecular biology hoped (Commoner 2002, 39–47). In like manner, Darwin and his successors were able to make significant initial progress by understanding evolution reductionistically. But the pioneers simplified the problem greatly. They focused on the physical aspects of organisms and ignored the sentient and rational aspects of higher animals.

Most biologists are hesitant to reject neo-Darwinism before they have in hand an alternative theory capable of guiding their research. In itself this attitude might seem to be a reasonable one. But with regard to evolution a normal scientific attitude has been pushed beyond reasonable bounds. Darwinism is unique among scientific theories. As Mayr has claimed, it has probably had even more influence upon the modern zeitgeist than relativity and quantum mechanics combined (2000, 79–80). The reason is not that it is more coherent or more solidly grounded in observation and experiment than those two. Rather, it is much less so. But Darwinism crystallized powerful trends in modern culture (J. Greene 1959, 1981, 1999). In regard to its impact on culture, Darwinism has resembled two other Victorian theories, namely, Marxism and Freudianism. I think that, like those two theories, it is partially based on illusion, but an illusion that many moderns have wanted to believe. I also think that it is going to be partially discredited as the other two have been already.[5]

Recall Einstein's remark that, although physicists are interested in philosophy, to professional philosophers they can sometimes seem to be unscrupulous opportunists. They cannot afford to be too consistent because even though they are looking for truth, they feel they must first satisfy the criterion of empirical adequacy. The same observation also applies to biologists. In the Parousia, adequacy with respect to the truth and adequacy with respect to empirical evidence will be revealed as being harmonious. But in this present age they sometimes quarrel. When they do so, scientists usually side with empirical adequacy. Somewhere Mayr remarked that he had always been very interested in philosophy. That may well be true, but his interest was characterized by a strong emphasis on its immediate practicality and usefulness in furthering his scientific work. As a result, he, and many other neo-Darwinists, see both truth and empirical adequacy mainly in terms of objective data and ignore important subjective aspects of their own experience as human persons. Philosophically speaking, and in reality as well, this is a great mistake. In 1926, Einstein stunned Heisenberg by telling him that even though he had used positivism to great effect in 1905, he now believed it to be nonsense.[6] As we saw above, Heisenberg himself, who was something of a positivist in his early years (the ones in which he was most successful as a physicist), later spoke in a more metaphysical vein about Aristotelian potentialities.

It seems to me that neo-Darwinists have identified empirical adequacy with truth more than many great scientists did in the past. As a result they are pushing their scientific hypothesis beyond the natural boundaries of their science and are trying to take over territory that has traditionally belonged to philosophers and theologians. But careful reflection on the matter reveals the radical difference between being material, being alive, being sentiently aware, and being intellectually aware. To react blindly to other entities is quite different from responding to them like a living organism; simply to be alive is quite different from being sentiently aware of what is happening; to be sentiently aware of what is happening is quite different from understanding the experience intellectually.

Because the objective sciences have been very successful in many ways, some of its practitioners choose to minimize the importance of these distinctions and neglect their own subjective experience of existing on several irreducibly different levels. They think that what science is unable to handle must be unimportant, and they devise theories that are directly contrary to humanistic and philosophical truths that would be evident to them if they were to reflect and free themselves of their fixation on narrowly scientific values.

Darwin cast a flood of light upon a wide variety of problems in biology. Some of them had already been recognized as problems by his contemporaries; others were shown to be such by Darwin himself or by his successors. He provided answers to some questions and suggested what seemed to be possible ways of finding answers to others. Thus, he so transformed the character of biology that even those who disagreed with him had to function within the new context he had set. In short, he created a new and dominant paradigm for the science of biology, somewhat as Newton had done for physics. But, as in the case of Newton, success was bought at the price of accepting without adequate reflection concepts that are only partial, approximate truths. In the twentieth century, physicists were surprised by the advent of relativity and quantum mechanics. At present, evolutionary biologists are resisting the possibility that their science needs a similar revolution.

Modest versus Ambitious Darwinism

In his book *The Advancement of Science*, Philip Kitcher distinguishes between "minimal" or, as I call it, "modest" Darwinism and the more "ambitious" theory that modern biologists normally mean when they speak of "neo-Darwinism" (1983, 27). As we have seen, minimal, or modest, Darwinism reigned among biologists for the sixty or seventy years after the *Origin*. Its principal thesis was descent with variation from a common ancestor. The cause of variation was often supposed to be teleological in character. But during the 1930s the more ambitious, nonteleological Darwinism known as "neo-Darwinism" became dominant and has continued to be dominant up to the present. Now, however, this ambitious kind of Darwinism is being challenged from many sides.

For Christians, the essential point at issue is not the generally accepted belief that evolution (that is, modest Darwinism) has occurred, but rather the nature of its causes. As I have said, modest Darwinism is a "theory of descent with modification," whereas neo-Darwinism is a "theory of descent with modification through natural selection."[7] The latter phrase comes from Darwin himself but, as Mayr remarked, "how separable the two theories actually were was demonstrated when almost every knowledgeable biologist adopted the theory of common descent soon after 1859 but rejected natural selection. They explained descent instead by Lamarckian, finalist, or saltational theories" (1991, 90).

For the Christian tradition it is far more important to distinguish between modest Darwinism and ambitious Darwinism rather than between evolution and anti-evolution. Most Christians familiar with modern biology have no problem about modest Darwinism. The latter is compatible with Christian doctrine, and to many like myself it is quite attractive from a theological point of view. Around the time of the Second Vatican Council the writings of Pierre Teilhard de Chardin became very popular among Christian believers. He combined modest Darwinism with a strong teleological and Christian emphasis, a view whose general tenor remains very attractive to many. Teilhard was criticized by Roman authorities at the time, but Pope John Paul II (1996) seemed to hold a position rather like Teilhard's.[8] In summary, modest Darwinism is no problem for most orthodox Christians familiar with biology. However, neo-Darwinism very definitely is a problem.

Unfortunately, in defending some sort of Darwinism many biologists pay comparatively little attention to the distinction between modest and ambitious Darwinism, that is, between Darwinism as a valid chronicle and Darwinism as a specific kind of history. But even though they do not make the distinction, many of their arguments resemble the *Origin* itself inasmuch as the most convincing ones support only modest Darwinism while those for ambitious Darwinism are more vulnerable than their authors realize.

Let us recall W. H. Newton-Smith's "pessimistic induction" (1981). Newtonian physics was the most solid, long-lived, well-accepted major theory in the history of modern science, but today it is no longer regarded as the "truth" pure and simple. In spite of that striking example of the precariousness of scientific theories, many biologists talk about ambitious Darwinism as though it is evidently true. To me this belief seems quite naïve. Neo-Darwinism is certainly an intellectual scheme that has been found helpful—so far—in dealing with empirical evidence.

Yet there are convincing philosophical and theological reasons for thinking that, with respect to ontological truth, it is highly inadequate. Therefore I contrast realism with constructive empiricism and conclude that, even though the latter has much to say for itself, in the end it is philosophically inadequate. Even though science aims at truth, empirical adequacy is its immediate goal. If scientists attain that immediate goal they are liable to think that they have arrived ipso facto at the truth and may continue thinking so until strong experimental evidence convinces them otherwise.

One of the founders of the modern synthesis, Theodosius Dobzhansky, remarked years ago, "Nothing in biology makes sense, except in the light of evolution."[9] But rejecting ambitious Darwinism and falling back on modest Darwinism would not turn off the light in the biological world. It would merely mean that the causal factors driving evolution are not yet fully understood. If that statement were to be accepted, the empirical evidence supporting the fact of evolution would remain essentially the same, and questioning the truth of neo-Darwinism would open a whole new world. Variation and selection may be two of the important causes of evolution, but they are not the only important ones.

The Two Darwinian Claims

As we have seen, there are two fundamental and distinct Darwinian claims. The first is that evolution has actually occurred; the second is that it occurred mainly because of variation and natural selection. The two claims are quite different in character as well as in the strength of the evidence and the quality of the arguments supporting them. As to the first Darwinian claim, that is, the actual occurrence of modest evolution, I find the evidence biologists present in favor of it to be quite persuasive. There is no point in my rehashing evidence that biologists have already explained quite well, but it may help if I explain briefly some of the theological and philosophical reasons that support my opinion.

First, it is worth noting, as I have already, that orthodox Christianity has no objection to the first Darwinian claim. In his "Address to the

Pontifical Academy of Sciences" on October 22, 1996, Pope John Paul II stated that in the past fifty years

> new knowledge has led to the recognition of the theory of evolution as more than a hypothesis. It is indeed remarkable that this theory has been progressively accepted by researchers, following a series of discoveries in various fields of knowledge. The convergence, neither sought nor fabricated, of the results of work that was conducted independently is in itself a significant argument in favor of this theory.[10]

However, the Pope also made it clear that he had very serious objections to the second Darwinian claim, at least in the form in which it is usually presented. As he said shortly later in the same address,

> rather than the theory of evolution, we should speak of several theories of evolution. Consequently, theories of evolution which, in accordance with the philosophies inspiring them, consider the spirit as emerging from the forces of living matter or as a mere epiphenomenon of this matter, are incompatible with the truth about man. Nor are they able to ground the dignity of the person.[11]

Thus, the term "evolution" is quite ambiguous. Neo-Darwinian evolution does not recognize that there are distinct and irreducible ontological levels in the world. It sees evolution merely as change on the same level of being and value. Orthodox Christians recognize a cosmic hierarchy that comprises, at the very least, two irreducible levels, human and subhuman. Indeed, I would suppose that many think that there are at least several, and perhaps many additional levels. In this view, evolution is more than mere change. It is also ontological progress. Given the fact that there is a cosmic hierarchy, it is quite unreasonable to suppose that the world's ascent up that hierarchy was due only to chance and necessity. Evolution must be a teleological process, one that has aimed at a goal from the very beginning.

Teleology and the Cosmic Hierarchy

Neo-Darwinists ignore the cosmic hierarchy, yet understanding it is essential in order to understand evolution truly. The development of

Earth's biosphere is a historical ascent that has developed successively from mere material existence, to vital existence, to sentient existence, and finally to rational and spiritual existence. Viewing the biosphere as a whole, one sees that evolution is essentially progressive. The emergence of higher levels adds more value to the reality of the whole. To be alive is more valuable than merely existing; to be sentient is more valuable than merely being alive; to be intelligent is more valuable than merely being sensate. In its ascent the biosphere retained what it had already acquired in the past. When the rational level emerged, nature preserved merely material entities, living entities, and sentient entities that had developed earlier. Indeed, it had to, because the higher rational level it brought forth depends upon the continuing existence of the lower ones. Not only do human beings still have to eat, but they also value the beauty and coherence of the entire hierarchy. When it reached the rational level, the biosphere acquired a value that surpasses all the qualities it had before, namely, rationality. By rationality I mean, of course, not the ability to do logic after the manner of a computer, but the ability to know and to love in a human way. It is because of these abilities that human dignity far surpasses that of any other material being.

Not only has the biosphere ascended to higher and higher ontological levels; it has done so in virtue of its own activity. Its activity is teleological. From the beginning it was oriented by an immanent principle in virtue of which it always wanted to reach a goal, a *telos*. Indeed, the same is true of every operation of nature and of all natural beings. To exist is also to be an agent acting for an end.

Science can tell us about abstract laws but, as Polanyi and Rahner have shown, such abstractions would be meaningless were it not for an underlying tacit understanding that enables one to grasp their significance. Mere succession is not equivalent to real causality. In being aware of ourselves existing and interacting with other beings, we are tacitly aware of what it means for any agent to influence others and to be influenced by others.

It is true that some biologists try to saw off the logical limb on which they are sitting. Having gotten interested in the biological entities they encounter in the world, they proceed to abstract the logical pattern of natural law that they find in the real behavior of such entities and then forget that this pattern would be quite meaningless and uninteresting were it not viewed in the light of their tacit understanding of being and action, both their own and that of the objects they study. They are implicitly contradicting themselves and their own interests, but they do not look within themselves deeply enough to notice the fact.

Before Descartes it was easy to believe that every agent acts for an end. Why else would an agent act? What else would "action" mean but for an actor to strive to reach a goal? As the medievals believed, Man (i.e., men and women) is the measure of all created things. The things beneath us should be understood in terms of ourselves, not vice versa. But the mathematical logic of Descartes and the world machine of Newton made it difficult for some modern people to accept the analogy of being and the teleology that goes with it. In order to see the progressive aspect of evolution one must be able to recognize the importance of transcendental values like being, unity, goodness, truth, and beauty. A person who is unable to do so cannot recognize the fact that human beings are worth more than microbes. Thus an eminent biologist like Lynn Margulis can speak as though the world of microbes is just as important and valuable as that of human beings. She writes:

> One widely held unstated assumption is the great chain of being.... For the Greeks, the chain joined a panoply of gods at the top to, in descending order, men, women, slaves, animals, and vegetables. A substratum of rocks and minerals occupied the lowest link. The Judeo-Christian version allowed slight modification.... These ideas are rejected as obsolete nonsense by the scientific worldview. All beings alive today are equally evolved.... There are no "higher" beings, no "lower animals," no angels, and no gods. The devil, like Santa Claus, is a useful myth. Even the "higher" primates, the monkeys and apes, in spite of their name (primate comes from Latin, Primus, "first") are not higher. We homo sapiens and our primate relations are not so much special entities: rather, we are newcomers on the evolutionary scene. (Margulis 1998, 3–4)

Could Margulis defend many of the absolute statements she makes? I think not, at least not in a rational way. Mayr was willing to admit the reality of evolutionary progress, provided that one understands the term in the qualified way he considered proper, which excludes genuine teleology (2001, 212–16). I would guess that he represented the average opinion of biologists on the question of evolutionary progress. Even though he might have agreed with me that Margulis's language is unfortunate, he seemed to think that scientific knowledge is the supreme arbiter of truth. Like Margulis, he had no rational argument against a humanistic and philosophical insight that is quite obvious in itself, namely, that because of their essential power to know and to love, rational beings possess an absolute dignity that surpasses that of all other material entities.

Apparently some neo-Darwinians are willing to accept the fact that there are different "stages" in evolution but do not want to admit that those stages differ in their ontological value. They do not admit what Pope John Paul II called "the truth about man," namely, his preeminent dignity in relationship to all other material beings. Yet Steven Weinberg and other physical cosmologists insist that the universe has no intrinsic meaning. How different is this cosmic despair from the hopeful attitude that has long characterized Western civilization!

The Glory of God Is Man Fully Alive

But let us postpone for the moment further discussion of the second Darwinian claim and return to the first. Many orthodox Christians, and apparently Pope John Paul II in particular, think modest Darwinism quite consonant with their faith. According to one of the Fathers of the Church, St. Irenaeus of Lyons (ca. 130–200), "the glory of God is man fully alive" (*Adversus haereses* 4.20.7). God created human beings not for his own advantage, but in order to give them a share in his own happiness. Irenaeus's aphorism can and should be expanded to read that the glory of God is the whole Creation fully actualized. The lower entities of the cosmic hierarchy were made for the sake of human beings, but they also possess their own being and their own ontological value. The glory of God is the full perfection not only of human beings but also of the rest of the world with which we are inextricably connected.

In his Letter to the Romans, St. Paul tells us that "the creation waits with eager longing for the revealing of the children of God; for the creation was subjected to futility, not of its own will but by the will of the one who subjected it, in hope that the creation itself will be set free from its bondage to decay and will obtain the freedom of the glory of the children of God" (Rom. 8:19–21).

The glory of God has not yet appeared in its fullness, nor will it until the world has been radically reformed. It will be divinized and fulfilled when the Holy Spirit takes possession of it, heals the wounds inflicted on it by sin, and makes it a reflection of God's greatness, power, and beauty.

God is his own sufficient reason for existing. The world cannot supply its own sufficient reason but must find it in God. Nevertheless, it can share in God's supreme dignity by being a partial cause of its own perfection. God gives it the power to cooperate with him by evolving from an initial, largely potential state, to one of full actuality. We see this happening in the development of some human persons when they grow in dignity and nobility of character by responding to the challenges and opportunities of life. Analogously, the whole world attains the perfection God desires for it by cooperating with him in actualizing the potential he gave to it in the beginning.

Scripture scholar Xavier Léon-Dufour writes:

> Coming as it does from God's hand, the world is a continual manifestation of the goodness of God. In his Wisdom, God has organized it in unity and harmony as a true work of art [Prov 8:22–31; Job 28:25ff]. His power and divinity in some fashion [Wis 13:3ff] are made so manifest through sensible creation that man, looking upon the universe, is at a loss to express his admiration [Ps 8; 19:1–7; 104]. (1995, 677)

Authentic science manifests the wisdom and power of the Creator more clearly than was possible in previous ages. Before science, believers were already able to rejoice in God's wisdom and power by contemplating his works. But today they can do so even more by virtue of science's more detailed picture of how he did and does it. God is the primary cause who empowers secondary causes and processes, and, in particular, the evolutionary process. It is the same artist who is at work in both the scientific and the prescientific pictures, but his wisdom and power can now be admired even more than before. They are so great that he can even empower creatures to take part in their own perfecting. The history of the world is a cosmic drama, a great work of art that is both spatial and temporal. Evolution is an essential element in this drama.

Notes

1. Evolution cannot be studied directly by the customary methods of science, by experimentation as inference from the particular to the general, by results to be confirmed in further experimentation, by the method of induction. It is a historical event that occurred once in the distant past, and only the outcomes are observed. This form of inference has been called abduction, a term used by the American philosopher Charles Sanders Peirce, meaning inference from effect to cause, also called inference to the best explanation. Probability theory is used to estimate the chance of a particular cause of a given observed outcome as compared with some other hypothetical cause(s) of the same outcome (Hacking 2001, 16–17; Dembski and Meyer 2000, 223–28).

2. See the discussion of probability and information theory in Dembski 2002, 125–29.

3. Ayala distinguishes between the two in "The Evolution of Life: An Overview" (1998, 22).

4. Somewhere Francis Crick has written that the origin of life on Earth may well be due to the seeding here of a rational species from some other planet. However, this explanation seems to be quite far-fetched. Crick still has to explain how rationality was first introduced into the universe. Does he imply that the world is eternal and that a rational species was able to survive the Big Bang?

5. I do not mean that any of the three is totally discredited. I believe that all three pointed out important aspects of the modern problematic, but they presented oversimplified solutions that aroused unwonted enthusiasm on the basis of dubious assumptions.

6. Weinberg, *Dreams of a Final Solution*, 180, 299n; quoting Heisenberg, *Encounters with Einstein, and Other Essays on People, Places and Particles*, 114.

7. Mayr, *One Long Argument*, 90, quoting Darwin's *Origins* [1859], 459. Modest Darwinism is much like a chronicle, whereas ambitious Darwinism is definitely a theory.

8. See his Address to the Pontifical Academy of Sciences, October 22, 1996. However, I must add that Teilhard was lukewarm about the doctrine of original sin, whereas the Pope believed in it firmly.

9. T. Dobzhansky, as quoted by Mayr in *What Evolution Is*, 39.

10. The text of the address is available on the Internet: "Address to the Pontifical Academy of Sciences," no. 4, http://www.pas.va/content/accademia/en/magisterium/johnpaulii/22october1996.html.

11. On the op-ed page (A23) of the *New York Times* of July 7, 2005, the Catholic cardinal of Vienna, Christoph Schönborn, objected that many defenders of neo-Darwinism have claimed that the late Pope John Paul II accepted neo-Darwinism. As Schönborn says, "this is not true." Careful reading of what Pope John Paul II said to the Pontifical Academy of Sciences on October 22, 1996, as well as his other writings, shows clearly that he did not accept neo-Darwinism and that the correct interpretation of his words is that neo-Darwinism is wrong (in addition to n. 10 above, the address is also available at http://inters.org/John-Paul-II-Academy-Sciences-October-1996). Two days later, on Saturday, July 9, 2005, the heading of a first-page article in the *New York Times* said, "Leading Cardinal Redefines Church's View on Evolution." This also is not true. As Fr. Vincent Cushing remarks in his letter to the *Times* on July 13, 2005 (p. A20), Cardinal Schönborn is not redefining anything. Nevertheless, as a bishop, an excellent theologian, and an important editor of the *Catechism of the Catholic Church*, he is offering us his interpretation of Catholic doctrine. In my opinion, his July 7 comments are quite correct. But I do not agree with Fr. Cushing if he means that there is no Catholic teaching about evolution. As Cardinal Schönborn has explained, Pope John Paul II taught us about it, not infallibly but with a lesser degree of authority to which individual Catholics need to pay attention when they make up their own minds. I, of course, agree with both the late Pope and with Schönborn.

CHAPTER 9

The Intelligent Design Movement

Editor's Note

Since Richard Pendergast's death in 2012 there have been further developments in the intelligent design (ID) movement, and the subject remains of central importance. To preserve the continuity and cohesiveness of the author's thought, it seemed best to leave his text unchanged, and to add an "Editor's Update" at the end of the next chapter.

In this chapter I want to summarize the objections to ambitious Darwinism that have been raised by the adherents of "intelligent design" (ID), particularly Michael Behe, William Dembski, and Stephen Meyer.

Behe is a biochemist and professor of biology at Lehigh University in Pennsylvania. He is also a senior fellow of the Center for Science and Culture of the Discovery Institute in Seattle.[1] In 1996, Behe published a book entitled *Darwin's Black Box* in which he claimed that neo-Darwinism is unable to account for the origin of the many marvelous and enormously complicated biochemical mechanisms that have been discovered in the past half-century in living organisms and their cells. In early 2007, he developed his ideas further in a second book, entitled *The Edge of Evolution*. In this book he aims to show that the powers of variation and natural selection are definitely limited—so limited that the causes of evolution must also be due to a further factor, namely, "intelligent design."

Like Behe, William Dembski is also a senior fellow of the Center for Science and Culture. He is the author or coauthor of a number of books in which he uses information theory to explore and criticize ambitious Darwinism, particularly, one entitled *No Free Lunch*.[2] He holds two doctorates, in mathematics and philosophy, as well as a master's degree in divinity. He was the director of the Polanyi Center at Baylor University until faculty objection to the work of the center caused the university to close it down.[3]

Meyer is a senior fellow and the director of the Center for Science and Culture. He has a Ph.D. in the history and philosophy of science from Cambridge University (UK) and has published numerous essays on the subject of intelligent design, and a book, *Signature in the Cell: DNA and the Evidence for Intelligent Design* (2009).

Irreducible Biochemical Mechanisms

The discovery of the chemical structure of DNA in 1953 by James Watson and Francis Crick was probably the most important scientific event of the last half of the twentieth century. At first it was thought that this discovery reinforced neo-Darwinism, but as Behe pointed out in his first book, *Darwin's Black Box*, in time the realization dawned that the genomes of higher animals are even more complex than had been supposed. According to Behe, the discoveries of biochemistry in the past fifty years have intensified a basic problem about Darwinism that had been pointed out by skeptics from the very beginning. Darwinists spoke about the process of evolution in relatively general, abstract terms, but they have never known precisely how the system works in detail. It is true that since Darwin's time evolutionary theory has become much more detailed and concrete. However, during the same period the fields of biochemistry and molecular biology have developed.[4] According to Behe, the enormously detailed information about the operations of living organisms discovered since the mid-1950s has

> paralyzed science's attempt to explain their origins. There has been virtually no attempt to account for the origin of specific complex biomolecular systems, much less any progress. Many scientists have gamely

asserted that explanations are already in hand, or will be sooner or later, but no support for such assertions can be found in the professional science literature. More importantly, there are compelling reasons—based on the structure of the systems themselves—to think that a Darwinian explanation for the mechanisms of life will forever prove elusive.[5]

Behe argues that numerous biochemical structures, especially structures he calls *irreducibly complex systems*, are so complex that the whole history of the universe is too short for random variation and natural selection alone to have produced them. Darwin and his successors had little conception of the complexity of modern organisms and the extreme interdependence of the functioning of their parts. In the light of modern biochemistry, the Darwinian hypothesis of their gradual evolution, especially irreducibly complex ones, seems to Behe to be quite unlikely.

As he says, in science the devil is often in the details. An attractive and exciting but general and abstract hypothesis can run head-on into stubborn facts hard to explain. Behe quotes Darwin's statement that "if it could be demonstrated that any complex organ existed which could not possibly have been formed by numerous, successive, slight modifications, my theory would absolutely break down" (Darwin 1988, 154; quoted by Behe 1996, 39). He then goes on to describe several mechanisms that he believes could not have originated by means of "numerous, successive, slight modifications." They are (1) the cilia and flagella which enable cells and microorganisms to move themselves or to move other things in relationship to themselves; (2) the mechanism responsible for blood clotting; (3) the mechanism that transports proteins within cells, and (4) the immune system.

What is an "irreducibly complex system" (ICS)? Behe defines it as "a single system composed of several well-matched, interacting parts that contribute to the basic function, wherein the removal of any one of the parts causes the system to effectively cease functioning" (1996, 39). It seems to him that an ICS had to arise "in one fell swoop" because a system lacking just one of its parts would not have worked at all. According to neo-Darwinism, evolution is a "Blind Watchmaker." It can see no value in nonfunctional precursors, and if chance brought one into being, natural selection would eliminate rather than enhance it.

But is it really true that an ICS could not be produced indirectly, rather than directly? In other words, is it possible for evolution to take some other mechanism that has a different function, or perhaps no function at all, and by means of a slight change turn it into an ICS? To Behe this seems to be unlikely. The irreducibly complex systems he considers are highly specialized. A precursor that lacks one of the essential parts of an ICS would not be useful to the organism. Assuming that evolution is a Blind Watchmaker that cannot imagine new creative possibilities, under that hypothesis it would never have built something useless in itself. The fact that they might be useful in the future would count for nothing.

In 2007, Behe published his second book, *The Edge of Evolution*. This new book may be even more significant than his first. The "edge" he refers to is the demarcation line between what Darwinian evolution can do, and what it cannot do. To find out what Darwinian evolution can and cannot do, Behe uses information from a number of sources, including (1) the ancient scourge, malaria; (2) the sickle cell disease that limits it; (3) the HIV virus and the disease it eventually causes, that is, AIDS; (4) the laboratory bacterium called *E. coli*; and (5) certain fish found in the Antarctic region. Behe is convinced that there is an immense gap between what Darwinian evolution has been shown to do and what Darwinists have claimed.

But not all biochemists, and much less all evolutionary biologists, agree with Behe. According to the biologist Simon Conway Morris (who by no means seems to be a materialist),

> while we should not underestimate the difficulty in explaining how such a flagellar motor might have evolved, everything else we know about evolution indicates that the pathway to construction will involve the twin processes of cobbling together and co-option, with at least some of the proteins being recruited in quite surprising ways from some other function elsewhere in the cell. This is not to deny that the

question as to how the flagellar motor was assembled is still unsolved, but in principle its origin should ultimately be no more inscrutable than explaining any other complex organic structure. (2003, 111)

It seems that the majority of modern biologists assume that neo-Darwinism must be right. Behe and his colleagues have replied to the many objections alleged against their theory. To me, a nonbiologist, their answers seem to be reasonable (see Behe 2007; Dembski 2002, esp. chap. 5; 2004; Meyer 2009). But perhaps it will be some time before a definitive verdict on the theory of intelligent design is forthcoming. Behe, Dembski, Meyer, and their colleagues are attacking a well-established scientific theory, and it is not likely to be overthrown quickly or easily. It seems that all they can reasonably hope for at present is to convince the community of biologists that there are grounds for questioning the validity of neo-Darwinism. If they can do that, in due time the natural skepticism of a new generation of young scientists may do the rest.

However, recall that back in Darwin's time, the eminent physicist Lord Kelvin argued convincingly that the lifetime of the Earth was too short to allow Darwinian evolution to occur. Only with the discovery of radioactivity in 1900 was it shown that Kelvin was wrong, and Darwin apparently vindicated.

Nevertheless, at a 1966 conference sponsored by the Wistar Institute in Philadelphia, a group of eminent physicists and mathematicians expressed their skepticism about the scientific validity of arguments in favor of neo-Darwinism (Moorhead and Kaplan 1967). Just as Darwin was unable to answer Kelvin's criticism, so in 1966 biologists were unable to counter their opponents' mathematical objections. Nevertheless, they still felt that there was something wrong with them. Were they right, just as Darwin was right in regard to Kelvin's objection? My opinion is that, on the basis of scientific reasons alone, no one really knows for sure. Indeed, just as the certainty of so many neo-Darwinists is based upon their so-called naturalistic philosophy, so my own certainty that neo-Darwinism is wrong relies in part on philosophical and theological arguments rather than strictly scientific ones.

As mentioned earlier, at present there is a dispute between particle and solid-state physicists. Some of the former accept reductionism; some of the latter claim that complex phenomena can be explained only by additional forces that arise among large numbers of particles (Laughlin and Pines 2000, 28–31; Laughlin et al. 2000, 32–37). It seems to me that in this dispute the solid-state physicists are right. The particle physicists accept the philosophical postulate that all complex systems are consequences of basic laws already found on the lowest level of nature. This postulate may please particle physicists like Steven Weinberg, but it does not satisfy solid-state physicists like R. B. Laughlin or David Pines. If physicists cannot deduce precisely on the basis of particle physics the behavior of comparatively simple systems, how can biologists deduce from basic principles the behavior of the extremely complex systems they study?

In their article "The Spandrels of San Marco and the Panglossian Paradigm," the late Stephen Jay Gould and his colleague Richard Lewontin criticized the facile way in which some neo-Darwinians concoct Darwinian histories.[6] As they pointed out, some of these histories resemble the unlikely stories of Dr. Pangloss in Voltaire's satire *Candide*. Both Gould and Lewontin were neo-Darwinists, but they were also critical ones. Apparently, Lewontin recognizes clearly that arguments for neo-Darwinism are partially based on his materialistic philosophy:

> We take the side of science *in spite of* the patent absurdity of some of its constructs, *in spite of* its failure to fulfill many of its extravagant promises of health and life, *in spite of* the tolerance of the scientific community for unsubstantiated just-so stories, because we have a prior commitment, a commitment to materialism. It is not that the methods and institutions of science somehow compel us to accept a material explanation of the phenomenal world, but, on the contrary, that we are forced by our *a priori* adherence to material causes to create an apparatus of investigation and a set of concepts that produce material explanations, no matter how counter-intuitive, no matter how mystifying to the uninitiated. (Lewontin 1997, 31)

Lewontin certainly would not agree that his statement proves intelligent design or denies neo-Darwinism. Nevertheless, it does support the thesis that neo-Darwinism is partially based on presuppositions that are philosophical rather than strictly scientific.

Students of the history of life on Earth resemble students of human history (see Meyer 2000). The latter are often in danger of falling into the trap of telling just-so stories. How did it come about that the United States was caught completely by surprise at Pearl Harbor? This happened less than a hundred years ago, let alone a hundred million. Yet people still argue about it. In historical matters it is wise to be cautious. Unfortunately, in our present era many people who do not understand the issues raised by neo-Darwinism are not cautious.

Probability and Information Theory

In detective stories and in everyday life as well, people sometimes need to decide whether a puzzling event was due to natural law, chance, or design. They often do so by estimating the odds for each explanation. Did she fall, or was she pushed? And if she fell, was her fall accidental or unavoidable? To say she was pushed is to attribute her plunge to design. To say her fall was accidental or unavoidable is to attribute her plunge respectively to chance or necessity. More generally, given an event, object, or structure, we want to know: Did it have to happen? Did it happen by accident? Did an intelligent agent cause it to happen? In other words, did it happen by necessity, chance, or design (Dembski 2000, 17)?

With the help of probability and information theory Dembski estimates the mathematical odds for biological evolution. To do so he has developed what he calls "complex specified information" (CSI). Roughly speaking, CSI is a particular sort of intelligibility inherent in material systems. He claims to prove that it cannot be generated by conventional Darwinian mechanisms alone. With Behe, he agrees that random variation and natural selection can and do generate some information. But he claims that they cannot do so beyond the limits defined by CSI. When it comes to CSI there are no free lunches.

To explain his basic ideas, Dembski uses numerous examples. One is the case of Nicolas Caputo (Dembski 2002, 55–58). For forty-one years

Caputo was the County Clerk of Essex, New Jersey, and a Democrat. Each year he had to conduct a supposedly chance lottery to determine which party would get the top ballot line in the state elections. Strangely, the Democrats won for forty of those forty-one years. Caputo claimed that the method he used was to put tokens representing the two parties in a container. Presumably, the Republican and Democratic tokens were equal in number and indistinguishable, under the conditions of the lottery. Then he swished the container around until they were well mixed. After that one token was selected in a blind, seemingly equi-probable way. If done properly this is a standard and effective way of making a random choice. Caputo claimed that the unusual results were simply due to chance.

However, the New Jersey Supreme Court did not agree. It noted that "the chances of picking out the same name 40 out of 41 times were less than 1 in 50 billion." Due to legal considerations Caputo was not accused of anything but the Court suggested unanimously that the manner in which the drawings were conducted be changed so as to prevent "further loss of public confidence in the integrity of the electoral process." The moral of the story is that events of very small probability hardly ever happen and if there is a plausible explanation of how such an event may have been brought about by design, then design is a more reasonable explanation than chance. It is conceivable that Caputo was honest and the results of his drawings were indeed due entirely to chance. However, under the circumstances described, accepting a political outcome whose antecedent probability was one in fifty billion would seem to reflect very poor judgment indeed. Hardly any intelligent adult really believed Caputo's story.

Chance and necessity are not the only possible ways of explaining events. According to Dembski, it is likely that in the case of evolution what happened was due in part to design rather than just chance or necessity. We know that with virtual certainty because of the striking conjunction between the very small probability of such an event happening by chance, and a plausible explanation of how and why such an antecedently unlikely event could have been brought about by design.

Dembski calls this plausible explanation of how and why the Democrats happened to win Caputo's raffle forty out of forty-one times a "specification." A specification is a certain pattern to which an event conforms. However, in order to contribute to a design inference, a specification must be "detachable." In other words, the pattern should not be dependent upon the event itself.

An example of a detachable specification is a "predesignation," as Dembski calls it. A predesignation is a specification that is made before the event. Dembski illustrates the point with the story of an archer who shoots a number of arrows at a wooden wall some distance away. After doing so he goes to the wall and paints targets around the arrows so that they are all sticking in a bull's-eye. He then announces that he is a champion archer. No one will believe him because his specification was made after the event and is not independent of the event of his shooting the arrows. His specification is a "fabrication" rather than a "detachable specification" because he made it up after the event in such a way as to conform with the event. But suppose another archer paints a target on the wall, thus predesignating the point at which he will aim. Then he shoots a number of arrows at it and if he succeeds in hitting the bull's-eye every time, people will believe that he is indeed a champion archer.

One does not need to know a detachable specification in advance. It may be that it is discovered only after the event. But whether the pattern gets known before or after the actual event, its characteristics do not depend upon knowledge of what actually happened. In either case it is a "detachable" specification.

There are other points that are also important in evaluating the significance of data. One is illustrated by medical tests. Such tests are usually accurate. However, they are not perfect and sometimes they give rise to false positives or false negatives. A false positive occurs when the test says the patient has the suspected disorder, whereas he does not. A false negative occurs when the test says the patient does not have the disorder, whereas he does. It is possible for Dembski's complexity-specification criterion for detecting intelligent design to give rise to false positives or false negatives. It would be nice to make both impossible, but since his criterion depends upon technical details of the statistical theory, that can't be done. Therefore he recommends biasing the criterion in such a way as to make false positives very unlikely. This is done mainly by demanding very small probabilities before judging that the event in question did not happen by chance. As a result, more false negatives are likely to occur. In other words, when the criterion says it is detecting design it is nearly always right, whereas when it says it does not detect design, design may still be there.

Dembski sums up his approach by means of an "explanatory filter." He writes:

> Whenever we infer design, we must establish three things: *contingency*, *complexity*, and *specification*. Contingency, by which we mean that an event was one of several possibilities, ensures that the object is not the result of an automatic and hence unintelligent process. Complexity ensures that the object is not so simple that it can readily be explained by chance. Finally, specification ensures that the complex and unlikely object exhibits the type of pattern characteristic of intelligence. (Dembski 2002, 25–26)

Thus the filter is like a flow chart with three nodes, each of which poses a question. Is the event or entity in question contingent? If so, is it also complex? If so, is it also specified? If the answer to all three questions is yes, it is probably designed. Otherwise, one assumes that the event was not due to design.

The design inference is partly negative in character. It is an inference to some cause that is neither a natural law nor chance. It is also based on the philosophical belief that everything has a sufficient cause and that the nature of an effect tells us something about the nature of the cause. In many cases the context suggests that the cause must be an intelligent agent, but of itself the design inference does not establish anything more than that. To find out more precisely the nature of the cause of the event in question, further information or more reasoning is needed.

In the context of evolution, the design inference is like a bridge that has one end in science and the other in philosophy and theology.[7] The power and intelligence of a designer responsible for the origin and development of intelligent life on Earth would have to be such that in our culture the question of God occurs to many people immediately. However, precisely as a scientific explanation the design inference explains directly only the near side of the bridge, the side that deals with the material world that science deals with. The inference detects objective intelligibility in some event or situation, and this in turn implies an intelligent designer. However, the inference and its conclusion do not specify the nature of the designer. I think that this distinction is important to Dembski because at the present time the oversevere separation between Church and State now prevalent in the United States requires God to be kept out of public education.

A critic might argue that, although there are always many things that the natural laws known to science cannot explain, the very purpose of science is to discover new natural laws that will explain as much as possible. Therefore it is unscientific to give up and postulate something like intelligent design, which relates not just to this world but also to something beyond the world.

However, impossibility theorems are well accepted in science. Dembski believes one can identify some seemingly improbable phenomena, for example, Behe's irreducibly complex biochemical mechanisms, which are unlikely to be due either to chance or to the laws of nature. Therefore, he thinks one must either accept the unpalatable conclusion that science cannot account in any way for some of the data within its proper domain, or else conclude that intelligent design is a third mode of explanation in science just as it is in everyday life. Obviously, he believes the latter choice is the better one. Science can point to something beyond itself without ceasing to be science.

Why did some scientists and philosophers of science decide that intelligent design could not be part of science in any way? Indeed, before Darwin it was part of science or else one of its presuppositions. In the realm of ordinary life as well as in the human sciences, it is easy to understand that intelligent human design is often an important factor in a situation. Anyone who reads detective stories or history knows that. Nor does one have to be a religious person to admit that superhuman intelligence and power might conceivably be important in explaining the objective properties of the world.⁸ As Dembski says, science should be able to study natural processes whether or not their cause is natural. So even though many agnostics hold that science by its very definition excludes any connection whatever with superhuman intelligent entities, there seems to be no reason for accepting such an arbitrary postulate. Those who accept it are diminishing the freedom and scope of science itself.

> Although truth is one, it has proven helpful to divide up human knowledge into the intellectual disciplines of theology, philosophy, the physical and biological sciences, the human and social sciences, and so forth. But one understands none of them fully and correctly unless one understands to some extent their connections, or at least their possible connections, with one another, as well as with the spontaneous knowledge from which they all spring. In order to understand properly and fully the nature of science, one must realize that it is not completely independent of other disciplines. It has "boundary conditions" that determine its proper place in our overall understanding of the world. By itself it cannot determine fully its boundary conditions. Therefore the relationship between science and other major disciplines, especially Christian philosophy and theology, should be looked into somewhere in a comprehensive science course. It is all the more important to do so in order to counteract the hubris that has crept into the thinking of some scientists and scholars who speak as though science determines the boundary conditions with all other rational disciplines without being determined by them to any great extent. There is no reason to claim that the cause of a material phenomenon has to be purely natural or material. To do so is a philosophical assumption, not a scientifically established fact.

Dembski's work is essentially mathematical. He uses statistical methodology to show how extremely rare events lead to inferring design in specified complexity. He employs information theory aiming to show that Darwinian algorithms are unable on their own to produce complex specified information (CSI), his marker for design. This is highly technical work, basically a scientific controversy of specialists.⁹

The Multiverse

Beside the usual biological arguments with regard to intelligent design, there is still another one worth mentioning. In chapter 11 of his book *Just Six Numbers*, Martin Rees explains that the present structure of the universe seems to depend on the fine-tuning of six fundamental physical quantities. But he does not accept the explanation of theists like John Polkinghorne that the fundamental constants we measure are what they are because the Creator made them so. Instead Rees prefers the speculative hypothesis that, beyond the horizon of our visible universe, fundamental laws and constants vary enormously. Supposedly, in these vastly distant regions beyond the sight of even our most powerful telescopes, things are quite different from what they are here. Supposedly, we exist in a local universe whose conditions allow us to exist. If we didn't we wouldn't be calculating probabilities or doing anything at all. Therefore, he thinks, the fine-tuning of the basic physical constants of our visible universe proves nothing. In such a universe there might be a very large set of different domains, each of which has its own basic laws and physical constants (Rees 2000, chap. 11; Smolin 1997). Let us call this kind of universe a "multiverse." In such a multiverse almost anything is bound to happen somewhere at some time.[10]

Dembski and Meyer think that this multiverse hypothesis is not scientific or empirical. In calculating probabilities they stop at the boundaries of the visible universe we know. If the universe extends far beyond our sight, there is no reasonable way of taking that possibility into account when one calculates probabilities. They believe that in doing so its advocates are giving up rationality and making untrammeled chance the universal explanation of everything. They think that this argument can be boiled down to the following crass form:

Premise 1: Alternatives to chance are for whatever reason unacceptable for explaining some event—call that event X.

Premise 2:	With the probabilistic resources available in the known universe, chance is not a reasonable explanation of X.
Premise 3:	If probabilistic resources could be expanded, then chance would be a reasonable explanation of X.
Premise 4:	*Let there be more probabilistic resources.*
Conclusion:	Chance is now a reasonable explanation of X.

(Dembski 2002, 86)

As Dembski explains, the term *probabilistic resources* "describes the number of relevant ways an event might occur." If one can somehow increase the number of ways in which success can be achieved, its probability becomes greater. By making probabilistic resources sufficiently large it becomes certain that success will be achieved somewhere at sometime.

On the op-ed page (A13) of the *New York Times* for Saturday, April 12, 2003, physicist Paul Davies had a letter in which he discussed this matter. In his opinion,

> extreme multiverse explanations are therefore reminiscent of theological discussions. Indeed, invoking an infinity of unseen universes to explain the unusual features of the one we do see is just as ad hoc as invoking an unseen Creator. The multiverse theory may be dressed up in scientific language, but in essence it requires the same leap of faith.

However, the "leap of faith" such explanations demand is not really genuine supernatural faith, which is based on authentic experience of God. Rather, it is based upon a decision to exclude the very possibility of God from the scientific worldview. Such an exclusion was unknown to those who started modern science and developed it for centuries.

Rees seems to be an atelic naturalist. Within that horizon there is no Creator. Given that philosophical position, the concept of a multiverse is perhaps the only obvious explanation available to him. But for Dembski, Behe, and Meyer, as well as for many others, to believe that sheer chance should dominate one's worldview is not reasonable. Rather than doing that, it seems better to believe that the multiverse hypothesis is implausible and that its originators should go back to their mental drawing boards.

Notes

1. See the website, http://www.discovery.org.

2. Besides *No Free Lunch* (2002) he is also the author of *The Design Inference* (1998), *The Design Revolution* (2004), and other books.

3. According to an article by John Wilson in *Christianity Today*, October 23, 2000, "Baylor's dismissal of Polanyi Center director Dembski was not a good move."

4. Behe compares living organisms with complex modern machines. To people unfamiliar with electronics a computer is simply a mysterious black box that somehow or other performs quasi miraculous feats. Before the past fifty years the inner workings of cells and some systems of cells were often like black boxes to evolutionists, who did not really know how they worked. They merely supposed that they did what evolutionary theory required.

5. Behe 1996, x. Of course, critics have now pointed out articles that they think are examples of progress in explaining the evolutionary origin of biochemical mechanisms. However, their examples seem to me quite nebulous.

6. Gould and Lewontin 1979, *Proceedings of the Royal Society of London* B205: 581–98. In spite of their criticisms, Gould (now deceased) and Lewontin are supporters of neo-Darwinism.

7. The bridge is the logo of the Center for Theology and the Natural Sciences in Berkeley, California (CTNS).

8. Of course the nonreligious person envisaged in that statement is not prejudiced against God or his existence.

9. It should be emphasized that Behe and Dembski are serious scientists. On the other hand, many of their opponents are also quite competent in those fields. At present many people are deciding this scientific dispute at least partly on philosophical or religious grounds.

10. In the May 2003 issue of *Scientific American* (pp. 41–51), Max Tegmark develops the multiverse concept in a way that is logical but also seems quite impossible.

CHAPTER 10

The Nature of Evolution

Seeking the Truth

Darwin hypothesized that random variation and natural selection are the only major factors that caused evolution. But today proponents of intelligent design (ID) present a rational, mathematical procedure for estimating the probability of neo-Darwinism. They claim to have shown that it is very small, so small that it is virtually impossible. It is important for scientists to continue exploring whether or not this claim may be true—for if it is, Darwin's hypothesis must be rejected.

Evolution depends upon a vast set of background conditions. No one really knows explicitly all the many factors, but perhaps one can guess the major ones. Darwin assumed that there are two, namely, random variation and natural selection. But ID theorists claim that besides random variation and natural selection, intelligent design is also important and that it is necessary to deal with it as a factor. Neo-Darwinists ignore intelligent design and weave Darwinian histories that involve only random variation and natural selection. In doing so they ignore the possibility of alternative histories that are just as coherent as their own. Indeed, they are even more coherent because they make it possible to see the relationship between biology and the meaning of a world that includes biology.

In ordinary life situations, intelligent design is often an important factor. Then why should it not be important in the case of evolution too? One might claim that we do not know any intelligent being that could have designed the entire biosphere of planet Earth. But this objection leaves out the possibility of God or superhuman beings subordinate to him. If one is really looking for the truth of the matter, such a possibility must be considered. Ambitious Darwinism assumes that science alone can explain evolution, whereas modest Darwinism acknowledges the possibility that other rational disciplines—and, in particular, Christian philosophy and theology—may have something important to say about it. An ambitious Darwinist may believe that "cobbling together" and "co-option" can account for evolution, but a modest Darwinist may reply that these processes are simply too weak to account alone for the enormous differences between the levels of the cosmic hierarchy.

An ambitious Darwinist and a modest one may not disagree at all about the lineages of various modern organisms. But the modest Darwinist may well ask the ambitious one, "What is the evidence that the transitions in the lineage we are discussing are due solely to random variation and natural selection?" At present there is no possibility of explaining exactly how irreducible systems are put together. How, then, can one claim that the mechanisms of random variation and natural selection alone are sufficient? Maybe the odds that a certain system came from another one are influenced not only by random variation and natural selection but also by teleology.

In section 5.10 of his book *No Free Lunch*, Dembski sketches how to calculate the odds for random variation and natural selection alone to cause the evolution of one of Behe's irreducible mechanisms. He claims that these odds are so small that almost certainly something else is needed, namely, intelligent design. Not every feature of an evolved entity has to be designed. The ID theorists single out irreducibly complex systems in particular because they believe that their essential components had to evolve together, and therefore the odds for their doing so are much smaller than the odds of a process whose components evolved one by one.

As noted in chapter 8, evolution, a historical event, cannot be studied by the customary methods of science, by experimentation to infer the general from the particular, by induction. It occurred once in the distant past, and all one can do is argue from effect to cause, by what has been called abduction or inference to the best explanation. Probability theory is used to estimate the chance of a particular cause as compared with some other hypothetical cause of observed outcomes. This requires careful study and analysis of the outcomes in question (Hacking 2001, 16–17; Dembski and Meyer 2000, 223–28). In the nineteenth century, Darwin did not prove his thesis with certainty. All he could do was to say that intuitively it seemed to him to be true. He believed that random variation and natural selection sufficed to produce our present biosphere and, in particular, the human race.

The change in Western culture that had begun in the Enlightenment was progressing briskly by this time. Darwin himself experienced it in his own life. He began as a typical lukewarm Victorian Christian and apparently ended as a saddened agnostic. His religious faith lacked the strength necessary to mobilize his powerful intellect to understand and dissolve the conundrums proposed to him by his environment, his own insights, and his personal experience of evil in the world.

As ID theorists have pointed out, the biochemical and mathematical complexities discovered in recent decades were completely unknown at the time. Now, just as in the time of Darwin, we are being offered two conflicting stories, "ambitious Darwinism" and a teleological account of evolution. Undoubtedly there are some critics who will assert that there is no teleological account of evolution that will hold water. However, in the next and final part of this book, I will present one that seems to work quite well, and as far as I can see also meets the requirements of Christian orthodoxy.

Around the 1930s the continued decline of Christian faith in the West, together with the development of genetics and probability theory, made neo-Darwinism more attractive to many biologists. However, the basic situation is still the same. No one has yet been able to prove that random variation and natural selection alone are able to produce evolution. The opponents of ID claim that there *may* have been very complicated processes that *may* have caused evolution without any teleology. Yet they overlook the fact that the opposite is also possible. To many, ID theorists present a more plausible account than neo-Darwinism. Science alone cannot determine its own boundary conditions. Truth is one, and to attain it one must take account not only of science but also of other rational disciplines. In the present case Christian philosophy and theology are important, and science must take account of them. In his much-discussed article in the *New York Times*, Christoph Schönborn, the Catholic cardinal of Vienna, asserted that philosophically it is clear that "the immanent design evident in nature is real" (Schönborn 2005, p. A23). I think he is quite right.

In the beginning scientists did not deny that there are entities beyond the domain of science that cause phenomena within that domain. This had begun to change by the time of Darwin, and by the 1930s and 1940s many biologists were feeling what the neuroscientist Antonio Damasio has called the "vertiginous feeling that no problem can resist the assault of science if only the theory is right and the techniques are powerful enough" (Damasio 1999b, 112).

Nowadays some scientists—according to Edward J. Larson and Larry Witham (1999), the great majority of distinguished scientists—think it is no longer necessary to suppose that God, or any superhuman being, is a factor in the affairs of the universe. They think that the way to discover objective truth is to make use of scientific methods only. The idea that a process as fundamental as evolution is due in part to something beyond the horizon of science is repugnant to them, and so they find it difficult to evaluate intelligent design impartially. Nevertheless, for a Christian scientist it is not difficult to suppose that God or superhuman beings may be a factor. It is a question of evidence and the criteria that establish evidence. Some modern scientists are thinking within a scientific box that limits their imagination, and so it seems impossible for them to even consider intelligent design or anything like it as a possibility. But science itself is not materialism. A scientist who is not a materialist will recognize the possible existence of entities that lie beyond science and acknowledge that such entities may possibly produce effects within the domain of science itself that science cannot explain. If he is also a fervent Christian, he may know from personal experience of God that he is real.[1]

No doubt he will also recognize that historically mankind has sometimes attributed purely natural phenomena to supernatural causes. Hence a scientist should not give up too easily in explaining puzzling phenomena and try first to account for them scientifically. However, there are limits to such efforts. If there is a preponderance of evidence suggesting that in the case of some phenomenon (for example, evolution) a superhuman cause is at work, a scientist should accept it.

Because in biological evolution there is little opportunity for direct experimentation of the type that has been helpful in physics and chemistry, this makes it hard to discover all the principal factors that have governed it. An evolutionary theorist has to work with the structure and behavior of the present-day biosphere and then deduce from it its past structure and behavior. Such an enterprise is a daunting one at best. It is much harder to formulate a valid history than a valid chronicle.

I admire Darwin because, in spite of the difficulties, he seems to have guessed correctly a great deal about what happened in the course of evolution and discovered two of the factors that may have governed it, namely, random variation and natural selection. His work was tremendously fruitful, and it enabled him and his successors to explain many difficult problems in a plausible way. However, even though he found two of the important factors that govern evolution, he neglected a third, even more important one, namely, teleology.

Teleological Evolution

According to Ernst Mayr, there are five different processes or phenomena that have been referred to as "teleology" in the extensive literature of biology and philosophy (Mayr 2004, 49). They are (1) teleomatic processes, (2) teleonomic processes, (3) purposive behavior, (4) adapted features, and (5) cosmic teleology. An example of a *teleomatic process* is the flowing of a river to the sea. A *teleonomic process* is one that is caused by an intrinsic, computer-like program. *Purposive behavior* has to do with Aristotelian final causes that move intelligent animals to act. An *adaptive feature* of a living entity is one that in the past was often regarded as an example of how God harmonizes natural entities to one another, but is now regarded by many as an adaptive result of natural selection. Finally, *cosmic teleology* is pretty much what I myself intend when I simply speak of "teleology." Mayr believed that the first four can be explained by modern science, and that the fifth, cosmic teleology, does not exist. His reasons for believing this are his a-priori belief that the most important evidence worth considering is scientific evidence (Mayr 2001, 82).

I, of course, believe that cosmic teleology is real. It is the influence of the future on the present. As I discussed in chapter 7, the future is the set of live potentialities, or propensities, which are now attracting the action of present causes. These future potentialities exist fully in the mind and will of the Logos, and partially in the present and past reality of the cosmos. I call them telic causes. They are not exactly the final causes of Aristotelian-Thomistic philosophy but, as I have noted previously, the two are related to one another. Unfortunately, Darwin's neglect of cosmic teleology has borne bitter fruit, perhaps not yet on the scientific level but certainly on the level of the general culture. Like Einstein, who made some serious mistakes, he too was a remarkable scientist, but was far from being infallible.

At about the time when most evolutionary biologists were being persuaded to accept neo-Darwinism, physicists managed to find an algorithm, QM, which predicts an extraordinary number of phenomena very accurately. But the problem of interpreting QM is difficult. It turns out that QM and Darwinism are similar to one another inasmuch as both are difficult to interpret. Both have two very different interpretations. The Copenhagen interpretation stands to my modified version of Cramer's ideas in somewhat the way that ambitious Darwinism stands to modest Darwinism. The Copenhagen interpretation of QM enables one to get along for the time being within the realm of physics, but it distorts the boundary conditions between physics and philosophy. Similarly, ambitious Darwinism enables one to get along for the time being within the realm of biology, but it distorts the boundary conditions with Christian philosophy and, most of all, with Christian theology. But, unlike the Copenhagen interpretation, ambitious Darwinism impinges directly upon the nature and dignity of human beings, and as a result it is causing a great deal of religious, social, and cultural damage. It seems that the brilliant successes of modern science have in this case led many people, especially evolutionary biologists, into serious error.

One may ask how it is that a view useful in science can sometimes be a human disaster. The possibility is ultimately rooted in the distinction between empirical adequacy and ontological truth. Empirical adequacy can be a false adequacy, one that is adequate for the time being within certain limits, but very inadequate in dealing with broader issues. Nevertheless, in the long run, empirical adequacy and truth converge. Perhaps even now ID may be a sign of a coming convergence.

Scientists, and especially evolutionists, need to pay attention to the boundary conditions of their science. Neglecting teleology is a bad mistake. Without it the Watchmaker would be blind and, as Dembski seems to have shown, would have wandered in a shifting fitness landscape till the end of the world. If Behe, Dembski, and Meyer are correct, neo-Darwinism is wrong. Furthermore, if my interpretation of QM is correct, neo-Darwinism also clashes with quantum physics.

In his book *Scientific Man: The Humanistic Significance of Science*, Enrico Cantore describes the situation that now confronts us:

> What is science as far as its relevance to man living in the scientific age? Science is the drama of contemporary man. The term must be taken rigorously. According to the dictionary, drama is a dynamic human situation the outcome of which hangs in a precarious balance. In other words, drama is a process involving persons and is characterized by the tension between two possible outcomes: human success or failure. But the condition of man living in the scientific age fits exactly the definition of drama given. That is to say, since science has become a predominant factor of our civilization, contemporary man is faced with the threat of social and cultural failure unless he succeeds in becoming more human through science. (Cantore 1977, 177)

After almost 150 years, ambitious Darwinism is still at best a precarious intellectual hypothesis even for an agnostic scientist. The ID hypothesis seems better. The mathematics of probability and information theory seem to lean in its direction, and for that reason I prefer it even within a strictly scientific horizon.

Critique of Intelligent Design

But is it possible that, just as neo-Darwinists' philosophical and religious presuppositions lead them to assert their atelic naturalistic theory with certainty, so ID theorists' opposite philosophical and religious presuppositions may be leading them to assert their position with the same sort of certainty? The scientific debate about evolution is being heated up by an underlying religious conflict between theists and atheists. Could both parties be wrong?

I believe that Behe, Dembski, Meyer, and their colleagues have managed to be more impartial than their opponents. Even if in the end their arguments turn out to be defective, they have at the very least shown those of their opponents to be equally so. Many of the latter hold neo-Darwinism with such certainty on the basis of philosophical and theological presuppositions that a great number of people, including myself, believe to be flat wrong. Ideally science, philosophy, and theology cannot contradict one another. Nevertheless in this imperfect world the actual science, philosophy, and theology practiced by imperfect human beings sometimes conflict, and there is no abstract or ideal way of settling such disputes. Each of them must be judged on its own merits. In the Galileo case of the seventeenth century, the theologians were mistaken in many ways. Today, with regard to evolution, neo-Darwinists deny important philosophical and theological concepts, particularly, the notion of teleology.

Nevertheless, on the other side of this dispute, ID theorists sometimes give one the impression that living organisms are accidental systems of atoms and molecules that divine influences are pushing and pulling from without. Do they, like Newton and Paley, think of God as a master mechanic who designs and constructs extraordinary machines? I hope not, although reading some ID literature may give one that impression. In contrast, the Christian tradition portrays God as a Creator who imparts to his creatures as much of his own being as they can receive.

They are not pushed or pulled but rather empowered. Thus, I fear that in opposing neo-Darwinism, ID theorists may be accepting a false philosophical horizon.

But whatever the case may be, what they say can be regarded as accepting some of their opponents' principles for the sake of argument, and then demonstrating that those principles do not prove their case. Random variation and natural selection are not enough by themselves. As in ordinary life, in the case of evolution intelligent design is also necessary. In such an argument one accepts some of the opponent's principles in order to show that they are false or insufficient. It is false to believe that living organisms, sentient animals, or intelligent human beings are machines, or that the postulates of modern theories are sufficient to explain their properties. Indeed, even inanimate entities are not machines.

"Intelligent design" does not mean exactly the same as "teleology"; however, the two concepts overlap. God's design for the world is one of love, which produces beings that are not machines but elementary, living, sentient, and intelligent beings oriented toward a goal, a telos, that is good and perfect, namely, the possession of God himself. Behe, Dembski, Meyer, and their colleagues at the Discovery Institute are trying to reach modern scientists in ways that the latter can understand. Perhaps for the time being it is better for them not to say much explicitly about the cosmic hierarchy and the kind of influences its higher levels exert upon the lower ones. They conclude, on the basis of their opponents' own premises, that the latter's conclusions do not follow. They point out that within the domain of science there are phenomena that science cannot explain, ones that must be explained by other disciplines with different and broader horizons. Their work is important because it is hard for our contemporaries, dazzled as they are by the remarkable successes of modern science and technology, to rely on the classical arguments from design for the existence of God unless it is exemplified in terms of science.

ATELIC NATURALISM

In this book I have used the term "neo-Darwinism" in the orthodox sense defined in the 1930s and 1940s and referred to since then as "the modern synthesis." That seems to be the sense in which, according to Lynn Margulis, "neo-Darwinism . . . is in a complete funk."[2] To Margulis, neo-Darwinism in that sense is now "little more than a 'quaint, but potentially dangerous aberration' that needs to be tossed out in order for science to answer 'basic questions' like why stasis is so prevalent in the fossil record, and how one species can evolve from another" (quoted in Mann 1991, 378).

In the same sense, but in less colorful language, another prominent biologist, Stuart Kauffman, has written, "[T]hirty years of research have convinced me that this dominant view of biology [i.e., strict neo-Darwinism] is incomplete" (Kauffman 1995, vii). Kauffman believes that matter is endowed with a basic power of self-organization that must be taken into account.

Margulis, Kauffman, and their colleagues are in the minority.[3] But if neo-Darwinists were to accept their opinions, neo-Darwinism would merely become a neo-neo-Darwinism that would escape, at least partially, their objections. Nevertheless, the new theory would still face many of the same difficulties that strict neo-Darwinism does today. Even though the ideas of Margulis and Kauffman cast doubt upon the exclusive primacy of random variation and natural selection in evolution, they are, like most of the neo-Darwinists they criticize, atelic naturalists. Although they are not strict neo-Darwinists, they are still hypnotized by the belief, so common among scientists, that science is the most important kind of human knowledge. If it is, then we cannot know anything above and beyond the material and natural. But why do they believe that? What would be wrong if science could not only explain some natural phenomena naturally but could also discover facts that point beyond nature? After all, if there were no such transcendent realities, then nature and the sciences that study it would have no intrinsic meaning.

Atelic naturalists often reply that divine revelation (as well as Christian theology and philosophy) is either obviously false, or at least highly unlikely. I think that, in saying that, they are relying on extra-scientific philosophical presuppositions of their own—ones that I believe, for numerous reasons, are really quite unreasonable. If atelic naturalists are not necessarily atheists, they have at least been influenced by atheistic elements in our intellectual milieu.

Neo-Darwinism is a special case of atelic naturalism. Much of Behe's, Dembski's, and Meyer's criticism of neo-Darwinism also applies to the views of Kauffman and Margulis. Random changes, whether many and small, or fewer and large, cannot generate complex specified information. They are subject to Dembski's law of conservation of information. However, as he says, there are mechanisms by which complex specified information (CSI) once generated is transmitted and moved around in the biosphere. Kauffman and Margulis, without realizing it, have been attempting to trace the information paths of CSI that are inherent in the teleological nature of the universe. Their work helps elucidate the true object of biology, which is not the impossible problem of explaining in a scientific way the generation of CSI, but rather the genuinely scientific problem of discovering how CSI, which should simply be accepted as given by science, has taken on its present form.

Atelic naturalistic explanations of evolution are, like that of the neo-Darwinists, inadequate. The created world did not bring itself into being, nor has it generated the intelligibility that is necessarily inherent in its being. Each level of the cosmic hierarchy is irreducible. The higher ones are not caused entirely by the lower ones, even though the lower ones are presuppositions for the higher. There is more in the higher levels than there is in the lower. The human soul, especially, has qualities that lower entities lack entirely.

Perhaps many contemporary scientists have gone astray because even though it is a good thing in itself, knowledge, like all good things, brings with it moral temptation for fallen human beings. Power, prestige, health, beauty, wealth, pleasure, and also knowledge—indeed, perhaps especially knowledge—tempt us, each in its own way. The temptation that comes with knowledge is the temptation to intellectual pride. We are the children of Adam and Eve, who wanted to decide for themselves, here and now, about good and evil. Unfortunately, if the survey of Larson and Witham (1999) is correct, many modern scientists, especially many of the most able, do not seem to understand this vitally important truth.

Earlier I quoted some remarks of Pope John Paul II to the Pontifical Academy of Sciences in 1996. There he said that now evolution is "more than a hypothesis." But shortly, in the same address, he also added that there are several theories of evolution. Some "are incompatible with the truth about man. Nor are they able to ground the dignity of the person."[4] It seems clear to me that both neo-Darwinism and neo-neo-Darwinism are two of those theories.

Much of what I have said thus far in this book depends more on our natural human faculties than on Christian revelation. But the project that has long attracted my interest is finding a theory of evolution that would be adequate, not from a merely natural and scientific point of view but also from a Christian philosophical and theological one. In the next and final part of this book I will sketch such a theory.

Notes

1. Besides the classical works of people like Teresa of Avila, John of the Cross, Ignatius Loyola, and others, there are many modern encounters of the human race with God. I myself have visited Medjugorje in the former Yugoslavia, where Our Lady has been appearing to some young visionaries since 1981. Such experiences, like the experience of Alexis Carrel at Lourdes, mentioned in chapter 1, often change a person's attitude.

2. Quoted in Mann, "Lynn Margulis: Science's Unruly Earth Mother," *Science* 252 (April 19, 1991), 378–81, here 379. Margulis is famous for her theory of the evolution of the modern, eukaryotic type cell of which all animals, plants, and fungi consist. The crucial steps in this evolution are thought to have been the formation of symbiotic organisms. When one prokaryotic bacterium attempted to assimilate another, it failed to do so. As a result the two organisms formed a symbiotic system beneficial to both. In time both organisms adapted to one another and eventually gave rise to one system consisting of two subsystems. For more details, see the works by Margulis and her colleagues in the reference list.

3. In partial contrast to Margulis's opinions, Niles Eldredge has remarked, "I don't think she's wrong... [but] I think she's being simple-minded. That view of neo-Darwinism is a cartoon" (quoted in Mann 1991, 379). In his foreword to the 2002 book of Margulis and Sagan entitled *Acquiring Genomes*, Ernst Mayr made quite clear his disagreement with some of their ideas, but at the same time he agreed with and approved of others.

4. See his address to the Pontifical Academy of Sciences, October 22, 1996. See 131nn10–11 above.

Excursus

Editor's Update on Intelligent Design

William Dembski published a book in 2014, two years after Richard Pendergast's death, that I believe is important to include in the present discussion. I have also found two interviews with Dembski on the Internet that I think will be helpful in understanding the ID situation, and I will give a brief summary of these. I will then add some comments of my own to complete this update.

William Dembski's 2014 Book

Dembski's new book is titled *Being as Communion: A Metaphysics of Information,* and he presents it as the last volume of a trilogy rounding out *The Design Inference: Elimination of Chance through Small Probabilities* (1998) and *No Free Lunch*: *Why Specified Complexity Cannot Be Purchased without Intelligence* (2002).

The theme of the book was inspired by the eminent physicist John Wheeler, who proposed the idea that information, not matter, is the primary substance of the world, that it is the concept that can finally unify the sciences. In 1990 he said:

> It from bit. Otherwise put, every "it"—every particle, every field of force, even the space–time continuum itself—derives its function, its meaning, its very existence entirely—even if in some contexts indirectly—from the apparatus-elicited answers to yes-or-no questions, binary choices, bits. "It from bit" symbolizes the idea that every item of the physical world has at bottom—a very deep bottom, in most instances—an immaterial source and explanation; that which we call reality arises in the last analysis from the posing of yes–no questions

and the registering of equipment-evoked responses; in short, that all things physical are information-theoretic in origin and that this is a participatory universe. (Wheeler 1990, 5)

Intelligent design is the study of patterns in nature that are best explained as the product of teleological causation. But Dembski notes that ID's conclusions are not credible in the materialistic culture that dominates so much of contemporary intellectual life. He therefore developed what he calls the metaphysics of information to provide the setting and to substantiate the results of the other two volumes. Information as the primary entity is partially manifested in matter, which is, however, secondary to it, leading to a real, but nonmaterialistic, basis of the universe. Dembski calls himself an informational realist. Referring to the title of the book, he explains his metaphysics as follows: "To exist is to be in communion, and to be in communion is to exchange information. Accordingly, the fundamental science, indeed the science that needs to ground all other sciences, is a theory of communication" (Dembski 2014, xiii).

His book *Being as Communion*, presenting his previous information-theoretic material in this broad framework, contains extensive documentation from the history of science and philosophy. The main result, aiming to demonstrate the failure of Darwinism as a complete evolutionary theory, is first given as the Law of Conservation of Information stated by the Nobel laureate biologist Peter Medawar: "No process of logical reasoning—no mere act of mind or computer-programmable operation—can enlarge the information content of the axioms and premises or observation statements from which it proceeds" (Medawar 1984, 79). This is the well-known property of the axiomatic-deductive method of mathematics. Dembski and his colleagues believe that this result can be extended to evolutionary computing, to show that searches cannot output more information than was in their input already at the start.

Relevant to the present discussion is Dembski's response to the critique of some theologians that ID has an external-design view of teleology, that it considers God a sort of master mechanic. Dembski insists that "intelligent design is compatible with a non-mechanistic conception of organisms." But these "criticisms are understandable because intelligent design advocates, myself included, haven't always been as clear as we might in our use of design terminology, not clearly distinguishing external design from intelligence or teleology more generally" (2014, 64). For Dembski as a theist, the source and guide of information is the Logos of Christian theology. He emphasizes, however, that religious belief is not a prerequisite for ID results, that this is a controversy within science. He invites nonmaterialist naturalists to engage in dialogue, such as the philosopher of science Thomas Nagel, author of *Mind and Cosmos: Why the Materialist Neo-Darwinist Conception of Nature Is Almost Certainly False* (2012). Professing to be an atheist, Nagel yet selected Stephen Meyer's *Signature in the Cell: DNA and the Evidence for Intelligent Design* in 2009 for "Books of the Year" of the *Times Literary Supplement*.

First Dembski Interview

I found a further relevant update on the Internet, an interview with William Dembski titled "How Is the Intelligent Design Movement Doing?" posted on September 8, 2016.[5]

Dembski considers the trilogy discussed above as the appropriate summary of his two decades of work as one of the founders of the intelligent design movement, known largely as the mathematician and philosopher behind ID. In response to the question about progress in the encounter with Darwinism, he said, "I would say that we have by far the better argument. Indeed, the Conservation of Information results described in my book *Being as Communion* seem to me to show that Darwinism cannot succeed as a complete theory of evolution, and that it requires smuggling in hidden sources of information that are best perceived as the product of intelligence." As for social and cultural impact, given the hostility of the dominant materialistic worldview "we may have truth on our side, but we are still marginalized."

Dembski believes it progress that, despite the charges of opponents, ID has largely been able to shift the discussion of biological origins from a religion vs. science controversy to a controversy of science vs. science.

There are two strands in the ID scientific research program. One is molecular biology, as represented by the Biologic Institute and its journal *Bio-Complexity*. The other is the purely information-theoretic strand, as represented by the Evolutionary Informatics Lab at Baylor University, where Dembski himself had been doing his work. (This program has since been shut down by the university, as discussed below.)

Despite the scientific promise, the future of ID is uncertain, with the all-out hostility of the culture leading to lack of funding for research and the supply of young talent entering the field.

Second Dembski Interview

This interview with William Dembski is the most comprehensive that I have found on the Internet. It was published by TheBestSchools.org in January 2012, updated in May 2014, and again in January 2019.[6] It is autobiographical and also gives a detailed history of the ID movement and its leading advocates.

Intelligent design research has been labeled a "pseudoscience" by those who control this part of the Internet. One may wonder why they are doing this, given that William Dembski and his colleagues hold advanced degrees in science from leading universities, state their hypotheses in scientific terms, and publish their results in academic books and peer-reviewed scientific journals.

According to the interview, as of 2007 more than one hundred professional scientific societies had issued formal denunciations of intelligent design. Dembski believes their motivation to be largely political. He recalls the denunciation of intelligent design by the AAAS (American Association for the Advancement of Science, publisher of the journal *Science*), of which he was then a member: "When my colleagues inquired who was behind their denunciation and what materials they had read that convinced them to issue it, it became clear that the materials were unread and the denouncers didn't understand what they were denouncing."

Dembski holds doctorates in mathematics and philosophy. He became interested in ID as a postdoctoral fellow at MIT, questioning the mathematical results of a Darwinian author. Although a believer, he is emphatic that Christian faith is not a prerequisite for accepting the validity of his results. If they don't hold up scientifically, they are worthless anyway. His approach has always been through mathematics, probability theory, and what he calls evolutionary informatics, the method he considers the theoretically most powerful ID challenge to date against Darwinian evolution. It is based on classical information theory, created at Bell Labs by the American mathematician Claude E. Shannon (1916–2005), published in 1948 in the *Bell System Technical Journal*, then in 1949 in book form as *The Mathematical Theory of Communication*, with an overview by Warren Weaver (Shannon and Weaver 1949).

Dembski was hired by Baylor University in 2000 to found and lead the Michael Polanyi Center for intelligent design research. But, after a highly successful and visible international conference entitled "The Nature of Nature," the university yielded to faculty pressure and closed the center within the first year. Later Baylor also shut down the evolutionary informatics program, Dembski's collaborative research with a senior colleague in engineering using the Baylor server.

> Following the national publicity of the Polanyi Center episode, Dembski's chances for an academic career were essentially gone. Also holding a master's degree in divinity, he qualified for a position at an evangelical seminary. Since 1996 he has found support and an intellectual community at the Discovery Institute in Seattle, a private institution best known for its Center for Science and Culture, an ID initiative.

After twenty-five years in intelligent design, having authored or edited over twenty books, William Dembski is taking a break to become an entrepreneur in the field of education. He is pleased with his work in ID and repudiates none of it. But, weary of the isolation and endless controversy, he is excited about his plans of developing educational materials, content, products, and software. He believes that education can and should be more effective, and that we have the technology to make a difference. His dream is free K–12 education worldwide. He sees as the greatest challenge to our freedom the centralization of power. We live in a technocratic age, where the elite are in charge, making the decisions for us. To work toward breaking their power is William Dembski's aim. The motto of this new phase of his life is the statement by the Stoic philosopher Epicurus: "Only the educated are free."

Commentary

To see the ID story in historical context, I will include here two events from the recent past.

A giant of twentieth-century science, British mathematician Ronald A. Fisher (1890–1962) was the founder of both modern statistics and genetics. He created the basis of the modern synthesis by showing Gregor Johann Mendel's laws of inheritance to be the essential mechanism for Charles Darwin's theory of evolution (Fisher 1930). But, as a Christian, Fisher saw no conflict between science and his own faith. In a 1955 radio address on the BBC entitled "Science and Christianity: Faith Is Not Credulity," he referred to his own work as "the study of the mode of inheritance of the heritable characteristics of animals, plants, and man" and spoke of the evil of misleading the public to believe that science is the enemy of religion. He urged scientists to acknowledge the limits of their own discipline:

> In order to know, or understand, better, it is necessary to be clear about our ignorance. This is the research scientist's first important step, his *pons asinorum*, or bridge which the asses cannot cross. We must not fool ourselves into thinking that we know that of which we have no real evidence, and which, therefore, we do not know, but can at most accept, recognizing that we still do not actually know it. (Fisher 1974, 51–52)

In 1977 we presented an international symposium at the Memorial Sloan-Kettering Cancer Center entitled "Medical Research: Statistics and Ethics," the proceedings of which were published in *Science* (Miké and Good 1977). We had invited some prominent scientists to explore issues concerning assessment of the masses of information generated by advances in technology and the need for meaningful interaction with the media and the public. The code of the scientist and its relationship to ethics were discussed in a lecture by Nobel laureate physiologist André Cournand, winner of the Prize in medicine for the development of cardiac catheterization. Cournand related the definition of principles of the code of the scientist in 1942 by sociologist of science Robert K. Merton as underlying the normative structure of science (Merton 1973) and gave his own formulation as follows: intellectual integrity, objectivity, doubt of certitude, tolerance, and communal spirit. With these as his starting point, Cournand reflected on related work in the field. He saw the potential of a worldwide scientific community that could provide guidance for the future development of science, and "the possibility of a humane world order based on the cooperation of a community of scientists and its public" (Cournand 1977, 700).

And where are we today?

In the ID drama of the last two decades we have been observing the scientific community—my community—betray its own basic principles to serve an ideology, in a frantic effort to save the reigning paradigm.

But the truth will prevail. The challenge now is for young scientists attracted to the aims of the ID movement to unite and to proceed with courage, despite the scorn and rejection of the mainstream scientific community, to help build an accelerated research program and then let the evidence lead the way.

Notes

5. See http://seanmcdowell.org/blog. The interview was conducted by Sean McDowell, a Christian apologist with whom Dembski had coauthored a book on intelligent design. Dembski also described his new interests focusing on the connection between technology, education, and freedom, and commented on the reception of the ID movement within various Christian communities.

6. See https://thebestschools.org/features/william-dembski-interview. The interview was conducted by James A. Barham of TheBestSchools.org, an online ranking organization of schools from secondary through graduate school levels. The interview also covered Dembski's experiences related to fundamentalism in the evangelical faith community.

PART FOUR

Theology and Evolution

11 • Evil, Original Sin, and Evolution
12 • The Future of Mankind

CHAPTER 11

Evil, Original Sin, and Evolution

The fourth part of this book has two chapters: chapter 11 presents an interpretation of evolution that I believe does justice to both science and theology. I claim that evolution has been guided by the teleological influence of the intelligent "cosmic powers" or "angels" to whom the development of the universe was entrusted by God in the beginning. The evil that now afflicts the human race (and, indeed, the whole universe) is attributed to the hatred of the devil and the other fallen angels that follow him (Wis. 2:24). This idea may seem absurd to anyone who believes in neo-Darwinism. However, I invite such an individual to entertain it as a hypothesis and see if it does not fit the facts better than other theories do.

Finally, in chapter 12 I speculate, rather briefly, about the future of Mankind. God created this vast universe that we see about us in all directions. We and our planet Earth are a very small part of it. Our biological race is especially important only because the second person of the blessed Trinity (the Logos) has become incarnate here among us. My belief is that God's saving love and power are intended not only for the rational beings on Earth but also for any that may exist anywhere in the universe.

The Problem of Evil

In Christian theology, the benevolent and omnipotent God is the principle of unity and order in the world. How is it, then, that the world has so much disorder and suffering? And why are organisms, and indeed the whole biosphere, so clumsily designed? The world is good and beautiful but it is also evil and ugly. In a Christian culture the existence of good is the subject of praise and thanksgiving, but intellectually it can be taken more or less for granted as something obvious in view of the Creator's perfect goodness. However, the problem of evil is difficult. Someone has said that evil is the great rock on which Christian faith founders. The classic formulation of the problem was given by Epicurus and reformulated in modern times by David Hume:

> Is he willing to prevent evil, but not able? then is he impotent. Is he able, but not willing? then is he malevolent. Is he both able and willing? Whence then is evil? (Hume [1779] 1993, 74)

The atheistic claim is that divine omnipotence, divine goodness, and the existence of evil are incompatible. Christians know, of course, that this cannot be true. Their faith in God is founded on divine revelation and personal religious experience, not on abstract reasoning. Nevertheless, the question remains, how can atheistic skepticism be refuted in a coherent, strictly intellectual way? Before Darwin many thought that this had already been done by the doctrine of original sin. I believe that doctrine is indeed the keystone of the answer to the problem of evil, but in our age it needs to be reformulated in a way that takes account of modern science. Otherwise, in an age of science the Christian worldview loses some of its convincing force.

Evil is, of course, a problem not only for Christians but also for every human being. However, it is especially acute for Christians because they believe that the world was created "out of nothing" and is now sustained by an infinite and omnipotent God who is love itself. But how can omnipotent love that is responsible for everything permit the atrocious evils we see in the world? Indeed, how can God tolerate the many clumsy designs one finds in the biosphere? Darwin devoted an entire book to such mechanisms in the case of orchids. These contrivances are from one point of view extremely ingenious, but as Stephen Jay Gould pointed out,

> [o]rchids were not made by an ideal engineer; they are jury-rigged from a limited set of available components. Thus, they must have evolved

from ordinary flowers.... Odd arrangements and funny solutions are the proof of evolution—paths that a sensible God would never tread but that a natural process, constrained by history, follows perforce. (Gould 2001, 670; in Pennock 2001)

As Gould said, prima facie evolution seems to be more like an ingenious tinkerer than an omniscient and omnipotent designer. At one time the Christian explanation of evil seemed fairly persuasive to most Western people. I do not mean, of course, that they found it easy to put up with evil. No one can. But, unlike agnostics and atheists, they were able to situate it in a positive context that made it easier for them to endure it. This context was essentially constituted by faith, but faith was supported by a seemingly rational and coherent understanding of evil. Nowadays, however, the discoveries of modern science, especially evolution, cast doubt upon the validity of that traditional understanding. As a result, Christians find themselves left with a naked faith that is harder to sustain because of their inability to rationalize evil as well as before.

Consequently, it is worthwhile trying to formulate an adequate modern understanding of evil and original sin. Christian tradition has the resources to do so. In fact, I believe that the traditional explanation requires only updating and some additional clarification of the issues.

The Doctrine of Original Sin

Roman Catholic doctrine about evil is stated in various authoritative texts, notable among which are the solemn profession of faith of the Fourth Lateran Council (1215) and the decree of the Council of Trent (1546) on original sin (Neuner and Dupuis 1982, nos. 19, 507–13). The Lateran Council intended to affirm directly the traditional doctrine of the one God who is the sole principle of the universe and created it out of nothing, as well as the doctrine that moral responsibility for sin is entirely due to creatures. Thus, it tells us that evil entered into the world through the sin of the angels, and that the human race sinned at their instigation.

Although the explicit teaching of this decree was concerned more with moral rather than physical evil, it was aimed against heretics of the day, the Cathars, who believed that matter is ontologically evil and was created by the evil god, Satan. In combating this heresy the Council Fathers must have had in mind the teaching of Genesis that the world as God first made it was "very good" (Gen. 1:31). In that context the implication is that matter is not evil of itself but has been corrupted by sin (Quay 1981).

The decree of the Council of Trent on original sin focused on the fall of the human race, which was attributed, of course, to the sin of the first man, Adam. Like Lateran IV, this Council was mainly concerned with moral rather than physical evil. However, it stated explicitly that the sin of Adam left the human race subject to suffering and death and in a worse condition in body as well as in soul. This teaching is coherent with the theory of original sin that had been worked out by Augustine and others. Without spelling out the precise connection between moral and physical evil in general, Trent seemed to imply that human suffering is due to the sin of Adam. In any event this was the common belief of theologians before the modern period.

However, since Darwin difficulties have arisen. As I have been implying, modern science has shown us how deeply rooted physical evil is in the fundamental constitution of matter. The fundamental structure of this world originated long before the human race existed. Therefore it is hard to believe that all the physical evil that afflicts humanity was due to human sin. Indeed it is easy to understand how one might think that sin is due to prior physical evil, which was in turn due to the will of the Creator himself.

Karl Rahner and others have tried to update the theory of original sin in a way that preserves the essential elements of the traditional doctrine (Rahner et al. 1968–70, 4:328–34). But some have taken a more radical approach to the problem. Noteworthy was the attempt made by a school of Dutch theologians (Hulsbosch 1961; Schoonenberg 1965; Smulders 1967; Wildiers 1968), who at about the time of the Second Vatican Council developed hints suggested by Pierre Teilhard de Chardin (1961, app.). This radical approach takes seriously the new knowledge science has given to us about the history of the universe. As Teilhard pointed out, evil seems to be not a mere accident in the universe but a necessary element in the structure of the system. Apparently, it is something written into the basic laws of nature and the history of cosmic and biological evolution. To say with the traditional account of original sin that at the beginning of our race God intended to exempt us from evil means that he planned to work a never-ending series of miracles in order to avoid the consequences of the system that he himself set up. His intentions, written into the nature of the world and the fundamental physical laws that govern it, are, according to the radicals, in conflict with the traditional account of his providential intentions toward humanity. Furthermore, supposing that he intended to exempt humanity from evil, why did he not carry out his decision? Surely the sin of one or a few human beings does not seem to be an adequate reason for not doing so. Once again the traditional theory makes the providential guidance of God appear contradictory and inconsistent.

Therefore, according to the radical revisionists, we must assume that evil does not come from sin but from the physical nature of the world. It is inevitable. Our dream of perfect happiness must be projected into the future rather than the past. Perfection is the goal of development, the supreme achievement of the evolutionary project in which God, the world, and humanity are involved. It is not something that was real in the beginning and was lost, but the hope that inspires us in our striving for the future. The ancient theory of original sin was the best explanation of evil at a time when the human race had a static worldview. But now, supposedly, it is counterproductive and obscures the greater and more inspiring explanation that is ours, thanks to the dynamic worldview science has given to us. Thus, it is argued, dynamic science has given the human race the great gift of a dynamic theology that enables us not to blame God for evil but to praise him for sustaining us in the painful but magnificent project of spiritual progress in which we are engaged.

It is well remembered that before the Second Vatican Council the conservative mentality of Rome rejected the thought of Teilhard, apparently without much understanding of the issues. In the more open climate that followed the Council, the position of the radical revisionists was able to get a hearing, but it was not officially accepted. On the other hand, the cogency of their position did not allow it to be forgotten. It is said that many Catholic intellectuals, perhaps even a majority, no longer believe in the traditional theory of original sin. (I have never taken a poll, but I believe that many claim this to be the fact.) Official doctrine and the beliefs of many of the Catholic intelligentsia seem to be in conflict on this point, and this situation is not good for the health and unity of the Church.

Many will conclude that the magisterium of the Church should change its mind and thus reestablish harmony between traditional doctrine and scientific reason. However, I believe that there are excellent reasons for not doing so. The doctrine of original sin is inextricably linked with the problem of evil. If one eliminates original sin, one is left with no satisfactory explanation of evil. Some radical revisionists will doubtless reply that there is no need to answer the problem of evil anyway. It is a mere pseudo problem, so why worry about it? But it is hard to think that the problem of evil is a mere pseudo problem. Earlier ages believed the existence of evil to be a real and serious one. Original sin is at least a partial explanation of it, and one of the factors responsible for the growth of modern atheism is the weakening of belief in that doctrine. I believe that to reject original sin is to forget part of the revelation that gives us truth about the world that science can never discover. What is needed is not rejection but a deeper understanding of original sin, one that, as we shall see, is compatible with a proper understanding of modern science.

Teilhard believed that the order of the world as revealed by science requires the existence of natural evil, "not by accident... but through the very structure of the system" (Teilhard 1961, app.). Yet the Bible seems to suggest the opposite. It seems that in the beginning God intended men and women to live in a world free of both physical and moral evil. As we saw above, at the end of the sixth day of Creation the Creator "saw everything he had made, and indeed, it was very good" (Gen. 1:31). Then, in the second chapter of Genesis, we see God putting Adam and Eve in a lovely garden that had no evil. It was only in the third chapter that evil was introduced by their disobedience to a divine command. In the book of Wisdom we are told that "God did not make death and he does not delight in the death of the living" (Wis. 1:13). It was "through the devil's envy [that] death entered the world (Wis. 2:24)." Thus, in the biblical perspective, natural evil should not exist. It is in opposition to God's original intention and it comes from sin—that is, from the perverse free decisions of creatures.

Attributing natural evil to God may change one's attitude toward him in an unfortunate way. If one thinks that he is its origin, one may be inclined to agree with Albert Camus's metaphysical rebel that God is "the father of death and . . . the supreme outrage" (Camus [1951] 1956, 24), or with Ivan in Dostoevsky's novel *The Brothers Karamazov*, that he is not just and one should not accept this universe of his in which the innocent suffer. Yet, as Christians believe, God is love itself. He loves all his creatures and he hates all the evils that afflict them, including natural evils. Is he not much more sympathetic than Ivan Karamazov to innocent children who suffer such evils? A person who loves God will be likely to think, at least prima facie, that he created a world without natural evil and that all its present ills are due to the sins of creatures, first the sins of Satan and other demons, and later those of human beings who have followed the demons.

But there is a distinction between God's absolute will and his conditional will. The future of any free being includes alternatives, including evil choices that God permits but does not want. He wants rational beings to love him freely rather than simply being compelled to do what he wants them to do. Human beings are truly free, and the evil we do is our responsibility rather than God's. God sees the physical evils resulting from sin as genuine evils but nevertheless tolerates them as instruments for good. They are genuine evils because they reflect the evil of their sinful origin. Yet those consequences of sin are not chosen either by God or by the beings who suffer them now, and with God's help they can be overcome and work for good in the end.

The objection can be raised that, if God can use evil for good in the present order of the world, why could he not have made use of it in his original plans for the world? I reply in terms of a medical metaphor.

Surgery can be very beneficial for a patient suffering from cancer, but to operate on a healthy one is malpractice. The evil of surgery opposes the cancer that is already there. But in the case of the healthy, there is no evil to be opposed. In the present sinful world order, evil can be limited by evil. Though one evil can oppose another evil, it is not in itself a source of good. In an order that has no evil, it would be absurd to introduce it. It should not be introduced when there is no evil to be opposed by it. A loving parent would not allow a surgeon to attack his child with a scalpel if it were not necessary.

In his remarkable book entitled *The Prophets*, Rabbi Abraham Heschel contrasts the portrait of Yahweh drawn by the Old Testament prophets with the concept of God constructed by philosophers and theologians ([German 1936] 1962, vol. 2, chap. 1). The prophetic portrait is based on intimate personal experience, the philosophical and theological concept on seemingly profound but abstract and sometimes defective thinking. "What is the primary content of prophetic experience, the thought immediately felt, the motive directly present to the prophet's mind?" (1962, 1:23). Heschel tells us that "divine pathos is the key to inspired prophecy" (1962, 1:24). God experiences "pathos" and conveys a certain participation of it to the prophets. Although Heschel attempts to define divine pathos, I believe he would claim that its meaning is best understood by prayerful meditation on the inspired writings of the prophets themselves. I add that for Christians it is best understood by prayerful meditation on the personal attitudes of Jesus. We read time and time again in the Gospels how he healed people who needed his help. And as he told us, to see him is to see the Father (John 14:9).

Roughly speaking, pathos means something like conscious intelligent feeling in a world that has gone astray. It is a complex act that includes perception, intellectual understanding, affective response, and personal resolve. Though pathos is not simply suffering, in the present world it involves suffering. It is a response of the whole person. Divine pathos and divine suffering are as exalted above the human as is divine existence. The Jewish scriptures portray the relationship between Yahweh and Israel as one of intimate personal love, indeed, in a certain sense a marriage relationship. The Lord rejoices and suffers in that relationship. The ontological gap between the two parties is infinite, and yet somehow it is bridged by infinite divine love. Because that love relationship between God and humanity is not what it ought to be, God suffers. Yet he is faithful and intends, if we are willing, to heal us and bring us to fulfillment.

God's original commands to angels and human beings were for their own good. He wanted human beings not to try to reason (and fail, of course) why he was telling us what to do, but rather to rely on his wisdom and affection for us. Alas, Modern Man is relying on our own supposedly adequate intelligence rather than his. Paul was certainly right in saying that all things work together for those who love God (Rom. 8:28). But it certainly is not better for those who do not love him.

It would seem that there is a karmic law in this universe by which the good offered to those who do evil is somehow transferred to those who do good. God was not surprised about what happened in his Creation. He knew from the beginning what the possibilities were, and besides being infinitely loving, he is also infinitely just. In a world without sin there would have been no suffering because creatures would have chosen to love him from the beginning. Had they chosen to serve him rather than themselves, the good offered to the world would have been distributed in a different way than it is now. Now we learn only by painful experience where our true good lies.

Ideas about angels, demons, and, in particular, Satan, developed during the Old Testament and intertestamental periods and were taken over by Jesus and the New Testament writers. Many sayings of Jesus, including some of the characteristic or "difficult" ones most likely to be authentic (Matt. 24:36; Luke 15:10), take the existence of angels for granted. Especially noteworthy is Jesus's career as an exorcist, about which there can be no reasonable doubt (Perrin 1967, 65). In Luke 11:20 (par. Matt. 12:28), Jesus uses his power of exorcism to prove the validity of his proclamation of the kingdom of God he preached, as well as to illustrate its nature. It entails the overthrow of the rule of Satan. In all the Gospels Jesus shows himself aware that he is locked in a struggle with Satan. His followers share in that struggle. The consciousness of being engaged in spiritual warfare against superhuman powers was an important part of the awareness and the spirituality of the early Church.

The opposition between Christ and Satan is particularly emphasized in the Gospel of John. Satan is the center of solidarity in sin, the father of those who refuse to believe in Jesus. He is a "murderer from the start ... a liar and the father of lies" (John 8:44), in contrast to Jesus, who is life and truth itself. Satan is at the center of the darkness that opposes Jesus the light (John 12:35–36; 13:27–30). The ministry of Jesus is a struggle with Satan, which reaches its climax in the Paschal Mystery when Satan is overcome and cast out (John 12:31; 14:30; 16:11; 17:15). In John, Satan is not only the one opposed to Christ, but he also absorbs the functions of the Pauline cosmic powers, sin and death. John's dualism passes over created structures that oppose the reign of God to focus on their ultimate source, the Adversary par excellence.

The biblical belief in the reality of angels and demons was essentially unquestioned in the Church until modern times. As we have seen, important testimony to this belief was given by the Fourth Lateran Council, which taught that "Man ... sinned at the suggestion of the devil" (Neuner and Dupuis 1982, 19). Also very important is the testimony of many saints through the centuries. They speak of their own experience of their struggles against the personal powers of evil who attacked them just as they had attacked Jesus. Especially noteworthy is the teaching of Ignatius Loyola about the need to recognize the influence of evil spirits upon us in order to discern clearly the will of God (Ignatius Loyola, *Spiritual Exercises,* nos. 313–36). The experience of these great human beings, who are keenly aware of the spiritual dimensions of human existence, must be taken seriously. Their common testimony about aspects of the world that are largely beyond the experience of the average person provides some of the best evidence we have about the proper way of interpreting the Scriptures. The reality of their struggles with Satan makes it clear how the words of Jesus about the personal nature of evil are to be understood. He was not merely accommodating his language to the culture of the times but was telling us about the real spiritual warfare in which our race is involved. He was calling to our attention the enemy who is out to destroy us—and may well do so if we insist on regarding him as an empty myth.

Belief in the existence and role of angels and demons has a certain philosophical and aesthetic appeal. St. Thomas Aquinas held that because God, who is purely spiritual, created the universe to participate in his own truth, goodness, and beauty, it is therefore fitting that there be creatures which do so in a more purely spiritual way than we who are a mixture of the spiritual and the material (Davies 1992, 55–56). In a similar vein, Karl Rahner believed that, whenever we find in the world forms of unity and coherence, of beauty and value, that go beyond the human in scale, depth, and intensity, we have reason to wonder whether there may not be some superhuman created spiritual principles at work (Rahner 1983, 267).

But because God himself is also a superhuman spiritual principle of coherence and unity, it is difficult to distinguish his influence from that of the good angels. However, distinguishing it from that of the demons is much easier. It is in the atrocious evil that afflicts our human world that we see most clearly what is at its center—malevolent beings who are not God but are more powerful and intelligent than we. We of the twentieth and early twenty-first centuries should be (but often are not) better able than other generations to recognize this.

When one reflects upon the sins of ordinary people, people seem to commit sins not so much from sheer malice as from weakness and the inability to resist temptation. As Ricoeur has pointed out, this intuition is expressed in the Genesis image of the serpent.

> If we follow the intention of the serpent theme all the way to the end, it must be said that man is not the absolute evil one, but the evil one of second rank, the evil one through seduction; he is not the Evil One, the Wicked One, substantivally, so to speak, but evil, wicked adjectivally; he makes himself wicked by a sort of counter-participation, counter imitation, by consenting to a source of evil that the naïve author of the biblical tale depicts as animal cunning. To sin is to yield. (Ricoeur 1967, 259)

Our sin is dependent, "Adamic" evil. The sin that entered the world in the beginning was evil of another sort, "Satanic," absolute evil. It could be committed only by a being stronger and more self-sufficient than ourselves, one whose power and intelligence provided him with the basis for an act of absolute pride, the evil act that had no evil antecedents. (Some Christian spiritual writers have conjectured that Satan's sin was to refuse allegiance to the coming Messiah, one who would possess a human nature that seemed to him to be much inferior to his own.)

In the appendix of *The Phenomenon of Man* that I cited above, Teilhard also speculated that, in spite of evil being a necessary feature of the present world, it may also be true that there may have been some "catastrophe or primordial deviation" that resulted in "a certain *excess*" of evil. I believe that his speculation is partially correct. The original disaster, due to the sin of Satan and his demons, has been made even worse by their seduction of the human race.

Christian teaching about the origin of evil comes to us largely in terms of "myth." I understand myth, in accord with the definition of Norman Perrin, as "a complex of stories—some no doubt fact, and some fantasy—which, for various reasons, human beings regard as demonstrations of the inner meaning of the universe and of human life" (Perrin 1976, 22). The myths given to us in the word of God express the truth but sometimes in an ambiguous way with regard to their literal significance. For these expressions of truth have two aspects, a formal and a material aspect. This is in analogy with the formal and material causes of Aristotle. According to the latter, a statue is the union of a material cause, namely, the stone or other material it is made of, and a formal cause, which is the shape imposed upon the stone by the sculptor. Similarly, let us say that the material aspect of a truthful expression conveys concrete facts about the world, while its formal aspect is its abstract significance. When we express the truth, our expression can embody these two aspects in varying degrees and in different ways. Almanacs tell us many facts about the world but convey comparatively little about their pattern. In contrast, great poetry can convey profound truth formally, but without revealing its material aspects to any notable degree.

With regard to the myth of original sin, formal truth is very important, but the status of its material aspect is ambiguous. In particular, the precise significance of the figure of "Adam" is ambiguous. Is he a historical individual, or a historical group, or the entire species in its early evolution ("mankind evolving"), or a biblical "corporate personality," or a personified abstraction ("everyman")? Again, was the "fall" of our race an event that occurred at a definite moment, or at least in a short period of time, or was it a whole evolutionary epoch, or something in between? Were the deleterious consequences sustained by our race spiritual or physical or social or some combination of these? Were these harmful consequences transmitted to Adam's descendants by spiritual or physical or social processes? Did evolution and genetics play a role, or did what happened take place on a higher plane that is unknown to science?

We can think of these and other questions as defining the dimensions of a space of questions within which the full truth must be sought. To answer these questions we must interpret the biblical myths, notably those of Genesis 3 and Romans 5, and authoritative Church interpretations like those of the Fourth Lateran and Trent Councils.

As I said above, the biblical texts are often myths that convey very important formal truth to us while remaining relatively ambiguous as to their literal truth. Church pronouncements through the centuries attempt to clarify those texts, but more with regard to formal than to material truth. They themselves are sometimes, if not myths, at least myth-like. In my opinion, we do not possess a high degree of certainty about the material aspect of the biblical teaching on original sin, and we convey its formal aspect in terms of the rather ambiguous material one. The myths of the beginning are true, just as the myths of the end are true. But we know no more about the material circumstances of original sin than we do about those of the Last Judgment. The fall of the human race must be understood as part of the fall of the universe. It is not the full explanation of evil, nor does the human race bear full responsibility for its sin. Human beings are responsible for human sin, but at the same time our conduct is partially excusable. Hence, unlike the fallen angels, we can be redeemed.

One can argue that God's omnipotent will cannot be resisted and that therefore evil must be a part of his original plan rather than something opposed to it. The answer is that God is love and love is omnipotent, not in a mechanical way but in a way characteristic of love. Love desires love in return. But love is essentially free, and even omnipotent love cannot guarantee a free return of love. An omnipotent lover can only overcome barriers that might prevent the beloved from loving him. That God does. He reveals himself to the beloved as fully as possible and seduces her in any way that he can. But love is dangerous, and even divine love can be disappointed. Nevertheless, God can make use of the disappointment to prevent further evil and to produce good that otherwise would not be possible. Thus Christ accepted the evils of the present era and by doing so achieved eternal glory. His saving work is not only an example and an inspiration but also a source of power for us in our own struggles. By union with him in his sufferings we participate in his redemptive role and his eternal joy.

The Role of the Cosmic Powers in Evolution

Besides the problem of evil there is also the problem of good. More specifically, besides the evil superhuman beings we call demons, or bad angels, there are also the good ones. The first thing about angels in general is that they exist. According to the *Catechism of the Catholic Church*: "The existence of the spiritual, non-corporeal beings that Sacred Scripture usually calls 'angels' is a truth of faith. The witness of Scripture is as clear as the unanimity of Tradition" (no. 328).

The good angels are servants of God, and because of their love for him they are friends and servants of the human race. The Scriptures tell us that they are messengers of God to human beings; that they protect us physically and spiritually, especially against Satan and his demons; that they enlighten us and pray for us. Before the modern period it was easy to believe in the existence of angels and demons. However, people also believed that the universe is static and that its natural structure is pretty much the same as when God originally created it. While a great deal of

Evil, Original Sin, and Evolution

attention was given to human history, and especially the history of salvation, the history of the physical world, beyond the bare fact of its creation, was unknown. So in those days the concept that the cosmic powers had anything to do with evolution was virtually unthinkable. But today, when the concept of evolution is commonplace, it requires no great step of the imagination to wonder whether there may be a connection between angels and evolution. Indeed, to me it seems almost inevitable to suppose that in the beginning the Father entrusted to the angels the development of the material Creation in which his Son would one day be born.

Unfortunately, to accept that idea would fly in the face of the reductionistic understanding of evolution now dominant in our culture. Nevertheless, I am proposing that not only do angels exist, but also that they are important in the evolution of the universe and of the human race in particular. The existence of evil in a world created by a loving, omnipotent God suggests that there must be creatures more powerful than Man who have disturbed the original order of Creation. It is clear that the present world order is a conflicted one in which good and evil not only co-exist but are even in violent conflict. The world is substantially good, but it has been injured by atrocious evil. When one reflects upon what happened in the twentieth century and what is threatening to happen in the twenty-first, it really should not be hard to believe in the reality of evil superhuman beings. Somewhere Carl Jung remarked that in the Hitler era he was surprised that many people did not believe in demons when every day in the street they were walking past individuals who were possessed by them.

At the same time, the way in which evil has been overcome in the past should make it equally easy to believe that there are also good beings more powerful than Man. In the light of the Judeo-Christian tradition and the Church's doctrine of original sin, I conjecture that the good of evolution is partially caused by good angels just as its evil is partially caused by evil ones.

The concept of the *natural* is much older than modern science, and it applies to more than the material aspects of the world that science studies. Angels have natures, and over the centuries many important

Christian theologians, including Aquinas and Rahner, have held that in some way they govern the material world. Within my evolutionary horizon, the course of evolution is partially governed by the good angels, albeit in the face of the opposition of Satan and his followers. Darwin correctly identified two important factors that govern the process, namely, random variation and natural selection. But he and his neo-Darwinian followers overlooked another, namely, the downward influence of the Logos himself, as well as that of angelic beings subordinate to the Logos but in some ways superior to human beings.

The practice of plant and animal breeders was important in the development of Darwin's thought. He drew an analogy between artificial selection and natural selection. Human breeders make use of teleological selection to shape natural random variation and thus produce useful changes within a given species. Darwin supposed that, over the vast ages of geological time, natural nonteleological selection shaped natural random variation in such a way as to produce the far more profound and intrinsically improbable changes necessary to produce the entire modern biosphere. The analogy is clear, but it is marred by the fact that Darwin's natural selection is blind whereas teleological selection by human breeders is highly purposeful. Darwin ignored that crucial difference between the two analogates, and so do his intellectual heirs.

For many contemporary biologists the foregoing discussion may seem bizarre. For the past seventy years or so neo-Darwinism has been the accepted opinion of the scientific community. Moreover, according to the survey published by Larson and Witham (1999), about 95 percent of the members of the biology section of the National Academy of Science who responded to their survey did not believe in the God of orthodox Christianity. I would guess that most of them do not believe in angels either. They think that phenomena within the domain of science should be explained by material causes only, and that it would be wrong to account for them by the existence of anything greater than ourselves.

But in areas other than biology, intelligent design is often important. Detectives, lawyers, judges, juries, insurance companies, quality-control engineers, communications specialists, cryptologists, astronomers looking for signs of intelligent life on other planets, and ordinary people struggling with ordinary situations often have to decide whether some kind of necessity, or chance, or intelligent design is at work (Dembski 2002, chap. 1). The same choice ought to govern our efforts in understanding biological evolution.

There is a great difference between a chronicle and a history. A chronicle tells one part of what happened; a history also explains why. Modest evolutionists tell us what happened, at least up to a point, whereas ambitious evolutionists claim that they are telling us not only what happened but also all the major factors that caused it. I believe that the chronicle of evolution that neo-Darwinists propose is probably correct. However, the hidden factors that caused it to occur are quite different. Darwin guessed important factors governing evolution, but he missed an even more important one, namely, teleology. My belief is that the positive causal influence of God and angels, on the one hand, and the negative influence of demons, on the other, are the ultimate factors that have shaped evolution. These factors are known to us with certainty only by supernatural revelation and are beyond the scope of science. People who do not believe in personal superhuman entities cannot know them and will continue to insist that intelligent design must be wrong.

Neo-Darwinism is a combination of what I have called "modest" Darwinism and a philosophical hypothesis that the universe can be understood solely in terms of itself. The founders of modern science believed that the universe cannot be understood without a transcendent element that human beings cannot understand fully. Yet today many modern scientists believe that the universe can be understood fully in terms of itself. In other words, they think that the world has its own adequate explanation and that there is no need of a transcendent element that comes from above and makes sense of what we call "nature." Yet in fact a person who believes this cannot make sense out of the world (Weinberg 1992, 255). Particle physicists cannot account even for the data of solid-state physics, let alone for the data derived from the far more complex systems of biology (Laughlin and Pines 2000, 28–31; Laughlin et al. 2000, 32–37).

As we have seen, human knowledge is divided somewhat arbitrarily into a variety of intellectual disciplines. Each discipline has a certain independence within its own proper domain, but each also has "boundary conditions" that govern the way it fits in with the others. Today some scientists assume they can employ their usual methods to solve any problem they are interested in, and feel no need for appreciating well-established conclusions from other intellectual disciplines, especially Christian philosophy and theology. Most of all, they do not consider divine revelation, the foundation on which Christian theology is based. The result is hubris on the part of some and resulting confusion in a culture that values both science and religion.

As intelligent design theorists seem to have shown, it is dubious that a largely random walk by the evolutionary process in the genetic landscape can hit upon the improbable material configurations proper to living organisms, let alone intelligent organisms. But, in spite of the fact that they ignore the teleological factor, Darwinists often talk as though the Blind Watchmaker is not really blind. It seems as though their chosen model of evolution is often overcome by an intuitive perception they are not willing to acknowledge (Greene 1999, 275–82).

What I am proposing is an analogy with human artificial breeding that seems to be better than Darwin's. Cosmic powers much older and more intelligent and powerful than Man have shaped the potential variation inherent in natural processes to produce the goals they desire, including the existence of the human race and its Messiah. In this case the analogy drawn from human breeders' artificial selection retains its teleological character and is not restricted in the way that Darwin's is. In other words, mutations and other alterations are not completely random but are molded by the cosmic powers. (I recall reading somewhere about a vision or a dream of a modern mystic, in which he or she saw an angel who had many arms. The angel was busily weaving a vast and complicated fabric.)

Just as God wants human beings to decide their eternal destinies by using the freedom he gives them, so he wanted the superhuman beings we call angels to decide their eternal destinies by choosing to use properly the freedom he had given them to govern the material world he had created along with them in the beginning (Neuner and Dupuis 1982, no. 19). Human beings use their freedom to promote or injure the well-being of other human beings. In like manner, the cosmic powers promoted or injured the whole order of the universe, including even the concrete humanity of the incarnate Logos himself.

Certainly, God, the Creator of the whole universe, plays the primary and decisive role in evolution. However, as Darwin and agnostics in general have made clear, the limited and imperfect character of the evolutionary process proves that God is not solely responsible for it. Human sin, original and actual, contributes to the massive evil in the world. Nevertheless, human beings are not powerful or malignant enough to be its principal causes. The malevolent influence of Satan and the other fallen powers has created the context of concupiscence and temptation in which human beings make their foolish and sometimes perverse choices. Nevertheless, the benevolent influence of the good angels supports the large-scale coherence, intelligibility, and beauty of the evolving world that makes human goodness possible. Cosmic evolution is a constructive project that has been and is still going on in the midst of a ferocious guerrilla war. Once one realizes the situation, one does not find it surprising that it has not gone smoothly.

Nevertheless, the last book of the Bible tells us that the final result of the long war in heaven is inevitable: "'It is I, Jesus, who sent my angel to you with this testimony for the churches. I am the root and the descendant of David, the bright morning star.' . . . The one who testifies to these things says, 'Surely I am coming soon.' Amen. Come, Lord Jesus!" (Rev. 22:16, 20).

CHAPTER 12

The Future of Mankind

Ignatius of Loyola, the founder of the Society of Jesus, loved to look at the stars. I do not know exactly what he thought, but like him I also am fascinated by them. As a person of the twenty-first century I am aware that they are like our own sun, and that a certain percentage of them also have planets, at least some of which may very well be like our own Earth.[1] In a universe centered on the incarnate Christ, I wonder what these Earth-like planets mean to the one who is the creator and savior of the whole universe. It seems possible that the same kind of intelligent life that has evolved here on Earth has also evolved elsewhere, and that God loves them with the same boundless divine love he has for us.[2]

The first phase in the history of the universe ended with the decisive defeat of Satan and his followers (Rev. 12:7–9). The second phase was the one of cosmic and biological evolution that produced the human race. This was the time when the world order we know was established, an order that is essentially good but is also marred by the evil of something like a guerrilla war. It is not the order that God wanted in the beginning, but, given the defection and positive interference of Satan and other demons, it is the best that is now possible.[3]

However, focusing on the evils of the present era would be wrong. It is true that God's original plan was the better one overall. He is the loving Father of all the intelligent beings he has created and continues to create. It is unthinkable that he wanted any of them to be lost. The biblical concept of predestination has been badly understood. According to Joseph Fitzmyer, it is meant to apply to collectivities like Israel and the Church, rather than individuals (Fitzmyer 1993, esp. 522). But since God's love has been definitively rejected by some of his creatures, the present sinful order of the world has advantages for those who continue to love him. As Paul says in his letter to the Romans, "We know that all things work together for good for those who love God" (Rom. 8:28). The power of God is such that in the end those who love him will be better off (though not necessarily in this mortal life) than they would have been in the beautiful and tranquil world he originally intended. As noted earlier, it would seem that there is a kind of karmic economy governing the world in such a way that the good rejected by those who do evil is somehow transferred to those who do good. Temptation sometimes results in moral disaster for some, but for others—the majority I hope—it results in virtue and greater strength of character (see Balthasar 1988).

The coming in the flesh of Jesus Christ introduced a new factor into Creation. As Satan had foreseen from the beginning, human beings are weak and fallible. The book of Genesis tells us of the initial failure of the human race and the seeming triumph of the deceiver. Nevertheless, God's plan proceeded. The people of Israel were chosen, and, even though some of them failed to meet the historical tests they endured, each time a purified remnant emerged. In the fullness of time this process culminated in a human person, Mary, the mother of God, who never failed him in the least. From her was born the Savior of the world, Jesus the Christ.

The New Testament tells the story of Jesus's birth, life, death, and resurrection. He is true God and true man, the second person of the Blessed Trinity, the Truth itself, who by his incarnation possesses a concrete human nature in a full and perfect way. In him, Satan, "the deceiver of the whole world" (Rev. 12:9), was at last confronted by the incarnate power and wisdom of God. By Christ's resurrection, human nature was glorified and the world re-created. As the Hallelujah Chorus of Handel's *Messiah* sings most beautifully, "the kingdom of this world is become the kingdom of our Lord and of his Christ." For those who believe, suffering and death now lead to resurrection.

After the resurrection and ascension of the Lord, on the day of Pentecost the Holy Spirit descended upon the apostles in power, and they immediately entered upon the mission the Lord had given them of converting the world to himself. But that mission has not yet been accomplished, and it is not certain to what extent it will be on the final day when the Lord himself comes again to complete it.

Before the sixteenth century, the "world" meant this planet, and the mission of Christians was thought to be limited to the Earth and the human race. Now we know that the universe is vast, and there may well be many planets like Earth in the universe. It is also possible that some of them are inhabited by rational animals that, according to Aristotle's definition of human nature, are fundamentally like us, even though they belong to other biological species. Now the question arises whether or not the mission of the Church is limited to the planet Earth. Are we destined to travel to the stars, or, if not, are we still to communicate to other races the gospel, or "good news," we have received? Or will more advanced races discover Earth and the history of the salvation God has accomplished here?

There is also another, prior question, which must first be answered. Is the incarnation of the Logos in Jesus of Nazareth the only incarnation? In other words, is it possible that the Logos has or will become incarnate in numerous intelligent species in different parts of the universe? In the Hindu religion many avatars are thought to have appeared in different places and in various guises here on Earth.[4] In contrast, Christians believe that at least on our planet there has been only one incarnation and that there will be no other. But what about the situation in other worlds that are so separated from ours by such enormous gulfs of time and space that it seems no information or causal influence can ever cross them? The Creator is interested in his whole Creation, and who is to tell him that he cannot create other rational biological species on other planets and reveal himself to them in whatever way he chooses? Doesn't this suggest that God can and will become incarnate elsewhere, much as he has here on Earth?

I for one do not wish to tell God what he can or cannot do. Nevertheless, I suspect that his actions and what he has already told us imply that the answer to the question about other incarnations is no. It seems to me that the human Jesus of Nazareth is the sole Redeemer and Lord of the entire universe. Our understanding of metaphysical terms like "person," "nature," "hypostatic union," and so forth do indeed stretch human intelligence to or beyond its limits. Reasoning about them seems to be perilous, and God has said nothing explicit about how our concepts apply to the question we are considering here. Nevertheless, the tenor of the revelation we have received seems to be against such a thing (see Col. 1:15–20). I believe that the entire universe is called to the supernatural destiny of union with the Trinity in one communion of love. There seems to be only one kingdom of God, one heaven, and one incarnate Messiah who governs it, one mother who is its queen. It is hard to reconcile multiple incarnations with the general tenor of Christian revelation. I find it more plausible to assume that the ordinary Christian point of view is correct and that multiple incarnations are not possible, or at least will not occur.

God's limitless love is concerned about the entire universe, not just planet Earth. The privilege of knowing and loving him is not meant only for members of our biological race but for all beings capable of receiving it. The mission originally given to the apostles may be meant to embrace the entire universe, not just our planet. Just as the Hebrew people were meant to share their relationship to God with the gentiles, so human beings may be meant to share their relationship to him with all other rational beings in the universe.

At one time Europeans speculated about the possibility that human beings might be living at the antipodes. However, most did not consider the possibility that they would ever meet such persons. Their scientific-technological knowledge and their accustomed time scale were too narrow to make the possibility seem likely. Nonetheless, it came about. Now we wonder about similar possibilities regarding rational beings existing in distant parts of the universe. If there are such beings, is it possible that our species will one day meet them, or at least communicate with them? An atheist like Carl Sagan thought we might at least communicate with some of them. It seems to me that Christians have all the more reason to think something similar.

Science and technology are in their infancy, and who knows what possibilities remain hidden in the future? The decisive factors are the wisdom of God and the centrality of Christ. Why would God create a universe so vast if he did not intend it to come somehow into relationship with Christ? Mere material structures, no matter how enormous, would be relatively pointless if they were not destined to be fulfilled in relationship to him. It is conceivable that God will use science and technology to enable the human race to share its faith with other rational beings throughout the universe. But whether or not that is true, in any event what Christ did here on Earth for us is meant for all. It may be that somehow or other, what has happened here will be spread ultimately to every rational creature in the universe.

That may well take a long time by our human standards. The current crisis of our civilization is indeed threatening us with widespread destruction and the temporary loss of values dear to us. If we do not repent, our generation may well experience terrible disasters. Nevertheless, I am convinced that in the long run God will not permit the permanent loss of the good news about his Son. The history of Christianity, like the history of human science, is itself only in its infancy. Who knows what remarkable possibilities may emerge in this vast universe in the course of the next few million, or billion, years?

At the end of his letter to the Romans, St. Paul speaks of "the revelation of the mystery that was kept secret for long ages" (Rom. 16:25). According to Xavier Léon-Dufour, the word mystery

> denotes nothing less than the object of the gospel: the realization of salvation by the death and resurrection of Christ, His implantation in history by proclaiming the Word. But this object is characterized as a divine secret, inaccessible to human intelligence without revelation (cf. 1 Co 14,2). (Léon-Dufour 1995, art.: Mystery, NT II)

Even though the divine secret itself was first revealed some two millennia ago, it was only in the twentieth century that its suitable natural setting became known to the human race. The remarkable scientific and technological progress of the past few hundred years has taught us that this setting is the story of the development of the vast universe that we now see stretching billions of light-years around us in all directions. But of itself this picture is like a painting of an empty landscape that cries out for the presence of a central figure that will give its otherwise impersonal magnificence human significance. That figure is Jesus the Christ, the incarnate Son of God.

That is why back in the 1960s the works of Teilhard de Chardin struck such a chord in the human psyche. In Teilhard's mind, the account of the development of Man, as well as of the entire universe, became not only a scientific account but also a modern "myth" which, recalling Norman Perrin's definition, is "a complex of stories—some no doubt fact, and some fantasy—which, for various reasons, human beings regard as demonstrations of the inner meaning of the universe and of human life" (Perrin 1976, 22). The history of the universe revealed by science has become the natural setting for the mystery of salvation. Today more than ever the seeming emptiness of this setting cries out for the supernatural mystery that gives us its ultimate significance.

Notes

1. Even if the probability that a given planet is like our Earth may be very small, nevertheless in such an enormous universe there must be many of them.

2. In the last chapter of my 1973 book, *Cosmos*, I discussed some of these topics. The present chapter is similar to my article in the *Heythrop Journal* 50 (2009): 833–45. Only after writing the present chapter did I become aware of an excellent essay by Christopher L. Fisher and David Fergusson, *Heythrop Journal* 47 (2006): 275–90, which discusses a number of other studies, particularly ones by Karl Rahner that I did not know about.

3. Can evil be real and genuine for human beings, but for God only apparent? It has been argued that, in the eyes of God, what we call evil actually enhances the overall goodness and beauty of the world, just as in human literature the sufferings of the hero serve to illustrate his nobility. But God's love for every rational creature cannot permit him to approve any sin, regardless of whatever amount of good it may produce.

4. One of the meanings of the general term "avatar" is the incarnation of a Hindu deity (as Vishnu). But only in the Christian religion has the metaphysical apparatus of substance, essence, nature, being, *esse*, and so on been worked out and applied in a consistent way. It seems likely that, if that were to be done in Hinduism, it would turn out to be a form of either modalism or docetism.

APPENDIX

Essence and Existence

Neither science nor philosophy is sufficient unto itself. In this age of science it seems clear that philosophy needs science in order to be anchored to concrete reality and avoid floating away into a speculative empyrean. But many do not appreciate fully that, without philosophical insight, science too can float away into a theoretical and mathematical empyrean of its own. Since the final interpretations of the meaning of scientific theories are at least partially philosophical, science depends upon philosophy to some extent. If the philosophy is explicit, it will have a better chance of being coherent. Otherwise it is likely to be riddled with unnoticed assumptions and inconsistencies.

My early training in philosophy was in the Aristotelian-Thomistic tradition, as it was understood by Etienne Gilson and other neo-Thomists. Since then I have also been influenced by the ideas of Karl Rahner, Michael Polanyi, Alfred North Whitehead, and others. In this appendix I explain briefly some of the concepts accepted by most, or at least many, contemporary Thomists, in addition to certain modifications of my own. I hope that seeing how I use these concepts in the main chapters of the book will help clarify them further.

The authors of popular books on physics often advise readers not to be put off by the mathematical equations they come upon. They are told to get the general idea and then go on. Often, concepts are clarified by the way they are used. In this book the reader encounters no equations but numerous concepts. However, analogous advice also applies here.

The Conception of Being

Metaphysics is the primary philosophical discipline that reflects upon and clarifies not only its own basic presuppositions but also those of all the others. The most fundamental presupposition of all is *being*, that is, everything that is or can be, whether actual or potential. Being, precisely as being, is what metaphysics takes as its object, whereas the other disciplines aim at understanding some limited domain of reality. Metaphysics aims to understand the whole and, in the light of the whole, to integrate all the aspects studied separately by the other sciences.

In his book *The Unity of Philosophical Experience* (1937), Etienne Gilson argues on the basis of history that metaphysics is inevitably doomed to fail if it overlooks or misunderstands its primary and foundational presupposition (namely, *being*). He shows that, since being is of itself unrestricted, it cannot be adequately understood by generalizing a more specialized point of view (such as, for example, Descartes's mathematical one). If I understand Gilson correctly, he thought that, in the abstract, philosophical reason would be capable of conceiving the authentic nature of being without the help of the Judeo-Christian revelation. Nevertheless, he also believed that historically Aquinas (b. ca. 1224–25, d. 1274) succeeded only by reflecting on the biblical revelation of the divine name, "I am" (Exod. 3:13–14, as well as the Gospel of John, passim).[1]

With the hindsight provided by divine revelation, one can show philosophically the truth of the Thomistic thesis about being. One approach originated with Joseph Maréchal and has been developed further by Karl Rahner, Emerich Coreth, and others (Coreth 1968). But even though I find their view coherent, I myself seldom find certainty on the basis of such subtle and complex philosophical arguments. In fact, I am struck by the fact that historically even great philosophers have been wrong in one or other important respect. As the philosopher Peter Lipton has remarked,

> Most philosophers, today and throughout the subject's history, adopt the rhetoric of certainty. They write as if the correctness of their view

has been demonstrated beyond reasonable doubt. This sometimes makes for stimulating reading, but it is either disingenuous or naïve. In philosophy, if a position is interesting and important, it is almost always also controversial and dubitable. (Lipton 2004, 4)

Philosophers often disagree with one another. There are many different schools of thought, and even within each school there are usually several different opinions. However, a Thomist has the advantage of being able to check his human reasoning against divine revelation. It is important to me that transcendental Thomism is supported not only by Gilson's historical approach but also by Christian theology, whose fundamental principles depend on divine revelation. With regard to the nature of being, the Thomistic account seems to me the only one that does full justice to the Christian doctrine of Creation. Here I present some brief, schematic reflections that I hope will help the reader understand my point of view in a provisional way. This should enable him to follow better the arguments I present. Often concepts become clearer and more plausible when they are used to deal with problems.

The ordinary usage in English, as well as in most Western languages, is suggestive.[2] It suggests that a being is some thing that is *be-ing*. In other words, the form of the word suggests that a being has a fundamental dynamism akin to action and that this dynamism is its act of existing. This act, or quasi act, is so fundamental that in performing it the be-er exists. If it were to stop be-ing it would no longer exist. It would become non-being, that is, nothing. Thus, the dynamic act of being is not accidental or peripheral in the constitution of the being. A runner is a runner in virtue of his act of running. But because running is accidental to the agent who runs, he does not disappear when he stops running. Ordinary actions begin and end without making the agent begin or end. But the act of existing is constitutive of the agent and so were he to stop be-ing he would become nothing. Thus, the act of existing is unique among acts. Other acts are accidental in character and they all depend upon the more fundamental act of being.

The *to-be* (or in Latin, *esse*) of an entity is constitutive of the entity. But how can a thing that of itself does not exist perform an act of existing and thus make itself real? It must be that a finite act of existing is a dependent act, which is possible only when it is supported and complemented by the action of a cause distinct from the be-er. The finite being's to-be, or *esse*, is not only an act of the finite being itself, but it is also in some way the act of its creative cause. For Aquinas, God is the infinite being who enables finite beings, which are first merely possible, to become fully real. God is being itself and he is capable of imparting to mere potentialities, which of themselves exist only in his mind, a real participation in his own actuality.

The term "participation" is reminiscent of Plato, who understood the reality of this limited world in terms of "ideas." For him there is a "really real" world of ideas like unity, goodness, truth, beauty, justice, and so on. That world is its own explanation, its own sufficient reason. Our merely dependent world "participates" in that transcendent one just as our feeble and incomplete truths participate in truth itself. But, for Aquinas, it is reality and not ideas that is at stake. Our limited reality is a participation in the infinite reality of God.

There are two fundamental questions one can ask about the world and about the individual entities and events that make it up, namely, *Is it?* and *What is it?* The two are related yet also radically different. The first is about existence, the second about essence. Essence is the *quiddity* or *whatness* of the thing; existence is its *esse*, its to-be or *quo est*, that by which it is. Essence and *esse* are not things but principles of being that together constitute real things. Of itself the first principle, essence, is a mere possibility. Originally it existed only in the mind of the Creator. The second principle, *esse*, is a participation in God's power to be.

Beside the main distinction in finite beings between essence and *esse* there is another distinction within essence itself. Finite beings are both changeable and unchangeable. I myself change constantly, yet at the same time I also endure. I am the same I who was once young and am now old. Therefore it seems that essence is the union of both *substance* and *accidents*. It is composed of something that always remains the same, which is called "substance," and other elements that come and go, which are called "accidents." My being is composed of essence and *esse*. At the same time, my essence itself is composed of substance and accidents. My *esse* actuates, mainly, my permanent substance, but it also actuates my changing accidents.

In his book *A Brief History of Time* (1988), Stephen Hawking explains how he hopes to define the essence of the universe in a mathematical way, but he says little about its existence. Nevertheless, toward the end of the book he asks, "What is it that breathes fire into the equations and makes a universe for them to describe?" (Hawking 1988, 174). He hopes his equations will lead humankind to understand *what* the world is. But then there will still remain the questions of *how* and *why* it is. I believe that any deep thinker, whether scientist or not, must sooner or later ask himself such questions and wonder how they are related to one another. From a Christian point of view, and in the light of the doctrine of Creation, the whatness of the world is in itself only a possibility in the mind of God. It becomes a reality only when the Creator, who is infinite and subsistent being itself, enables it to participate in his own reality and thus to possess its own, albeit finite, being.

Among finite beings, essence and existence, what is and that by which it is, stand to one another as potency to act, as possibility to actuality. The recognition that the two are really distinct is very important because it sets a fundamental context within which the development of metaphysics can proceed correctly and avoid innumerable blind ends. For that reason the real distinction between essence and existence is, according to Gilson, the greatest metaphysical discovery ever made.[3] With regard to God, the real distinction between essence and existence is illuminating in a negative way, by the very fact that it is not applicable. In him essence and existence are identical. He simply exists without limitation, and his proper name is *I Am* (Exod. 3:13). But in finite beings the distinction is real. Aquinas made use of the infinitive form, "to-be," to emphasize the dynamism of the act of existing. God *is esse,* the unlimited act of being, whereas finite beings merely participate in *esse* rather than being identical with it. What they are is that by which they are. Their essence limits the fullness of their being. The finite *esse* of a creature is not identical with the infinite *esse* in which the creature participates, nor is the *esse* of one entity the same as the *esse* of any other.

Unlike terms that are univocal, the term "being" is a highly analogous one. One can say that John is a man and James is a man. Even though they are not identical individuals, we are able to abstract from their individual essences an intelligibility that is the same in both. Their manhood as such can be considered apart from the elements that make them different and are therefore excluded from consideration. But we cannot abstract "being" from James or John the way we abstract "manhood" from them, because their "being" refers to the reality of everything about them, including their differences. The "manhood" of John is exactly the same as the "manhood" of James, but the "being" of John is not the same as the "being" of James. Nevertheless, the "being" of James and the "being" of John are not simply different, because they are alike inasmuch as they are both real beings. Thus, the analogous term "being" applies to every real entity, but in a different way for each. With respect to being, each existent is both irreducibly different from and at the same time like each of the others.

If one cannot know the being of James and John by abstracting it from them, then how does one know it? By making judgments about them. One judges that John is a being and one also judges that James is a being. But what is the basis by which these judgments are made? If each intelligible element of one being is different from each and every intelligible element of a second, how can the two be similar? The only explanation seems to be that all finite individuals are related, each in its own unique way, to a single reality that transcends them all and is the source of them all, namely, being itself. It is their participation in this one transcendent reality that makes all of them alike as beings. All of these relationships are different from the others with respect to their initial terms, but all have the same final term, namely, being itself.

If we judge that two things are analogously similar because of their analogous causal relationships to being itself, it seems that we must know being itself in some way. If we did not know it at all we could not grasp the similarity of the many diverse entities that relate to it. But we do not know being itself in any way we can explain easily. How can we both know it and not know it at the same time?

How this is possible has been made clearer for us moderns by Michael

Polanyi.[4] Polanyi was both an eminent physical chemist and an outstanding philosophical cosmologist. He might also be called a scientific phenomenologist, one who examined and analyzed in great detail scientific experience. He claimed that the kind of explicit knowledge we can express in words and other symbols emanates from a more fundamental tacit knowing that cannot be adequately expressed and often is not even adverted to at all. In his book *The Tacit Dimension*, he begins by pointing out that

> we can know more than we can tell. This fact seems obvious enough; but it is not easy to say exactly what it means. Take an example. We know a person's face, and can recognize it among a thousand, indeed among a million. Yet we usually cannot tell how we recognize a face we know. So most of this knowledge cannot be put into words. (Polanyi 1967, 4)

Through many other examples drawn from both science and human experience, Polanyi demonstrates the fact that explicit objective knowledge depends upon tacit subjective knowledge. Attention is focused upon focal, objective knowledge, while the background from which the objective knowledge arises is tacit and implicit rather than explicit. Sometimes the cognitive background can be made partially objective in a later mental act. Yet such objectification is never completely successful.

Polanyi's insight into the nature of human knowing derives from the practice of modern science. Nevertheless, long before Polanyi, Plato pointed out the importance of the distinction between tacit and explicit knowing in his dialogue the *Meno* (80d–86c). How is it possible to inquire about anything? If we ask about it we evidently do not know it. Yet we could not ask if we did not somehow know it already. Evidently every inquiry presupposes some heuristic anticipation of the answer to the question one seeks to answer. To account for our human power to inquire about the unknown, Plato suggested the myth that the known unknown we seek is something that we once knew clearly in a previous existence. This myth has a certain resonance with our common human experience of trying to recapture a memory we have temporarily forgotten. But of course we do not remember an existence prior to this one and have no satisfactory evidence in favor of its reality. Moreover, Christian tradition rules out reincarnation after death (*Catechism of the Catholic Church* §1013).

Other philosophers have held that we are born with fundamental innate concepts in virtue of which we are able to learn everything else. But if so, what enables us to know for certain that these innate ideas are correct? "Instinct" or "common sense" may compel the naïve to believe they are, but reflection reveals no compelling reason to support such beliefs.

I believe that the best explanation is that of transcendental Thomism. At the very beginning of his conscious existence, a human being becomes sensibly aware of a jumble of impressions about which he knows nothing in an explicit, intellectual way. But, as Aquinas insisted, "being is the first thing encountered by the intellect" (Gilson 1986, 196). The new person immediately judges that he is encountering something that is real. This can be possible only if a human person already possesses at the beginning a certain tacit, heuristic anticipation of reality that enables him to judge immediately that in the sensible impressions he receives he is encountering a real world. This fundamental judgment remains at the root of all the explicit understanding he attains in the course of his life. His fundamental heuristic anticipation of being embraces in a certain way all that he knows or can know intellectually either now or in the future. He can know any real thing in some way—either as lying within the grasp of his cognitive power or else as exceeding that power; either as an object lying within his intellectual horizon or else as belonging to a realm that lies beyond it. But in knowing that it lies beyond him he knows that it exists.

What Plato referred to metaphorically as a memory of a former life is in fact a tacit, unthematic knowing that is a necessary aspect of one's existence as a human person. For a human being, to be is to know in this tacit way. Whenever one interacts with the world, this tacit, potential knowledge gives rise to explicit, objective knowledge, as well as to subjective awareness of oneself as the subject and source of this explicit knowledge.

To put it in a slightly different way, tacit knowing is a heuristic anticipation of being itself, an anticipation in virtue of which I am able to inquire about and come to know the finite beings that participate in being. Being itself is like a limitless horizon that surrounds and supports the luminous realm within me where I encounter objects. The objects manifest themselves by acting upon my senses, but their sensible effects on me would mean nothing to me were it not for my tacit knowledge of being within which they are situated (Rahner 1978, esp. chap. 2; McCool 1975, chap. 1).

In speaking of a "horizon," as I just did, I am obviously using a metaphor. If someone stands on the peak of a high mountain and looks around, he finds he has a certain limited field of vision within which are situated all the things he can see from where he stands. His horizon, the distant circle where the dome of the sky appears to meet the earth or sea, is that which seems to limit his field of vision. It is also the near edge of the limitless realm that lies beyond it.

Clearly enough, one's point of view, field of vision, and horizon are closely related and dependent upon one another. One can draw an analogy between bodily vision and natural intellectual understanding. As knowers, we always have an epistemic point of view from which we can understand some objects but cannot understand others. But there is an ultimate epistemic boundary that includes all we can comprehend in an objective, explicit way. This ultimate horizon is also the appearance to us of the infinite mystery that exceeds our powers of explicit understanding. That mystery is in fact being itself, which is infinite and always exceeds our finite intellects. Being itself is what makes it possible for us to know finite beings in an explicit way. It is the unfathomable mystery that determines humanity's ultimate point of view and field of intellectual vision. Even people who have never heard of or thought about being itself still know it tacitly and rely upon it in everything they know and do. To be a human being is to be, as Rahner has said, "spirit in the world." As spirit, I am aware of being present to myself. I have not only a tacit knowing of my own finite act of being but also a heuristic anticipation of the infinite act of being in which I participate.

Though infinite being and infinite intelligibility are identical, finite being and finite intelligibility are not. One can exist without knowing anything explicitly. But to be a finite spirit is to participate in being itself to a sufficient degree that when one is actuated by the objective world, one can know oneself subjectively as the source of one's acts of knowing.

NOTES

1. Aquinas's Jewish predecessor, Moses Maimonides (1135–1204), came to much the same insight by reflecting on the same text from Exodus.

2. For brief introductions to the Thomistic concept of being, see Clarke, *The One and the Many*, chap. 2; and Klubertanz, *Introduction to the Philosophy of Being*, chap. 2.

3. Aquinas was not the first to accept the distinction between essence and existence, although he clarified and exploited it. See the *New Catholic Encyclopedia* 2003, 5:549 (art. "Essence and Existence").

4. Polanyi's masterwork is *Personal Knowledge* (1964). See also his books *The Tacit Dimension* (1967); *The Study of Man* (1959); and *Knowing and Being* (1969). Excellent introductions to his thought are Scott, *Everyman Revisited*; and Dulles, *Theological Studies* 45 (1984): 537–50.

Reference List

Aczel, Amir D. 2001. *Entanglement: The Greatest Mystery in Physics*. New York: Four Walls Eight Windows.
Amábile-Cuevas, Carlos F., Maura Cárdenas-García, and Mauricio Ludgar. 1995. "Antibiotic Resistance." *American Scientist* 83:324–29.
Anderson, P. W. 1972. "More Is Different: Broken Symmetry and the Nature of the Hierarchical Structure of Science." *Science* 177:393–96.
Aquinas, Thomas (Saint). *Commentary on Aristotle's De Anima*.
———. *Summa contra gentiles* (= C.G.).
———. *Summa theologica* (= S.T.).
Arraj, James. 1996. *The Mystery of Matter: Nonlocality, Morphic Resonance, Synchronicity and the Philosophy of Nature of Thomas Aquinas*. Chiloquin, OR: Inner Growth Books.
Artigas, Mariano. 2000. *The Mind of the Universe: Understanding Science and Religion*. Philadelphia: Templeton Foundation Press.
Augros, Michael. 2004. "Reconciling Science with Natural Philosophy." *The Thomist* 68:105–41.
Augustine (Saint). 1943. *The Confessions of St. Augustine*. Translated by J. F. Sheed. New York: Sheed & Ward.
Ayala, Francisco J. 1998. "The Evolution of Life: An Overview." In *Evolutionary and Molecular Biology*, edited by Robert John Russell, William R. Stoeger, S.J., and Francisco J. Ayala, 21–57. Vatican City: Vatican Observatory Publications; Berkeley: Center for Theology and the Natural Sciences.
Ayala, F., and T. Dobzhansky, eds. 1974. *Studies in the Philosophy of Biology*. Berkeley: University of California Press.
Baggott, J. E. 2004. *Beyond Measure: Modern Physics, Philosophy, and the Meaning of Quantum Theory*. New York: Oxford University Press.

Balthasar, Hans Urs von. 1988. *Dare We Hope "That All Men Be Saved"?* San Francisco: Ignatius Press.

Barr, James. 1977. *Fundamentalism*. London: SCM.

Barr, Stephen M. 2003. *Modern Physics and Ancient Faith*. Notre Dame, IN: University of Notre Dame Press.

———. 2006. "The Miracle of Evolution." *First Things* (February): 30–33.

Barrow, John D., and Frank J. Tipler. 1986. *The Anthropic Cosmological Principle*. New York: Oxford University Press.

Barth, Markus, and Helmut Blanke. 1994. *Colossians: A New Translation with Introduction and Commentary*. Translated by Astrid B. Beck. Anchor Bible 34B. New York: Doubleday.

Behe, Michael J. 1996. *Darwin's Black Box: The Biochemical Challenge to Evolution*. New York: Free Press.

———. 2007. *The Edge of Evolution: The Search for the Limits of Darwinism*. New York: Free Press.

Behe, Michael J., William A. Dembski, and Stephen C. Meyer. 2000. *Science and Evidence for Design in the Universe: Papers Presented at a Conference Sponsored by the Wethersfield Institute, New York City, September 25, 1999*. Proceedings of the Wethersfield Institute 9. San Francisco: Ignatius Press.

Bell, John S. 1987. *Speakable and Unspeakable in Quantum Mechanics: Collected Papers on Quantum Philosophy*. New York: Cambridge University Press.

———. 1989. "Against Measurement." In *Sixty-Two Years of Uncertainty*, edited by Arthur I. Miller, 17–31. New York: Plenum Press.

Bergant, Dianne, and Carroll Stuhlmueller. 1985. "Creation according to the Old Testament." In *Evolution and Creation*, edited by Ernan McMullin, 153ff. Notre Dame, IN: University of Notre Dame Press.

Berge, Claude. 1985. *Graphs*. North-Holland Mathematical Library 6.1. New York: Elsevier Science Pub.

Bethel, Tom. 1999. "Rethinking Gravity." *The American Spectator* (April): 20–23.

Bohm, David. 1951. *Quantum Theory*. Englewood Cliffs, NJ: Prentice-Hall.

———. 1953. "A Suggested Interpretation." *Physical Review* 85:166–79.

Bohm, D., and Y. Aharonov. 1957. "Discussion of Experimental Proof." *Physical Review* 108:1070–76.

Bohr, Neils. 1963. *Essays 1958/1962 on Atomic Physics and Human Knowledge*. New York: Wiley.

Bollobás, Béla. 1998. *Modern Graph Theory*. New York: Springer.

Brauer, Matthew J., and Daniel R. Brumbaugh. 1998. "Biology Remystified: The Scientific Claims of the New Creationists." In *Intelligent Design: Creationism and Its Critics*, edited by Robert T. Pennock, chap. 12. Cambridge, MA: MIT Press.

Brisson, Luc, and F. Walter Meyerstein. 1995. *Inventing the Universe*. Albany: State University of New York Press.

Brown, Raymond E. 1966, 1970. *The Gospel according to John: Introduction, Translation, and Notes*. 2 vols. Anchor Bible 29, 29A. Garden City, NY: Doubleday.

———. 1997. *An Introduction to the New Testament*. New York: Doubleday.

Bub, Jeffrey. 1997. *Interpreting the Quantum World*. Cambridge: Cambridge University Press.

Buckley, Michael J. 1987. *At the Origins of Modern Atheism*. New Haven: Yale University Press.

Callender, Craig, and Nick Huggett, eds. 2001. *Physics Meets Philosophy at the Planck Scale*. Cambridge: Cambridge University Press.

Campbell, Neil A., Jane B. Reece, and Lawrence G. Mitchell. 1999. *Biology*. 5th ed. New York: Addison Wesley Longman.

Camus, Albert. 1956. *The Rebel: An Essay on Man in Revolt*. New York: Vintage Books.

Cantore, Enrico. 1977. *Scientific Man: The Humanistic Significance of Science*. New York: ISH Publications. Distributed by International Scholarly Book Services, Forest Grove, Oregon.

Carrel, Alexis. 1994. *The Voyage to Lourdes*. Introduction by Stanley L. Jaki. Fraser, MI: Real-View-Books.

Casti, John L. 2002. "Science Is a Computer Program." *Nature* 417:381–82.

Catechism of the Catholic Church. 1997. 2nd ed. Vatican City: Libreria Editrice Vaticana.

Chalmers, David J. 1996. *The Conscious Mind: In Search of a Fundamental Theory*. New York: Oxford University Press.

Churchland, Patricia. 1986. *Neurophilosophy*. Cambridge, MA: MIT Press.

Churchland, Paul M., and Clifford A. Hooker, eds. 1985. *Images of Science*. Chicago: University of Chicago Press.

Clarke, W. Norris. 1962. "Causality and Time." In *Experience, Existence, and the Good: Essays in Honor of Paul Weiss*, edited by Irwin C. Lieb, 143–57. Carbondale: Southern Illinois University Press.

———. 1993. *Person and Being*. Milwaukee: Marquette University Press.

———. 1994. *Explorations in Metaphysics*. Notre Dame, IN: University of Notre Dame Press.

———. 2001. *The One and the Many*. Notre Dame, IN: University of Notre Dame Press.

Clauser, J. F., and M. A. Horne. 1974. "Experimental Consequences of Objective Local Theories." *Physical Review* D10:526–35.

Commoner, Barry. 2002. "Unraveling the DNA Myth." *Harper's Magazine* (February): 39–47.

Copleston, Frederick. 1985. *A History of Philosophy*. 9 volumes in 3. New York: Doubleday Image.

Coreth, Emerich. 1968. *Metaphysics*. Translated by Joseph Donceel. New York: Herder & Herder.

Cournand, André. 1977. "The Code of the Scientist and Its Relationship to Ethics." *Science* 198:699–705.

Coveney, Peter, and Roger Highfield. 1990. *The Arrow of Time*. New York: Fawcett Columbine.

Coyne, George. 1998. "Evolution and the Human Person." In *Evolutionary and Molecular Biology*, edited by Robert John Russell, William R. Stoeger, S.J., and Francisco J. Ayala, 11–17. Vatican City: Vatican Observatory Publications; Berkeley: Center for Theology and the Natural Sciences.

Cramer, John G. 1986. "The Transactional Interpretation of Quantum Mechanics." *Reviews of Modern Physics* 58:647–87.

Cranston, Ruth. 1988. *The Miracle of Lourdes*. Updated ed. New York: Image Books.

Crewdson, John. 2002. *Science Fictions*. Boston: Little, Brown.

Crick, Francis. 1981. *Life Itself: Its Origin and Nature*. New York: Simon & Schuster.

———. 1994. *The Astonishing Hypothesis: The Scientific Search for the Soul*. Parsippany, NJ: Simon & Schuster.

Crick, Francis, and Leslie E. Orgel. 1973. "Directed Panspermia." *Icarus* 19:341–46.

Cullman, Oscar. 1962. *Christ and Time*. Rev. ed. London: SCM.

Cushing, James T. 1994. *Quantum Mechanics*. Chicago: University of Chicago Press.

———. 1998. *Philosophical Concepts in Physics*. New York: Cambridge University Press.

Cushing, James T., Arthur Fine, and Sheldon Goldstein. 1996. *Bohmian Mechanics and Quantum Theory: An Appraisal.* Boston: Kluwer Academic.
Cushing, James T., and Ernan McMullin, eds. 1989. *Philosophical Consequences of Quantum Theory.* Notre Dame, IN: University of Notre Dame Press.
Damasio, Antonio. 1994a. *Descartes' Error.* New York: Grosset Putnam.
———. 1994b. "Descartes' Error and the Future of Human Life." *Scientific American* (October): 144.
———. 1999a. *The Feeling of What Happens.* New York: Harcourt, Brace.
———. 1999b. "How the Brain Creates the Mind." *Scientific American* (December): 112–17.
Darwin, Charles. (1859) 1964. *On the Origin of Species by Means of Natural Selection or the Preservation of Favored Races in the Struggle for Life.* Facsimile ed. London: Murray.
———. (1862) 1984. *The Various Contrivances by Which Orchids Are Fertilised by Insects.* Chicago: University of Chicago Press.
———. 1988. *Origin of Species.* New York: New York University Press.
Davies, Brian. 1992. *The Thought of Thomas Aquinas.* Oxford: Clarendon Press.
———. 2002. "Creationism and All That." *The Tablet* [London] (May 11, 2002): 16–17.
———. 2006. *The Reality of God and the Problem of Evil.* New York: Continuum.
Davies, Paul. 2003. Op. ed. *New York Times* (April 12, 2003): A13.
Dawkins, Richard. 1986. *The Blind Watchmaker.* New York: W. W. Norton.
———. 1995. *River out of Eden: A Darwinian View of Life.* New York: Basic Books.
———. 1996. *Climbing Mount Improbable.* New York: W. W. Norton.
Dembski, William A. 1998. *The Design Inference: Elimination of Chance through Small Probabilities.* Cambridge: Cambridge University Press.
———. 1999. *Intelligent Design.* Downers Grove, IL: InterVarsity Press.
———. 2000. "The Third Mode of Explanation: Detecting Evidence of Intelligent Design in the Sciences." In Michael J. Behe, William A. Dembski, and Stephen C. Meyer, *Science and Evidence for Design in the Universe: Papers Presented at a Conference Sponsored by the Wethersfield Institute, New York City, September 25, 1999,* 17–51. Proceedings of the Wethersfield Institute 9. San Francisco: Ignatius Press.

———. 2002. *No Free Lunch: Why Specified Complexity Cannot Be Purchased without Intelligence*. Lanham, MD: Rowman & Littlefield.

———. 2004. *The Design Revolution*. Downers Grove, IL: InterVarsity Press.

———. 2014. *Being as Communion: A Metaphysics of Information*. Farmdale, UK: Ashgate.

Dembski, William A., and James M. Kushiner, eds. 2001. *Signs of Intelligence*. Grand Rapids: Brazos.

Dembski, William A., and Stephen C. Meyer. 2000. "Fruitful Interchange or Polite Chitchat? The Dialogue between Science and Theology." In Michael J. Behe, William A. Dembski, and Stephen C. Meyer, *Science and Evidence for Design in the Universe: Papers Presented at a Conference Sponsored by the Wethersfield Institute, New York City, September 25, 1999*, 213–31. Proceedings of the Wethersfield Institute 9. San Francisco: Ignatius Press.

Dennett, Daniel C. 1991. *Consciousness Explained*. Boston: Little, Brown.

Denzinger, Henricus, and Adolfus Schönmetzer, eds. 1962. *Enchiridion Symbolorum*. 32nd ed. New York: Herder.

Depew, David J., and Bruce H. Weber. 1995. *Darwinism Evolving*. Cambridge, MA: MIT Press.

Dirac, P. A. M. (1930) 1958. *The Principles of Quantum Mechanics*. 4th ed. Oxford: Clarendon Press.

Dostoevsky, Fyodor. 1982. *The Brothers Karamazov*. Translated by David Magarshack. New York: Penguin Books.

Drake, Stillman, ed. 1957. *Discoveries and Opinions of Galileo*. Garden City, NY: Doubleday-Anchor.

Dreyfus, Hubert L. 1992. *What Computers Still Can't Do*. Cambridge, MA: MIT Press.

Dreyfus, Hubert L., and Stuart E. Dreyfus, with T. Athanasiou. 1986. *Mind over Machine*. New York: Free Press.

Dulbecco, Renato. 1997. *Encyclopedia of Human Biology*. 2nd ed., vol. 4. San Diego: Academic Press.

Dulles, Avery. 1984. "Faith, Church, and God: Insights from Michael Polanyi." *Theological Studies* 45:537–50.

———. 1994. *The Assurance of Things Hoped For: A Theology of Christian Faith*. New York: Oxford University Press.

———. 1996. *The Craft of Theology*. Expanded ed. New York: Crossroad.

Dych, William V. 1992. *Karl Rahner*. Collegeville, MN: Liturgical Press, Michael Glazier.

Edelman, Gerald. 1989. *The Remembered Present*. New York: Basic Books.

———. 1992. *Bright Air, Brilliant Fire*. New York: Basic Books.

Eigen, Manfred. 1992. *Steps towards Life: A Perspective on Evolution*. Translated by P. Woolley. Oxford: Oxford University Press.

Einstein, Albert. 1949. "Reply to Criticisms." In *Albert Einstein: Philosopher-Scientist*, edited by Paul Arthur Schilpp. Evanston, IL: Library of Living Philosophers.

———. 1994. *Ideas and Opinions*. Based on *Mein Weltbild*. Translated by S. Bargmann. New York: Modern Library.

Einstein, A., B. Podolsky, and N. Rosen. 1935. "Can Quantum-Mechanical Description of Physical Reality Be Considered Complete?" *Physical Review* 47:777–80.

Eldredge, Niles. 2000. *The Triumph of Evolution*. New York: W. H. Freeman.

Emmanuel of Medjugorje (Sr.). 1997. *The Amazing Secret of the Souls in Purgatory*. Santa Barbara: Queenship Publishing.

"The Emperor's New Theory: The Theory of Everything." 2002. *The Economist* (June 1): 79–80.

Espagnat, Bernard d'. 1976. *Conceptual Foundations of Quantum Mechanics*. Reading, MA: W. A. Benjamin.

Everett, Hugh. 1983. "'Relative State' Formulation of Quantum Mechanics." In *Quantum Theory and Measurement*, edited by J. A. Wheeler and W. H. Zurek. Princeton: Princeton University Press. Originally published in *Reviews of Modern Physics* 29:454–62.

Farrelly, M. John. 1964. *Predestination, Grace, and Free Will*. Westminster, MD: Newman Press.

Felt, James W. 2001. *Coming to Be: Toward a Thomistic-Whiteheadian Metaphysics of Becoming*. Albany: State University of New York Press.

Feynman, Richard P. 1985. *QED*. Princeton: Princeton University Press.

Finance, Joseph de. 1960. *Être et agir dans la philosophie de Saint Thomas*. 2nd ed. Rome: Gregorian University.

Fisher, Christopher L., and David Fergusson. 2006. "Karl Rahner and the Extraterrestrial Intelligence Question." *Heythrop Journal* 47.2:275–90.

Fisher, Ronald A. 1930. *The Genetical Theory of Natural Selection*. Oxford: Clarendon Press. 2nd ed. New York: Dover, 1958.

———. 1974. "Science and Christianity: Faith Is Not Credulity." In *Collected Papers of R. A. Fisher*, vol. 5, edited by J. H. Bennett, 351–52. Adelaide: University of Adelaide.

Fitzmyer, Joseph A. 1993. *Romans: A New Translation with Introduction and Commentary*. Anchor Bible 33. New York: Doubleday.

Flannery, A. 1981. *Vatican Council II*. Northport, NY: Costello.

Floridi, Luciano. 1999. *Philosophy and Computing*. New York: Routledge.

Folse, Henry J. 1989. "Bohr on Bell." In *Philosophical Consequences of Quantum Theory*, edited by James T. Cushing and Ernan McMullin, 254–71. Notre Dame, IN: University of Notre Dame Press.

Fraassen, Bas C. van. 1980. *The Scientific Image*. Oxford: Clarendon Press.

Frankl, Viktor. 1959. *Man's Search for Meaning*. Boston: Beacon Press.

Fredkin, Edward. 1990. "Digital Mechanics." *Physica* D 45:254–70.

Frye, R., ed. 1983. *Is God a Creationist?* New York: Charles Scribner's Sons.

Futuyma, Douglas J. 1998. *Evolutionary Biology*. 3rd ed. Sunderland, MA: Sinauer Associates.

Galileo. See Drake, Stillman.

Gell-Mann, Murray. 1994. *The Quark and the Jaguar*. New York: W. H. Freeman.

George, Timothy. 2003. "What God Knows." *First Things* (June/July): 7–9.

German Bishops' Conference. 1987. *The Church's Confession of Christ*. San Francisco: Ignatius Press.

Gigerenzer, Gerd, et al. 1989. *The Empire of Chance: How Probability Changed Science and Everyday Life*. New York: Cambridge University Press.

Gilkey, Langdon. 1965. *Maker of Heaven and Earth*. Garden City, NY: Doubleday Anchor.

———. 1981. *Religion and the Scientific Future*. Macon, GA: Mercer University Press.

———. 1985. *Creationism on Trial*. Minneapolis: Winston.

———. 1993a. *Nature, Reality, and the Sacred*. Minneapolis: Fortress.

———. 1993b. "Creationism: The Roots of the Conflict." In *Is God a Creationist?*, edited by R. Frye, 56–67. New York: Charles Scribner's Sons.

Gilson, Etienne. 1937. *The Unity of Philosophical Experience*. New York: Charles Scribner's Sons.

———. 1940. *The Spirit of Medieval Philosophy*. Translated by A. Donnes. New York: Charles Scribner's Sons.

———. 1952. *Being and Some Philosophers*. 2nd corrected and enlarged ed. Toronto: Pontifical Institute of Mediaeval Studies.

———. 1962. *The Philosopher and Theology*. Translated by Cécile Gilson. New York: Random House.

———. 1986. *Thomist Realism and the Critique of Knowledge*. Translated by Mark A. Wauck. San Francisco: Ignatius Press.

Gleick, James. 1992. *Genius*. New York: Pantheon Books.

Gold, T., ed. 1967. *The Nature of Time*. Ithaca, NY: Cornell University Press.

Goldschmidt, R. B. 1945. "Mimetic Polymorphism, a Controversial Chapter of Darwinism." *Quarterly Review of Biology* 20:147–64, 205–30.

Goldstein, Sheldon. 1998. "Quantum Theory without Observers." *Physics Today* (March): 42–46 (part 1); (April): 38–42 (part 2).

Goodwin, Brian. 1994. *How the Leopard Changed Its Spots*. New York: Charles Scribner's Sons.

Gould, Stephen Jay. 2001. "The Panda's Thumb." In *Intelligent Design: Creationism and Its Critics*, edited by Robert T. Pennock, chap. 31. Cambridge, MA: MIT Press. Revised ed. reprinted from *Natural History*, November 1978.

———. 2002. *The Structure of Evolutionary Theory*. Cambridge, MA: Harvard University Press.

Gould, Stephen Jay, and Richard C. Lewontin. 1979. "The Spandrels of San Marco and the Panglossian Paradigm." *Proceedings of the Royal Society of London B* 205:581–98.

Greene, Brian. 1999. *The Elegant Universe*. New York: W. W. Norton.

———. 2003. "The Future of String Theory." *Scientific American* (November): 68–73.

———. 2004. *The Fabric of the Cosmos*. New York: Alfred A. Knopf.

Greene, John C. 1959. *The Death of Adam*. Ames: Iowa State University Press.

———. 1981. *Science, Ideology, and World View*. Berkeley: University of California Press.

———. 1999. *Debating Darwin*. Claremont, CA: Regina Books.

Gribbin, John. 1995. *Schrödinger's Kittens and the Search for Reality*. New York: Little, Brown.

Griffin, David Ray. 1976. *God, Power, and Evil: A Process Theodicy*. Philadelphia: Westminster Press.

Hacking, Ian. 1983. *Representing and Intervening*. Cambridge: Cambridge University Press.

———. 2001. *An Introduction to Probability and Inductive Logic.* Cambridge: Cambridge University Press.

Hahn, Roger. 1986. "Laplace and the Mechanistic Universe." In *God and Nature*, edited by David C. Lindberg and Ronald L. Numbers, 256–76. Berkeley: University of California Press.

Harary, F., R. Z. Norman, and D. Cartwright. 1965. *Structural Models.* New York: Wiley.

Haroche, Serge. 1998. "Entanglement, Decoherence and the Quantum/Classical Boundary." *Physics Today* (July): 36–42.

Hartshorne, Charles. 1970. *Creative Synthesis and Philosophic Method.* LaSalle, IL: Open Court.

Haught, John F. 1995. *Science and Religion.* Mahwah, NJ: Paulist Press.

Hawking, Stephen. 1988. *A Brief History of Time.* New York: Bantam Books.

Hayes, Zachary. 1989. *Visions of a Future: A Study of Christian Eschatology.* Wilmington, DE: Michael Glazier.

———. 2001. *The Gift of Being.* Collegeville, MN: Liturgical Press.

Heelan, Patrick A. 1983. *Space-Perception and the Philosophy of Science.* Berkeley: University of California Press.

Heisenberg, Werner. 1962. *Physics and Philosophy.* New York: Harper & Row.

———. 1983. *Encounters with Einstein, and Other Essays on People, Places and Particles.* Princeton, NJ: Princeton University Press.

Herbert, Nick. 1985. *Quantum Reality.* Garden City, NY: Doubleday Anchor.

Heschel, Abraham J. 1962. *The Prophets.* New York: Harper & Row. German original 1936.

Hiebert, Erwin N. 1986. "Modern Physics and Christian Faith." In *God and Nature*, edited by David C. Lindberg and Ronald L. Numbers, 424–47. Berkeley: University of California Press.

Holt, R. A. 1973. "Atomic Cascade Experiments." Ph.D. dissertation, Harvard University.

Hooper, Judith. 2002. *Of Moths and Men.* New York: W. W. Norton.

Horgan, John. 1994. "Particle Metaphysics." *Scientific American* (February): 96–106.

———. 1995. "From Complexity to Perplexity." *Scientific American* (June): 104–9.

Hotz, Robert Lee. 1997. "A Study in Complexity." *MIT Technology Review* 100 (October): 22–29.

Huggett, Nick, ed. 1999. *Space from Zeno to Einstein*. Cambridge, MA: MIT Press.

Hulsbosch, A. 1961. *God in Creation and Evolution*. New York: Sheed & Ward.

Hume, David. 1993. "Dialogue concerning Natural Religion." *New York*: Cambridge University Press.

Hyers, C. 1983. "Biblical Literalism." In *Is God a Creationist?*, edited by R. Frye, 95–104. New York: Charles Scribner's Sons.

Ignatius of Loyola (Saint). 1951. *The Spiritual Exercises of St. Ignatius*. Translated by Louis J. Puhl. Chicago: Loyola University Press.

Irenaeus of Lyons (Saint). *Adversus haereses*.

Isham, Christopher J., and John C. Polkinghorne. 1993. "The Debate about the Block Universe." In *Quantum Cosmology and the Laws of Nature: Scientific Perspectives on Divine Action*, edited by Robert John Russell, Nancey Murphy, and C. J. Isham, 135–44. Vatican City State: Vatican Observatory; Berkeley: Center for Theology and the Natural Sciences.

Jacob, François. 1973. *The Logic of Life: A History of Heredity*. New York: Pantheon.

Jaki, Stanley L. 1980. *Cosmos and Creator*. Chicago: Regnery Gateway.

Jammer, Max. 1960. *Concepts of Space*. New York: Harper & Row.

———. 1966. *The Conceptual Development of Quantum Mechanics*. New York: McGraw-Hill.

———. 1974. *The Philosophy of Quantum Mechanics*. New York: Wiley.

John Paul II (Pope). 1988, 1995. "Message of His Holiness Pope John Paul II." In *Physics, Philosophy, and Theology: A Common Quest for Understanding*, edited by Robert J. Russell, William R. Stoeger, and George V. Coyne, p. m1. Vatican City State: Vatican Observatory.

———. 1994a. *Crossing the Threshold of Hope*. New York: Alfred A. Knopf.

———. 1994b. *Tertio millennio adveniente* (Apostolic Letter "On the coming of the third millennium"). November 10.

———. 1996. Address to the Pontifical Academy of Sciences. October 22.

———. 1998. *Faith and Reason*. Encyclical letter [*FR*].

Johnson, George. 2001. "New Contenders for a Theory of Everything." *New York Times*, December 4, 2001: F1, F5.

Johnson, Phillip E. 1991. *Darwin on Trial*. Washington, D.C.: Regnery Gateway.

———. 2000. *The Wedge of Truth*. Downers Grove, IL: InterVarsity Press.

———. 2001. "The Intelligent Design Movement." In *Signs of Intelligence*, edited by William Dembski and James Kushiner, chap. 1. Grand Rapids: Brazos.

Kadanoff, Leo P. 2002. "Wolfram on Cellular Automata." *Physics Today* (July): 55–56.

Kasper, Walter. 1995. *The God of Jesus Christ*. New York: Crossroad.

Kauffman, Stuart. 1995. *At Home in the Universe*. New York: Oxford University Press.

Kern, Lauren. 2000. "In God's Country," *Houston Press*, December 14.

Keynes, Randal. 2001. *Darwin, His Daughter, and Human Evolution*. New York: Riverhead Books, 2002.

Kipling, Rudyard. (1902) 1912. *Just So Stories*. Garden City, NY: Doubleday.

Kitcher, Philip. 1982. *Abusing Science*. Cambridge, MA: MIT Press.

———. 1993. *The Advancement of Science*. New York: Oxford University Press.

Kittel, Gerhard, ed. 1971. *Theological Dictionary of the New Testament*, vol. 7, ed. Gerhard Friedrich. Grand Rapids: Eerdmans.

Klubertanz, George. 1953. *The Philosophy of Human Nature*. New York: Appleton-Century-Crofts.

———. 1963. *Introduction to the Philosophy of Being*. 2nd ed. New York: Appleton-Century-Crofts.

Koestler, Arthur. 1969. "Beyond Atomism and Holism—The Concept of the Holon." In *Beyond Reductionism: New Perspectives in the Life Sciences*, edited by Arthur Koestler and J. R. Smythies, 192–232. New York: Macmillan.

Kraus, Elizabeth M. 1979. *The Metaphysics of Experience*. New York: Fordham University Press.

Kreeft, Peter. 1993. *Christianity for Modern Pagans: Pascal's Pensées*, edited, outlined and explained. San Francisco: Ignatius Press.

Kuhn, Thomas S. 1957. *The Copernican Revolution*. Cambridge, MA: Harvard University Press.

———. 1970. *The Structure of Scientific Revolutions*. 2nd ed. Chicago: University of Chicago Press.

Landau, L. D., and E. M. Lifshitz. 1977. *Quantum Mechanics*. 3rd ed. Oxford: Pergamon Press.

Larson, Edward J., and Larry Witham. 1999. "Scientists and Religion in America." *Scientific American* (September): 88–93.

Laudan, L. 1982. "Science at the Bar: Causes for Concern." *Science, Technology and Human Values* 7:16–19, no. 41.

———. 1983. "The Demise of the Demarcation Problem." In *Physics, Philosophy, and Psychoanalysis: Essays in Honor of Adolf Grünbaum*, edited by R. Cohen and L. Laudan, 111–27. Boston Studies in the Philosophy of Science 76. Dordrecht: Reidel.

Laughlin, Robert B., and David Pines. 2000. "The Theory of Everything." *Proceedings of the National Academy of Science* 97.1:28–31.

Laughlin, Robert B., et al. 2000. "The Middle Way." *Proceedings of the National Academy of Science* 97.1:32–37.

Leclerc, I. 1958. *Whitehead's Metaphysics*. London: George Allen & Unwin.

———. 1972. *The Nature of Physical Existence*. New York: Humanities Press.

Leggett, A. J. 1999. "Quantum Theory: Weird and Wonderful." *Physics World* 12 (December): 73–77.

Léon-Dufour, Xavier, ed. 1995. *Dictionary of Biblical Theology*. Updated 2nd ed. Gaithersburg, MD: Word among Us; Boston: St. Paul Books and Media.

Leslie, John. 1982. *American Philosophical Quarterly* 19 (April): 141–51.

Levine, Joseph. 1983. "Materialism and Qualia: The Explanatory Gap." *Pacific Philosophical Quarterly* 64:354–61.

Lewis, C. S. 1962. *The Problem of Pain*. New York: Macmillan.

Lewontin, Richard. 1997. "Billions and Billions of Demons." *New York Review of Books*, January 9, 1997, 28–32.

Lightman, A., and R. Brawer, eds. 1990. *Origins: The Lives and Worlds of Modern Cosmologists*. Cambridge, MA: Harvard University Press.

Lindberg, David C., and Ronald L. Numbers, eds. 1986. *God and Nature*. Berkeley and Los Angeles: University of California Press.

Lipton, Peter. 2004. *Inference to the Best Explanation*. 2nd ed. London and New York: Routledge.

Lonergan, Bernard J. F. 1964. *De Deo trino II: Pars systematica*, 186–93, esp. 193. Rome: Gregorian University.

———. 1968. "Metaphysics as Horizon." In *Metaphysics*, edited by Emerich Coreth, 197–219. Translated by Joseph Donceel. New York: Herder & Herder. First published in *Gregorianum* 44 (1963): 307–18.

———. 1972. *Method in Theology*. New York: Herder & Herder.

Mann, Charles. 1991. "Lynn Margulis: Science's Unruly Earth Mother." *Science* 252 (April 19, 1991): 378–81.

Margulis, Lynn. 1993. *Symbiosis in Cell Evolution: Microbial Communities in the Archean and Proterozoic Eons*. 2nd ed. New York: Freeman.

———. 1998. *Symbiotic Planet*. New York: Basic Books.

Margulis, Lynn, Michael Dolan, and Ricardo Guerrero. 2000. "The Chimeric Eukaryote: Origin of the Nucleus from the Karyomastigont in Amitochondriate Protests." *Proceedings of the National Academy of Sciences of the United States of America* 97 (13): 6954–59.

Margulis, Lynn, and René Fester, eds. 1991. *Symbiosis as a Source of Evolutionary Innovation*. Cambridge, MA: MIT Press.

Margulis, Lynn, and Dorian Sagan. 1986. *Microcosmos*. New York: Summit Books.

———. 1997. *Slanted Truths*. New York: Springer-Verlag.

———. 2002. *Acquiring Genomes: A Theory of the Origin of Species*. New York: Basic Books.

Maritain, Jacques. 1957. *Existence and the Existent*. Garden City, NY: Doubleday.

Marsh, Gerald, and Charles Nissim-Sabat. 1999. "Comment on 'The Speed of Gravity,'" *Physics Letters A* 262:257–60.

Maudlin, Tim. 1994. *Quantum Non-Locality and Relativity*. Cambridge, MA: Blackwell.

Maynard Smith, John. 1988. "Evolutionary Progress and Levels of Selection." In *Evolutionary Progress*, edited by M. H. Nitecki. Chicago: University of Chicago Press.

———. 1991. "A Darwinian View of Symbiosis." In *Symbiosis as a Source of Evolutionary Innovation*, edited by Lynn Margulis and René Fester, 26–39. Cambridge, MA: MIT Press.

Mayr, Ernst. 1982. *The Growth of Biological Thought*. Cambridge, MA: Belknap Press of Harvard University Press.

———. 1985. "How Biology Differs from the Physical Sciences." In *Evolution at a Crossroads*, edited by D. Depew and B. Weber. Cambridge, MA: MIT Press.

———. 1988. *Toward a New Philosophy of Biology*. Cambridge, MA: Harvard University Press.

———. 1991. *One Long Argument*. Cambridge, MA: Harvard University Press.

———. 1997. *This Is Biology: The Science of the Living World*. Cambridge, MA: Belknap Press of Harvard University Press.

———. 2000. "Darwin's Influence on Modern Thought." *Scientific American* (July): 78–83.

———. 2001. *What Evolution Is*. New York: Basic Books.
———. 2004. *What Makes Biology Unique*. New York: Cambridge University Press.
McBrien, Richard P. 1981. *Catholicism*. Minneapolis: Winston.
McCool, Gerald A., ed. 1975. *A Rahner Reader*. New York: Seabury.
McGinn, Colin. 1999. *The Mysterious Flame*. New York: Basic Books.
McKenzie, John L. 1965. *Dictionary of the Bible*. New York: Macmillan.
McMullin, Ernan. 1981. "How Should Cosmology Relate to Theology?" In *The Sciences and Theology in the Twentieth Century*, edited by A. R. Peacocke, 17–57. Notre Dame, IN: University of Notre Dame Press.
Medawar, Peter. 1983. *The Limits of Science*. New York: Harper & Row.
———. 1985. *Evolution and Creation*. Notre Dame, IN: University of Notre Dame Press.
———. 1989. "The Explanation of Distant Action: Historical Notes." In *Philosophical Consequences of Quantum Theory*, edited by James T. Cushing and Ernan McMullin. Notre Dame, IN: University of Notre Dame Press.
Merleau-Ponty, M. 1962. *Phenomenology of Perception*. Translated by Colin Smith. London: Routledge & Kegan Paul.
Mermin, N. David. 1993. "Hidden Variables and the Two Theorems of John Bell." *Reviews of Modern Physics* 65:803.
Mersch, Emile. 1938. *The Whole Christ*. Translated by John R. Kelly. Milwaukee: Bruce.
———. 1951. *The Theology of the Mystical Body*. Translated by Cyril Vollert. St. Louis: B. Herder.
Merton, Robert K. 1973. "The Normative Structure of Science." In *The Sociology of Science*, 267–78. Chicago: University of Chicago Press.
Metzinger, Thomas. 1999. "The Hint Half Guessed." *Scientific American* (November): 125–26.
Meyer, Stephen C. 1990. "Of Clues and Causes: A Methodological Interpretation of Origin of Life Studies." Dissertation, University of Cambridge.
———. 2000. "The Scientific Status of Intelligent Design." In Michael J. Behe, William A. Dembski, and Stephen C. Meyer, *Science and Evidence for Design in the Universe: Papers Presented at a Conference Sponsored by the Wethersfield Institute, New York City, September 25, 1999*, 151–211. Proceedings of the Wethersfield Institute 9. San Francisco: Ignatius Press.
———. 2009. *Signature in the Cell: DNA and the Evidence for Intelligent Design*. New York: HarperOne.

Miké, Valerie. 2000. "Seeking the Truth in a World of Chance." *Technology in Society* 22:353–60.

———. 2005. "The Ethics of Evidence: A Call for Synthesis." In *Encyclopedia of Science, Technology, and Ethics*, edited by Carl Mitcham, 1:lii–lx. 4 vols. Detroit: Macmillan Reference USA.

Miké, Valerie, and Robert A. Good. 1977. "Old Problems, New Challenges." *Science* 198:677–78.

Miller, Arthur, ed. 1990. *Sixty Years of Uncertainty*. NATO ASI Series. New York and London: Plenum Press.

Miller, Kenneth R. 1999. *Finding Darwin's God*. New York: Harper Collins.

Misner, Charles W., Kip S. Thorne, and John Archibald Wheeler. 1973. *Gravitation*. San Francisco: W. H. Freeman.

Monod, Jacques. 1974. "On Chance and Necessity." In *Studies in the Philosophy of Biology*, edited by F. J. Ayala and T. Dobzhansky. Berkeley: University of California Press.

Montano, Edward J. 1955. *The Sin of the Angels: Some Aspects of the Teaching of St. Thomas*. Washington, DC: Catholic University of America Press.

Moore, James R., ed. 1989. *History, Humanity and Evolution*. New York: Cambridge University Press.

Moorhead, Paul S., and Martin M. Kaplan, eds. 1967. *Mathematical Challenges to the Neo-Darwinian Interpretation of Evolution*. Philadelphia: Wistar Institute Press.

Morris, Simon Conway. 2003. *Life's Solution: Inevitable Humans in a Lonely Universe*. Cambridge: Cambridge University Press.

Nagel, Thomas. 2012. *Mind and Cosmos: Why the Materialist Neo-Darwinist Conception of Nature Is Almost Certainly False*. Oxford: Oxford University Press.

Neirynck, Jacques. 2003. *The Vassula Enigma*. Independence, MO: Trinitas.

Neumann, John von. See von Neumann, John.

Neuner, J., and J. Dupuis. 1982. *The Christian Faith in the Doctrinal Documents of the Catholic Church*. Rev. ed. New York: Alba House.

Neville, Robert. 1995. *The Cosmology of Freedom*. New Haven: Yale University. Press.

New Catholic Encyclopedia. 2003. 2nd ed. New York: McGraw-Hill.

Newton-Smith, W. H. 1981. *The Rationality of Science*. Boston: Routledge & Kegan Paul.

Nichols, Terence L. 1996. "Aquinas's Concept of Substantial Form and Modern Science." *International Philosophical Quarterly* 36:30–18.

Nielsen, Michael A. 2002. "Rules for a Complex Quantum World." *Scientific American* (November): 66–75.

O'Collins, Gerald. 1981. *Fundamental Theology*. New York: Paulist Press.

Overbye, Dennis. 2000. *Einstein in Love*. New York: Penguin-Viking.

Pagels, Heinz R. 1985. *Perfect Symmetry*. New York: Simon & Schuster.

Pais, Abraham. 1979. *Reviews of Modern Physics* 51:863–914, esp. 907.

———. 1982. *Subtle Is the Lord*. New York: Oxford University Press.

Pascal, Blaise. 1996. *Pensées*. Translated and edited by A. J. Krailsheimer. New York: Penguin.

Peirce, Charles S. 1931. *Collected Papers*, edited by C. Hartshorne and P. Weiss. Cambridge, MA: Harvard University Press.

Pelikan, Jaroslav. 1971–1989. *The Christian Tradition: A History of the Development of Doctrine*. 5 vols. Chicago: University of Chicago Press.

———. 1996. *Mary through the Centuries*. New Haven: Yale University Press.

Pendergast, Richard J. 1973. *Cosmos*. New York: Fordham University Press.

———. 1988. *A Vision for Our Times: In the Sadness of the Modern World*. Unpublished manuscript. Volume 3 in the Pendergast Series.

———. 1990a. "A Thomistic Process Theory of the Trinity." *Science et Esprit* 42.1:35–59.

———. 1990b. *The Living Universe: An Organic Theory of Mind and Matter*. Unpublished manuscript. Volume 4 in the Pendergast Series.

———. 1990c. *Creation, Evil, and the Trinity: A Christian Process Theology*. Unpublished manuscript. Volume 5 in the Pendergast Series.

———. 1991. "A Process Theory of Creation." *Science et Esprit* 43.2:135–60.

———. 1992. "A Process Christology." *Science et Esprit* 44.1:45–66.

———. 2007. *The Cosmic Hierarchy: The Universe and Its Many Irreducible Levels*. Unpublished manuscript. Volume 2 in the Pendergast Series.

———. 2008. "The Mass on the World." *Heythrop Journal* 49.2:269–82.

———. 2009. "Evil, Original Sin, and Evolution." *Heythrop Journal* 50.5:833–45.

———. 2011. "Quantum Mechanics and Teleology." *Heythrop Journal* 50.2:271–78.

Pennock, Robert T. 2001. *Intelligent Design: Creationism and Its Critics*. Cambridge, MA: MIT Press.

Penrose, Roger. 1989. *The Emperor's New Mind*. New York: Oxford University Press.
———. 1994. *Shadows of the Mind*. New York: Oxford University Press.
———. 2004. *The Road to Reality*. New York: Alfred A. Knopf.
Perrin, Norman. 1967. *Rediscovering the Teaching of Jesus*. New York: Harper & Row.
———. 1974. *The New Testament: An Introduction*. New York: Harcourt, Brace, Jovanovich.
———. 1976. *Jesus and the Language of the Kingdom*. Philadelphia: Fortress Press.
Phipps, William E. 2002. *Darwin's Religious Odyssey*. Harrisburg, PA: Trinity Press International.
Polanyi, Michael. 1959. *The Study of Man*. Chicago: University of Chicago Press.
———. 1964. *Personal Knowledge: Towards a Post-Critical Philosophy*. New York: Harper Torchbooks.
———. 1967. *The Tacit Dimension*. Garden City, NY: Doubleday-Anchor.
———. 1969. *Knowing and Being*. Edited by Marjorie Grene. Chicago: University of Chicago Press.
Polkinghorne, John. 1984. *The Way the World Is: The Christian Perspective of a Scientist*. Grand Rapids: Eerdmans.
———. 1985. *The Quantum World*. Princeton, NJ: Princeton University Press.
———. 1987. *One World*. Princeton, NJ: Princeton University Press.
Popper, Karl R., and John C. Eccles. 1977. *The Self and Its Brain*. New York: Springer-International.
Prestige, G. L. 1956. *God in Patristic Thought*. London: S.P.C.K.
Quay, Paul. 1981. "Angels and Demons: The Teaching of IV Lateran." *Theological Studies* 42:20–45.
Rae, Alastair I. M. 1986. *Quantum Physics: Illusion or Reality?* New York: Cambridge University Press.
Rahner, Karl. 1961. *On the Theology of Death*. Quaestiones Disputatae 2. New York: Herder & Herder.
———. 1966. *Theological Investigations*. Volume 4. Baltimore: Helicon Press.
———. 1978. *Foundations of Christian Faith*. Translated by William Dych. New York: Crossroad Seabury.
———. 1983. *Theological Investigations*. Volume 19. Translated by E. Quinn. New York: Crossroad.

Rahner, Karl, et al., eds. 1968–1970. *Sacramentum mundi.* 6 vols. New York: Herder & Herder.
Rees, Martin. 1997. *Before the Beginning: Our Universe and Others.* Reading, MA: Addison Wesley.
———. 2000. *Just Six Numbers: The Deep Forces That Shape the Universe.* New York: Basic Books.
Richard of St. Victor. 1979. *The Twelve Patriarchs, the Mystical Ark, Book Three of The Trinity.* Translated by Grover A. Zinn. Classics of Western Spirituality. New York: Paulist Press.
Ricoeur, Paul. 1967. *The Symbolism of Evil.* Boston: Beacon Press.
Rose, Steven. 1998. *Lifelines.* New York: Oxford University Press.
Routledge Encyclopedia of Philosophy. 10 vols. 1998. London and New York: Routledge.
Ruse, Michael. 2000. *The Evolution Wars.* Santa Barbara, CA: ABC-CLIO.
Russell, Bertrand. (1910) 1957. *Mysticism and Logic.* Reprint. Garden City, NY: Doubleday Anchor.
Russell, R. J., W. R. Stoeger, and G. V. Coyne, eds. 1988. *Physics, Philosophy, and Theology: A Common Quest for Understanding.* Vatican City State: Vatican Observatory. Distributed by the University of Notre Dame Press, Notre Dame, IN.
Sandbach, F. H. 1975. *The Stoics.* New York: W. W. Norton.
Savitt, Steven F., ed. 1995. *Time's Arrows Today.* New York: Cambridge University Press.
Schilpp, Paul Arthur, ed. 1949. "Reply to Criticisms." In *Albert Einstein: Philosopher-Scientist.* Evanston, IL: Library of Living Philosophers.
Schlegel, R. 1981. "The Return of Man in Quantum Physics." In *The Sciences and Theology in the Twentieth Century,* edited by A. Peacocke. Notre Dame, IN: University of Notre Dame Press.
Schönborn, Christoph. 2005. "Finding Design in Nature." *New York Times,* July 7, 2005: A 23.
Schoonenberg, Piet. 1965. *Man and Sin.* Translated by Joseph Donceel. Notre Dame, IN: University of Notre Dame Press.
Schrödinger, Erwin. 1978. *Collective Papers on Wave Mechanics.* New York: Chelsea.
———. 1980. *Proceedings of the American Philosophical Society* 124:323.
Scott, Drusilla. 1985. *Everyman Revisited.* Lewes, Sussex, UK: Book Guild.
Searle, John R. 1997. *The Mystery of Consciousness.* New York: New York Review of Books.

Shannon, C. E., and W. Weaver. 1949. *The Mathematical Theory of Communication.* Urbana: Southern Illinois University Press.

Shimony, Abner. 1978. "Metaphysical Problems in the Foundations of Quantum Mechanics." *International Philosophical Quarterly* 18:3–17.

Simpson, G. G. 1964. *This View of Life.* New York: Harcourt, Brace & World.

Singh, Simon. 1997. *Fermat's Enigma: The Epic Quest to Solve the World's Greatest Mathematical Problem.* New York: Walker.

Smolin, Lee. 1997. *The Life of the Cosmos.* New York: Oxford University Press.

———. 2000. *Three Roads to Quantum Gravity.* New York: Basic Books.

———. 2004. "Atoms of Space and Time." *Scientific American* (January): 66–75.

Smulders, P. 1967. *The Design of Teilhard de Chardin.* Westminster, MD: Newman.

Spaemann, Robert. 2012. *Über Gott und die Welt: Eine Autobiographie in Gesprächen.* Stuttgart: Klett-Cotta.

Stanley, Steven M. 1981. *The New Evolutionary Timetable.* New York: Basic Books.

Stapp, Henry P. 1993. *Mind, Matter, and Quantum Mechanics.* New York: Springer.

Strait, Peggy Tang. 1989. *A First Course in Probability and Statistics with Applications.* 2nd ed. New York: Harcourt Brace Jovanovich.

Tegmark, Max. 2003. "Parallel Universes." *Scientific American* (May): 41–51.

Teilhard de Chardin, Pierre. 1961. *The Phenomenon of Man.* New York: Harper Torchbooks.

Terhal, Barbara M., Michael M. Wolf, and Andrew C. Doherty. 2003. "Quantum Entanglement: A Modern Perspective." *Physics Today* (April): 46–52.

Theological Dictionary of the New Testament. 1971. Vol. 7, edited by Gerhard Friedrich. Translated by Geoffrey W. Bromiley. Grand Rapids: Eerdmans.

Tillich, Paul. 1961. *Systematic Theology.* Vol. 1. Chicago: University of Chicago Press.

Two Friends of Medjugorje. 1990. Words from Heaven. Birmingham, AL: Saint James Publishing.

van Flandern, Tom. 1998. "The Speed of Gravity—What the Experiments Say." *Physics Letters A* 250:1–11.

———. 1999. Reply to comment on "The Speed of Gravity." *Physics Letters A* 262:261–63.

Vawter, Bruce. 1983. "Creationism: Creative Misuse of the Bible." In *Is God a Creationist?*, edited by R. Frye. New York: Charles Scribner's Sons.

von Neumann, John. 1955. *Mathematical Foundations of Quantum Mechanics*. Translated by R. T. Beyer. Princeton, NJ: Princeton University Press. 1st German ed., Berlin: Springer, 1932.

Watson, James D., et al. 1987. *Molecular Biology of the Gene*. 2 vols. Menlo Park, CA: Benjamin/Cummings.

Weinberg, Steven. 1992. *Dreams of a Final Theory*. New York: Pantheon.

———. 1993. *The First Three Minutes*. Updated ed. New York: Basic Books.

Wells, Jonathan. 2000. *Icons of Evolution: Science or Myth?* Washington, DC: Regnery.

Wheeler, John. 1962. *Geometrodynamics*. San Diego: Academic Press.

———. 1990. "Information, Physics, Quantum: The Search for Links." In *Complexity, Entropy, and the Physics of Information*, edited by W. Zurek. Redwood City, CA: Addison-Wesley.

Wheeler, J. A., and R. P. Feynman. 1945. *Reviews of Modern Physics* 17:157.

———. 1949. *Reviews of Modern Physics* 21:425.

Whitehead, Alfred North. 1929. *The Aims of Education*. New York: Free Press.

———. 1959. *Symbolism: Its Meaning and Effect*. New York: G. P. Putnam's Sons.

———. 1967a. *Science and the Modern World*. New York: Macmillan, Free Press.

———. 1967b. *Adventures of Ideas*. New York: Macmillan, Free Press.

———. 1968. *Modes of Thought*. New York: Macmillan, Free Press.

———. 1979. *Process and Reality*. Corrected edition edited by D. Griffin and D. Sherburne. New York: Macmillan, Free Press.

Wick, David. 1995. *The Infamous Boundary*. Boston: Birkhäuser.

Wigner, Eugene P. 1960. "The Unreasonable Effectiveness of Mathematics." *Communications in Pure and Applied Mathematics* 13:1–14.

Wildiers, N. M. 1968. *An Introduction to Teilhard de Chardin*. New York: Harper & Row.

Wilson, Edward O. 1980. "Sociobiology." Cambridge, MA: Harvard University Press.

Wistar Institute. See Moorhead, Paul S., and Martin M. Kaplan.

Wolfram, Stephen. 2002. *A New Kind of Science*. Champaign, IL: Wolfram Media.

Yam, Philip. 1997. "Bringing Schrödinger's Cat to Life." *Scientific American* (June): 124–29.

Zee, A. 1986. *Fearful Symmetry*. New York: Macmillan.

Zeilinger, Anton. 2000. "Quantum Teleportation." *Scientific American* (April): 50–59.

Zurek, Wojciech H. 1991. "Decoherence and the Transition from Quantum to Classical." *Physics Today* (October): 36–44.

———. 1993. "Letters: Negotiating the Tricky Border between Quantum and Classical." *Physics Today* (April): 13ff.

PREVIEW 1

Contents of Volume 2: Expanded Edition

The Cosmic Hierarchy: The Universe and Its Many Irreducible Levels

Preface

PART ONE: SETTING THE SCENE

1 • Introduction
   1. The Present Crisis
   2. John Paul II on Science, Philosophy, and Theology
   3. Recalling Etienne Gilson
   4. Christian Cosmology
   5. The Faith of Scientists
   6. Different Ways of Knowing

2 • Creation and Evolution
   1. Creation and the Big Bang
   2. Simultaneity
   3. General Relativity
   4. Creationism and Neo-Darwinism
   5. The Christian Doctrine of Creation
   6. Consilience

3 • Philosophical Concepts
    1. Philosophical Cosmology
    2. Being
    3. Objective and Tacit Knowledge
    4. Critical Realism
    5. Intentionality
    6. Being and Action
    7. Final and Telic Causality
    8. Insights from Whitehead and from Systems Theory

4 • Critical Scientific Realism
    1. Scientific Realism and Empiricism
    2. Analogy and Verisimilitude
    3. Conceptual Models
    4. Explanatory Power
    5. Tacit Knowledge

Part Two: Hierarchical Structure

5 • The Cosmic Hierarchy
    1. Theories of Matter
    2. Mayr versus Weinberg
    3. The Emergence of Consciousness
    4. Beings within Beings
    5. Conclusion

6 • Reductionism and Consciousness
    1. Artificial Intelligence
    2. The Limits of Neuroscience
    3. A Neuroscientific Model of Consciousness
    4. The Nature of Consciousness
    5. Philosophical Discussion of Consciousness
    6. Conclusion

PART THREE: QUANTUM MECHANICS

7 • Basic Concepts of Quantum Mechanics
1. The Two-Slit Experiment
2. Superposition
3. Uncertainty and Complementarity
4. The Processes U and R
5. Entanglement
6. The EPR Thought Experiment
7. Bohm's Improved Experiment
8. Bell's Theorem

8 • Diverse Interpretations of Quantum Mechanics
1. The Copenhagen Interpretation
2. Hidden Variables
3. Many-Worlds
4. Consciousness
5. Spontaneous Localization and the Role of Gravity
6. Interpretations FAPP
7. Consistent Histories
8. The Propensity Interpretation
9. The Transactional Interpretation

9 • The Nature of Time
1. Past, Present, and Future
2. The Discreteness of Time
3. The Reality of the Past
4. An Objection
5. The Cosmic Tree
6. Cosmology and Eschatology
7. Predestination

10 • Quantum Mechanics and the Cosmic Hierarchy
    1. More on the Cosmic Hierarchy
    2. Reinterpreting Cramer's Interpretation
    3. Conclusion

11 • A Speculative Model
    1. The Level of the Elementary Entities
    2. Structure and Evolution of the Model
    3. Future Prospects

Part Four: Biological Evolution

12 • Modest and Ambitious Darwinism
    1. Neo-Darwinism
    2. Modest versus Ambitious Darwinism
    3. The Two Darwinian Claims
    4. Teleology and the Cosmic Hierarchy
    5. The Glory of God Is Man Fully Alive

13 • The Intelligent Design Movement
    1. Irreducible Biochemical Mechanisms
    2. Information Theory
    3. The Multiverse

14 • The Nature of Evolution?
    1. Seeking the Truth about Evolution
    2. Teleological Evolution
    3. Critique of "Intelligent Design"
    4. Atelic Naturalism

Part Five: Theology

15 • Evolution and Evil
    1. The Problem of Evil
    2. The Doctrine of Original Sin
    3. Ten Theses
    4. The Role of Cosmic Powers in Evolution

16 • Creation and the Trinity
    1. The Quest for Unity
    2. The Doctrine of the Trinity
    3. Transcendental Concepts
    4. The Interpersonal Model
    5. The Psychological Model
    6. Personalism and the Trinity
    7. The Trinity and the Act of Creation
    8. Creation Makes a Difference in the Trinity
    9. God's Immutability
    10. The Economic Trinity, Deification, Incosmation

17 • The Future of Mankind

Bibliography

Index

PREVIEW 2

Synopsis of Volume 2: Expanded Edition

FROM AUTHOR'S PREFACE. I have divided the chapters of this book into five parts. More of the details of each part are presented in their respective introductions. Here I discuss some of the main ideas of each.

SETTING THE SCENE. Part One (chaps. 1–4) is introductory in character. I present a number of rather traditional positions, including what is sometimes called "critical realism." My object here is not so much to convince readers as to persuade them that the topic is at least arguable and to go ahead assuming its truth in a provisional way.

HIERARCHICAL STRUCTURE. The second part (chaps. 5–6) first explains the nature of the *cosmic hierarchy*, a principal theme of the book as a whole. Then I use it to argue against the positions of people who defend reductionism, especially those who believe in the possibility of artificial intelligence or who think that the mind is reducible to the brain.

QUANTUM MECHANICS. In Part Three (chaps. 7–11) I explain the lower levels of the hierarchy, the ones that pertain to physics. First I outline some of the basic concepts and principal interpretations of quantum mechanics (QM). Then I discuss the nature of time and make use of it to show how QM should be interpreted. Finally, I propose a speculative scheme for the lowest level of the cosmic hierarchy that underlies the present "fundamental particles" of physics.

Quantum mechanics is certainly a remarkable algorithm that enables one to predict very accurately the trajectories of many physical systems.

Nevertheless, it is poorly understood because the philosophical horizon in which it has been interpreted takes insufficient account of the nature of time, the distinct levels of the cosmic hierarchy, and the role of teleology in natural processes. My own interpretation of QM is based on two earlier ones, one of which harks back to Heisenberg and has been developed by Henry Stapp, and the other of which originated with John Wheeler and Richard Feynman and was later developed by John Cramer.

BIOLOGICAL EVOLUTION. In Part Four (chaps. 12–14) I discuss biological evolution and the intermediate levels of the hierarchy that pertain to it. I begin by emphasizing the distinction between the fact of evolution and the neo-Darwinian theory about the mechanism of evolution. The fact of evolution is, or at least ought to be, quite acceptable to orthodox Christians who are reasonably familiar with contemporary evolutionary biology. In my view, evolution is a progressive step-by-step actualization of the successive levels of the cosmic hierarchy. Rather than a mindless wandering through the space constituted by the possible configurations of inanimate matter, it is progress in terms of ontological value. The mysterious cause of evolution, which the biologist Richard Dawkins calls "The Blind Watchmaker," is not blind at all. The nature of the interfaces between different levels of the hierarchy, in this case the ones that biology deals with, is crucial. In particular, the relationship of the level of human intelligence to the sensate and vital levels below it is very important for understanding the moral and religious aspects of our human existence.

As a result, I discuss at some length the work of William Dembski, Michael Behe, and their colleagues. On the basis of modern biochemistry and information theory they attempt to show that evolution can be adequately explained only by taking account of "intelligent design." Even though their mathematical and scientific arguments are still controversial, I believe they show quite clearly that neo-Darwinian theory relies on unproven philosophical assumptions.

THEOLOGY. Part Four leads to the theological concepts of Part Five (chaps. 15–17). I begin by discussing the relationship between evolution and the problem of evil. From its very beginning the theory of evolution has been entangled with personal moral and religious considerations. Darwin himself was very much influenced by his personal experience of evil in the world and the temptation it presents to Christian faith. Neo-Darwinians argue that the imperfections and evils that mar the evolutionary process show that it cannot be the work of a divine Creator, or even a superhuman designer of any sort. I show that, to the contrary, Christian tradition suggests a plausible synthesis of modern science with Christian orthodoxy.

As the book of Job attests, the existence of evil in the world has always been a serious challenge to Judeo-Christian faith. It was one of the important reasons why Darwin lost faith in God's goodness and omnipotence and came to explain biological evolution in a nonteleological way. It is still one of the reasons that make neo-Darwinism plausible to many people. But my claim is that an updated version of Christian doctrine about evil and sin is quite capable of answering the objections raised against it.

Next I discuss the Christian doctrine of Creation in connection with those of the Trinity and the Incarnation. It is clear that there must be a connection. The relationship between the three divine persons is the root of the omnipotent power of the triune God who is the Creator of the universe. Moreover, the unity of the universe is due to its unity with the second person of the Trinity, the Word who was made flesh. How are we to understand these mysterious connections? We cannot understand them fully, but we can hope to do so at least to some extent.

Finally, I conclude Part Five, and the book, by speculating on the future of the human race in the light of Christian belief in Jesus Christ and his mission. The divine revelation that St. Paul called the "mystery hidden for ages in God," one that had been given to him by revelation, has now in our age found its proper setting. That setting is our modern scientific discovery of the vast universe around us. This scientific view enables us to guess at the vastness of God's plan for the whole of his Creation.

Each of the five parts of the book contributes to a comprehensive understanding of reality. The first one lays down the metaphysical foundations; the second explains the overall structure of the whole; the third shows how its lower levels determine some of its basic principles; the fourth explains some of its higher levels and how they have evolved; the fifth deals with the ultimate divine source of the entire structure.

Curriculum Vitae: Richard J. Pendergast, SJ

March 24, 1927	Born in Brooklyn, New York, son of Thomas and Harriet (Fitzpatrick) Pendergast
1932–44	Attended St. Vincent Ferrer Grammar School and Brooklyn Preparatory School
1945–46	Service in U.S. Navy
1944–45, 1946–49	Completed B.E.E. in engineering at Manhattan College, Bronx, New York
July 30, 1949	Entered New York Province of Society of Jesus
1949–52	Novitiate and liberal arts studies at St. Andrew-on-the-Hudson, Hyde Park, New York
1952–55	Completed licentiate in philosophy at Saint Louis University, St. Louis, Missouri
1955–56	Taught physics at Brooklyn Preparatory School
1956–60	Completed Ph.D. in physics at Saint Louis University
1960–64	Completed licentiate in theology at Woodstock College, Woodstock, Maryland
June 20, 1963	Ordained to Roman Catholic priesthood
1964–65	Jesuit tertianship at Our Lady of Martyrs Shrine, Auriesville, New York
1965–66	Postdoctoral studies in physics at Loyola University, New Orleans, Louisiana
1966–70	Assistant professor of physics at Saint Peter's College, Jersey City, New Jersey

1970–71	Sabbatical at Jesuit School of Theology, Berkeley, California
1971–72	Associate professor of physics at Saint Peter's College In 1972 left academic track in physics for pastoral ministry and focus on science–faith studies. His book *Cosmos* was published in 1973.
1972–75	Chaplain and bioethics consultant at Saint Louis University School of Medicine
1975–76	Sabbatical at Jesuit School of Theology, Chicago, Illinois
1976–77	Director of spiritual retreats at Gonzaga Retreat House, Monroe, New York
1977–79	Priestly ministry to Catholic charismatic community, Newark, New Jersey
1979–83	Director of spiritual retreats at Loyola Retreat House, Morristown, New Jersey
1983–84	Sabbatical at Weston Jesuit School of Theology, Boston, Massachusetts
1984–85	Assistant pastor at St. Ignatius Church, Manhattan, New York
1985–91	Chaplain at Cenacle Retreat House, Ronkonkoma, New York
1991–2012	Pastoral minister and writer at Murray-Weigel Hall, Fordham University, Bronx, New York
June 24, 2012	Died in New York

Index

AAAS, 163
abduction, in the study of evolution, 130n1, 148–49
accidental, meaning of term, 33
accidental system, lacking unity, 100
accidents
    concepts as, 26
    natural, 31
    nature of, 30–31
    supernatural, 31–33
act of existing, 26–28, 37, 100
    being and, 197
    constitutive of the agent, 197
    and creative cause, 198
    as dependent act, 198
    future possibilities and, 106
    See also being; *esse*
Aczel, Amir, 85nn1, 4
    on Bell's theorem, 83–84
    on entanglement, 76–77
Adam
    significance of figure of, 181
    sin of, 172
adaptive feature, 151–52
agent, 105–6
Aharonov, Yakir, 82, 85n4

American Association for the Advancement of Science (AAAS), 163
angel(s)
    belief in, 184
    in the Bible, 177–78
    demons and, 178–79
    evolution and, 183
    existence of, 182
    immateriality of, 109n3
    natures of, 183–84
    ontological level of, 35n6
    presence of, 101
    sin of, 171
    See also cosmic powers; demons
angel(s), fallen
    and evil, 169
    influence of, on human beings, 187
angel(s), good, 182–83
Aquinas, Thomas. *See* Thomas Aquinas, Saint, 94
Aristotle, xv, xx, 9
    as basis for philosophy of Aquinas, xv
    concept of Scala Naturae, 114

Aristotle (*cont.*)
  and efficient cause, 19–20
  and final cause, 20, 151
  on formal and material causes, 180
  on fundamental motion of universe, 86
  on nature of material entities, 19
  on potentialities, 121
  on prime matter and substantial form, 19, 41–42
  static worldview of, xv
Aristotelian-Thomistic philosophy, 195
  beliefs of, 26–27
  on material beings, 20
Arnold, Matthew, 3
artificial intelligence (AI), xviii, 37–42
artificial selection
  and natural selection, 184
  See also natural selection; random variation and natural selection
Asimov, Isaac, 38
Aspect, Alain, 77, 84–85
atelic naturalism, 155–58
  divine revelation and, 156–57
  neo-Darwinism and, 157
atheists
  ambivalence of, xxii
  conflict of, with theists, 154
  on evil, 170
  influence of, on atelic naturalists, 156–57
atomism, philosophical, 19
atoms (Greek *atomos*), 19
Audi, Michael, on Copenhagen interpretation, 62
aufheben ("to sublate"), xix. *See also* sublation

Augustine, Saint, 34, 94
  and idea of spiritual substance, 25–26
  and problem of evil, 172
  on time, 86
Augustinian-Franciscan school, 20
Augustinian Neoplatonism, 20
avatar, meaning of, 193n4
Ayala, Francisco J., 13n3

Bailly, Marie-Louise, 17
behaviorists, and third-person states, 53
Behe, Michael, 146n9, 155, 234
  on intelligent design, 132
  and irreducibly complex systems, 134–35, 142, 148
  on living organisms compared with machines, 146n4
  and modern biochemistry, 132–34
  on neo-Darwinism, 132–36, 153–54, 157
  on problems with Darwinism, 133–36
  on sheer chance, 145–46
being
  act of existing and, 197
  analogy of, 127, 200
  as be-ing, 197
  composed of essence and *esse*, 198–99
  conception of, 196–204
  fundamental dynamism of, 197
  as object of metaphysics, 196
  teleology and, 127
  Thomistic account of, 197
  See also act of existing; *esse*; essence
being itself
  as mystery, 203
  as transcendent reality, 200

Bell, John Stewart, 75n5, 85n2, 88
   Bell's theorem, 77
   and Bohr's philosophy, 80
   on Copenhagen interpretation, 80
   on entangled particles, 104
   interactions studied by, 103
   See also Bell's theorem
Bellarmine, Robert Cardinal, 71
Bell Labs, xiii, 164
Bell's theorem, 66, 82–85
   cosmic hierarchy and, 95
   cosmic tree and, 95
   teleology and, 95–96
Benedict XVI, Pope (Joseph Cardinal Ratzinger), xxi, xxiv
   ref. 11
Big Bang, 67, 110n5
biochemical mechanisms, origin of, 146n5
biological evolution. *See* evolution
biology
   evolutionary, 11–12
   molecular, 7
   physics and, 24, 27–28
biosphere, 126
Blind Watchmaker, 153, 186, 234
   See also Dawkins, Richard
body
   relationship of human person to, 100
   soul and, 100–101
Bohm, David, 85n4
   on Copenhagen interpretation, 80
   deterministic theory of, 75
   EPRB experiment and, 77
   improved experiment of, 81–83
   on particle and wave, 103
   theory of quantum mechanics, 66

Bohr, Niels, 61
   on collapse of wave packet, 67
   complementarity principle of, 62
   and Copenhagen interpretation, 62
   and direct experience of ideas, 64
   positivist approach of, 81
   on quantum mechanics, 73, 80, 81
   on uncertainty principle, 78
Bonaventure, Saint, 20
Born, Max, 62
boundary conditions, xxx, xxxi, xxxi n3
   of intellectual specialties, 10–11, 95, 186
   between physics and philosophy, 152
   of science, 143
brain
   as material condition for spiritual operations of the soul, 23
   material with respect to the soul, 33–34
   soul formal with respect to, 33–34
Broglie, Louis de, 61, 76
   on Copenhagen interpretation, 80
   and hidden variable interpretation, 65
   on particle and wave, 103
   theory of the double solution, 65

Campbell, Christine, xxxi
Campbell, Murray, 39
Camus, Albert, on God as father of death, 175
Cantore, Enrico, on science, 153
Caputo, Nicolas, as probability example for Dembski, 138–40
Carrel, Alexis, 55
   at Lourdes, 17–18, 158n1

Casstello, Alicia, xxxi
Cathars, beliefs of, 171–72
Catholic Church
    and cosmology, xvi (*see also* cosmology: Christian)
    and relationship between science and religion, 7
    See also Church
causes, four kinds of, 20. *See also* Aristotle
Center for Science and Culture, 132–33
Center for Theology and the Natural Sciences (CTNS), 146n7
certainty, and faith, xxvii
Chalmers, David, 52–55, 57n5
chance
    evolution and, 117–18
    as explanation for events, 138–39
    governing universe, 23
    and necessity, 117–18
chaos theory, 35n3
Christ. *See* Jesus Christ
Christian faith, 170
Christology
    Pendergast's process and, xix
    See also Pendergast, Richard J.
Church
    mission of, 190
    relationship between Christ and, 33
    and State, separation of, 142
    See also Catholic Church
Churchland, Patricia, 46–47
Clarke, W. Norris, xxxi, 204n2
Clauser, John, 77
Commoner, Barry, on genome, 120
communication, verbal, 29–30
competition, meaning of, 115
completeness criterion, 78–79
complex specified information (CSI), 143, 157. *See also under* Dembski, William
computer
    compared to lever, 39–40
    reflecting intelligence of programmer, 40–41
    not substantial entity, 40–41
conjugate quantities, 91
consciousness, 22, 68–71
    awareness of one's own unity and, 28
    emergence of, 27–29
    human, 37–57
    nature of, 47–50
    philosophical discussion of, 50
    as property of subject, 47–48
    as qualitative property of the act of knowing, 48
    of self, of higher organisms, 25
    structure of, 43
    theory of Antonio Damasio, 42–47
Copenhagan interpretation, 65, 105
    fourth axiom of, 69, 71
    particle and wave and, 80, 103
    as pragmatic, 63
    Pyrrhic victory of, 81
    triumph of, 65
Coreth, Emerich, on being, 196–97
cosmic evolution. *See* evolution: cosmic
cosmic hierarchy, xviii
    evolution and, xvi, xxix, 118–19
    holism and, xix
    levels of, 23, 99, 233, 234
    and irreducible levels in the universe, 22, 157

Index

nature of, 233
   particles and waves and, 103–4
   teleology and, 125–28
   time and, 87–88
cosmic powers, 186–87
   conflict between good and evil, xxix
   evil and original sin and, xxii
   role of, in evolution, 182–87
   sin and death as, 178
cosmic teleology. *See* teleology: cosmic
cosmic tree, 91–93, 97nn7–8
   existence of world and, 97n8
   existing in mind of God, 92
   including all possible histories, 105
   many-worlds interpretation and, 93
   as timeless, 92
cosmology
   Aristotelian-Thomistic, 5
   Christian, xxviii, 10–11, 238
   eschatology and, 93–96
Council of Trent, 171–72, 181
Courant Institute of NYU, xiii
Cournand, André, 166
Coyne, George, xxxi
Cramer, John, 234
   on Copenhagen interpretation, 62
   and quantum mechanics, xviii
   transactional interpretation of quantum mechanics of, 73–75, 105, 107, 110n5
creation
   Christian doctrine of, 235
   out of nothing, 170
   St. Paul in Romans, 129

   Pendergast's process theory of, xix
   unity in, 7
Crick, Francis, 57n4
   on consciousness, 50–51
   and discovery of DNA, 120, 133
   on origin of life, 130n4
critical realism, 233
CSI. *See* complex specified information
Cunniffe, Helena, xxxi
Cushing, James T., 63, 65
Cushing, Vincent, on Catholic teaching about evolution, 131n11
Damasio, Antonio, 57nn2–3
   as materialist, 43
   on science, 51–52, 150
Darwin, Charles, xxix, xxi n2
   biology and, 121–22
   evil and, xxix, 235
   four insights of, 114
   as most influential scientist since Newton, 24–25
   on orchids, 170
   On the Origin of Species, 114–15
   on plant and animal breeders, 184
   random variation and natural selection and, 149, 151, 184 (*see also* natural selection; random variation and natural selection)
   religious faith of, 149
   teleology lacking for, 185
   theory of biological evolution of, 108

Darwinian histories, 137
   and intelligent design, 147
   meaning of, 117–18

Darwinism
    evolutionary biology and, 114
    illusion and, 120
    modern culture and, 120, 130n5
    modest versus ambitious, 122–24
    philosophy of science and, 114
    problems with, 132–46
    and quantum mechanics, 152–53
    two claims of, 124–25
    zeitgeist and, 114
Darwinism, ambitious, xxi, 113–31,
        148–149
    and boundary conditions with
        Christian philosophy, 152–53
    objections to, 132–33
    as precarious hypothesis, 153–54
Darwinism, modest, xxi, 113–31,
        148–49
    and Christian faith, 123, 128–30
    descent with variation from
        common ancestor, 122–23
Davies, Paul, on multiverse theory,
        145
Dawkins, Richard, xxix
    on Blind Watchmaker, xxix, 234
    as materialist, 26
Deep Blue, 38–39
Dembski, William, 146nn2, 9, 155,
        234
    and complex specified information
        (CSI), 138–42
    criticism of neo-Darwinism of,
        153–54, 157
    on idea of multiverse, 144–45
    on improbable phenomena, 142–
        43
    and inference of design, 142
    and information theory, 132–33,
        143
    law of conservation of information
        and, 157
    on mathematical odds for
        biological evolution, 138–42,
        143
    on necessity, chance, or intelligent
        design, 145–46, 185
    on odds for random variation and
        natural selection, 148
    on probabilistic resources, 145
Democritus, 19
demons
    angels and, xxix
    belief in, 179
    in the Bible, 177–79
    negative influence of, on
        evolution, 185
    sins of, 175, 180
Dennett, Daniel, on consciousness,
        51–52
Descartes, 70
    on being, 196
    mathematical logic of, 127
design
    and contingency, complexity, and
        specification, 141
    as explanation for events, 138–39
    inference of, 141–42
    intelligent (*see* intelligent design)
despair, cosmic, 128
determinism, and quantum
        mechanics, 108
devil
    evil and, 169
    See also demons; Satan
dignity, human, 6
Discovery Institute, 155
distance, symmetric definition of, 99

divine revelation
  atelic naturalists and, 156–57
  Thomistic philosophy and, 197
Dobzhansky, Theodosius, 124, 131n9
Dostoevsky, Fyodor, on God, 175
Dreyfus, Hubert, 42, 57n1
Dulles, Avery, 36n9
Dych, William V., 36n7

Edelman, Gerald, on consciousness, 50–51
Einstein, Albert, 61, 85n3
  deterministic worldview of, 79
  on entanglement, 76–77
  EPR experiment and, 76–83
  hidden variable interpretation and, 65
  on higher-level interactions, 103
  as metaphysical, 73
  on necessity, 23
  on physicists, 120–21
  and position of moon, 70–71
  positivism and, 121
  on quantum mechanics, 77–79
  theory of relativity of, 104
  as *Time*'s man of the twentieth century, 114
Eldredge, Niles, on Lynn Margulis, 159n3
embodiment, being and, 27
empirical adequacy
  distinguished from ontological truth, 153
  nature of reality and, 81
empiricism, and quantum mechanics, 63
energy, discrete from matter, 91
entanglement, 76–85
  Bell's theorem and, 83–84
  of related particles, 103–4
  Schrödinger's cat and, 69–70
  simultaneity and, 76–77
  teleology and, 95–96
entities
  becoming actual, 23
  beyond domain of science, 150
  complex material, 23
  elementary, 22
  higher-level, 22–23, 28, 100
  inanimate, 22
  indivisibles of, 98
  intermediate-level, 99–100
  living and nonliving, 22, 25
  lower-level, 22, 30, 100
  rational, 22
  sentient, 22
  simplification of, 23
  smallness of, 23
  substantial, 40–41
Epicurus, 165
  problem of evil and, 170
EPR thought experiment, 77–81
EPRB experiment, 77, 81–83, 103–4, 109n4
eschatology
  cosmology and, 93–96
  meaning of, 94
esse
  Christian concept of, 193n4
  cosmic tree and, 92–93
  distinguished from essence, 197–99
  existing, 26
  as principle of being, 198
  to-be, 197–98
essence, 25
  distinguished from *esse*, 197–99
  embodied in matter, 26

essence (*cont.*)
  existence and, 195–204
  meaning of, 198
  as principle of being, 198
  as union of substance and accidents, 198–99
Ethics of Evidence Foundation, xvii, xx–xxi, 239
Eucharist, xix
Everett, Hugh
  on collapse of wave packet, 67–68
  many-worlds interpretation of quantum mechanics and, 67–68
evidence, xvii
evil
  "Adamic," 180
  cosmic powers and, xxii
  entering world, 92
  linked with original sin, 174–75
  moral, 172
  natural, 175
  origin of, in Bible, 174–75
  personal powers of, 178
  physical, 172
  problem of, 169–71, 234–35
  radical view of, 172–73
  reality of, 193n3
  Roman Catholic doctrine of, 171–72
  "Satanic," 180
  superhuman beings, 183
  See also demons; Satan
evolution, xxviii–xxix, 11
  abduction and, 130n1, 148–49
  ambitious Darwinism and, 148 (*see also* Darwinism, ambitious)
  angels and, 183–84
  arguments for, 148–49
  background conditions for, 147–48
  biological, 138–39, 151
  as "Blind Watchmaker," 134–35
  branching, 114
  cause of, 234
  Christian belief and, 113
  Christian theory of, xxix, 122–23
  common descent and, 114–15
  cosmic, 86–87
  cosmic hierarchy and, xvi, xxix, 118–19 (*see also* cosmic hierarchy)
  cosmic powers and, xxii, 182–87
  fact of, 124–25
  genetics and, 115, 117–18
  gradual, 114
  holists and, 118–19
  mechanisms of, 118–19, 234
  modest Darwinism and, 148 (*see also* Darwinism, modest)
  moral and religious considerations of, 235
  as natural selection, 114
  nature of, 147–59
  non-constancy of species and, 114
  Pendergast's view of, xvi
  problem of evil and, 234–35
  progressive, 126
  random variation and natural selection and, 147–59 (*see also* random variation and natural selection)
  reductionist understanding of, 183
  teleology and, 49–50, 118–19, 125, 148–49, 151–54
existing, act of. *See* act of existing
existing (*esse*). *See* esse

faith
    absence of, in modern world, 3
    certainty and, xxvii
    Christian, 36n9
    erosion of, 3
    as gift of God, 36n9
    nature of, 181
    supernatural truth and, xxvii, 10
Fergusson, David, 193n2
Feynman, Richard P., 14–15, 17–18, 75n6, 234
    and electromagnetic wave theory, 73–75
    letter to wife after her death, 15–16
fides quaerens intellectum, 8
First Vatican Council, 9
Fisher, Christopher L., 193n2
Fisher, Ronald A., 165
Fitzmyer, Joseph A., on predestination, 180–89
Fordham University, xvii–xviii, xxxi
form (Greek *morphē*), 19
    Aquinas on, 20
    Franciscan school and, 20
    rational and sentient, 20
    soul as, 41
    virtual, 20–21
    vital, 20
Fourth Lateran Council, 181
    belief in devil and, 178
    on origin of evil, 171–72
Franciscan school, and holism, 35n1
Frankl, Viktor, on lack of meaning in life, 109
Freedman, Stuart, 77
freedom, of human beings, 175
Freudianism, and modern culture, 120, 130n5

Fry, Edward S., 77
functionalism, 54
future
    ambiguity about meaning of, 107
    Christian hope and, 97n9
    influence of, on present, 152
    as magnet for present, 95–96
    mode of being of, 89–90
    as potential, 87–88, 96, 105, 152
    relation of, to present, 107

Galileo, xxx, 10, 11, 49, 71, 154
genetics, and evolution, 115, 117–18
genomes, complexity of, 133
geographical isolation, and formation of new species, 116
Ghirardi, Gian Carlo, and modification of Schrödinger's equation, 71–72
Gilson, Etienne, xx, 195
    on being, 196
    on distinction between essence and existence, 199
    historical approach of, 197
Gleick, James, 14–15
God
    and angels, 185
    as being itself, 198
    belief in, 184
    as Creator, 154–55, 169, 188, 235
    design of, for world, 155
    enabling finite beings to become real, 198
    essence and existence identical in, 199
    evolution and, 185, 187
    as Father, 188
    glory of, 128–30
    as love, 182

God (*cont.*)
  pathos of, 176
  perfect goodness of, 170
  personal, 12–13
  plan of, for universe, 188–89
  presence of, 101
  as primary cause, 75, 88, 129–30
  as principle of unity and order in world, 169–70
  prophetic portrait of, 176
  relationship of, to humanity, 177
  will of, 175
Gödel, Kurt, incompleteness theorem, xvii
good, problem of, 182
Gospel of John, and struggle with Satan, 178
Gould, Stephen Jay
  on evolution, 170–71
  on neo-Darwinism, 137, 146n6
grace, 32
graph theory, 109n1
gravity, Schrödinger's equation and, 72
Greenbaum, Arline (wife of Richard Feynman), 15–16
Greene, Brian, on spacetime, 90
Greene, John C., 25
Gribbin, John, on Cramer's transactional interpretation, 110n5

Haberstroh, Father Harvey, xiv–xv
Hacking, Ian, on concept becoming reality, 77
Handel, G. F., 189
Hawking, Stephen, on essence of universe, 199
Hayes, Zachary, OFM, xxiv ref. 2

on eschatology, 94, 96
review of *Cosmos*, xvi
Hegel, G. W. F., xix, 5, 31
Heisenberg, Werner, 61, 78, 234
  and Copenhagen interpretation, 62, 80
  and notion of potentiality, 73
  positivism and, 63, 73, 121
  propensity interpretation of, 72–73
  uncertainty principle and, 62, 91
heritability, meaning of, 115
Heschel, Abraham, 176
hidden variables, 65–66, 77–79, 83–84
Hindu religion, 190, 193n4
history, cosmic, 92–93
Hitt, Gail, xxxi
Høffding, Harald, 63
holism
  Christian, 23–24
  consciousness and, 56–57
  cosmic hierarchy and, xix
  of Franciscan school, 35n1
  modern, 21–24
  problems of, 29
  and understanding structure of world, 29–34
Holt, Richard, 77
Holy Spirit
  believer's personal relationship with, 32
  faith and, 34
  as gift of Father and Son, 32
  supernatural grace and, 33
homunculus, 46–47
hope, Christian, 97n9
horizon
  metaphor of, 13–14, 203–4
  scientific, 14

Horne, Michael, 77
Hubble telescope, xx
hubris, of scientists and scholars, 143, 186
Hulsbosch, A., on evil, 172
human being(s)
    altruistic love and, 118–19
    bodies and, 101
    consciousness and, xviii
    freedom of, 175
    nature and dignity of, 153
    rational components of, 44–45, 118–19
    sins of, 179
    spiritual components of, 44–45
    spiritual warfare of, 178–79
    as substantial entities, 37
    vital components of, 44
    union of soul and body, 42
humanism, 6
human race
    fall of, 172
    and fall of universe, 181
    relationship of, to God, 177
    suffering of, and sin of Adam, 172
Hume, David, on problem of evil, 170
Huxley, Thomas, xxxi n2
hylomorphism, xviii–xix, 19, 22
    as inadequate, 41–42
    structure of the world and, 29–34

IBM, and Deep Blue, 38–40
Ignatius Loyola, Saint, 158n1, 188
    on influence of evil spirits, 178
immortality, personal
    belief in, 12–13
incarnation, 235
    and history of universe, 189

infamous boundary
    between quantum and classical realms, 68–70
information theory, 138–43
intelligence
    and substantial unity, 39
intelligent design (ID), xxi, 132–46, 234
    in areas other than biology, 184–85
    critique of, 154–55
    neo-Darwinism and, 147, 149–50
    as part of science, 142–43
    teleology and, 155
Irenaeus of Lyons, Saint
    on human beings, 128–29
irreducibly complex system (ICS)
    definition of, 134–35
Isham, Christopher
    on time, 89

Jaki, Stanley, 17
James, William, 63, 80
    hypersensible realities and, 64
    pragmatism of, 63–64
Jammer, Max
    on Copenhagen interpretation, 62
    and reality criterion, 78–79
Jesuits, xiv
Jesus Christ
    angels and demons and, 177–78
    biblical story of, 189–90
    coming again, 187
    as exorcist, 177–78
    as firstborn of creation, 106–7
    good news of, xxvii
    as incarnate Logos, 6
    incosmation of, 107
    mission of, 189–90

Jesus Christ (*cont.*)
   person's new existence in, 33–34
   struggle of, with Satan, 177–78
John of the Cross, Saint, 158n1
John Paul II, Saint (Pope), xxx
   Address to Pontifical Academy of Sciences, October 22, 1996, xxi–xxii, xxiv ref. 13, 125, 131n8, 131nn10–11, 158, 159n4
   Crossing the Threshold of Hope, 6
   on evolution, 125, 158
   Fides et Ratio, 9–10
   on human dignity, 6
   mass in Central Park (1995), xviii
   on modest Darwinism, 128
   on science and religion, xxviii, xxx–xxxi, 6–10
   and Teilhard de Chardin, 123
   on truth about man, 128
Jordan, Ernst Pascual
   and Copenhagen interpretation, 62
Jung, Carl, on demons, 183

Kant, Immanuel
   noumena and, 64
   phenomena and, 64
   philosophy of, 17
Kasper, Walter Cardinal, 216
Kasparov, Garry, 38–39
Kauffman, Stuart
   on neo-Darwinism, 156
   and teleological nature of universe, 157
Kelsey, Jan, xxxi
Kelvin, Lord William Thomson, 136
Kitcher, Philip
   on Darwinian histories, 117
   on ambitious Darwinism, 122–24

Klubertanz, 204n2
knowledge, human
   bringing temptation, 157
   divided into disciplines, 143
   nature of, 200–204
   tacit, 201–3
   transcendental Thomism explanation of, 202–4
Kubrick, Stanley, 38
Kuhn, Thomas
   on paradigms, 108–9

Labbe, Charlotte, xxxi
Lamarck, Jean-Baptiste, 114
   Lamarckian finalist theories, 123
language, inclusive, xxv, xxxi n1
language production, 29–30
Larson, Edward J., 150
   survey about faith of scientists, 12–13, 14, 157–58, 184
Laughlin, R. B.
   as solid-state physicist, 137
Leibniz, 54
Léon-Dufour, Xavier
   on goodness of God, 129
   on word "mystery," 192
Leuba, James H.
   survey about faith of scientists, 12–13
Leucippus, 19
Lewontin, Richard
   on neo-Darwinism, 137, 146n6
life
   lack of meaning in, 109
Lipton, Peter
   on certainty, 196–97
locality, 79
Logos, divine
   events latent in, 107
   existence of world and, 94

as firstborn of all creation, 24
governing whole universe, 96n2
as highest level of causality, 24
as incarnate, 169, 190–91
influence of, on evolution, 184
possibilities existing in, 105
telic causes in mind of, 105–6
unifying entire universe, 22
as unique entity that sublates all lower ones, 22, 87–89
See also Jesus Christ
Lonergan, Bernard
  on horizon, 13
  on sublation, 35n5
loop quantum theory, 90–91
Lourdes, France
  shrine to Virgin Mary at, 17
love
  God as, 182
  science and, 18
  union and, 8
Loyola Retreat House, xiv

machines
  as accidental systems, 37–38
  not conscious, 48
Maimonides, Moses, 204n1
Manhattanville College, xiii
mankind, future of, xxix, 188–93, 235
Mann, Charles, 158n2
many-worlds interpretation, 66–68
Maréchal, Joseph, on being, 196–97
Margulis, Lynn
  on neo-Darwinism, 156
  teleological nature of universe and, 157
  on theory of evolution, 158n2, 159n3
  on world of microbes, 127–28

Marxism, 120, 130n5
material beings, 19–21
materialists, 26
  arguments about evolution and, 119–20
  beliefs of, 26
  reductionist claims of, xxii
matter
  as body, 41
  discrete from energy, 91
  evil and, 172
  informed by soul, 41
  united with form, 19–20
Mayr, Ernst, 24–29, 131n9, 159n3
  as atheistic materialist, 25
  on Charles Darwin, 114
  on common descent and natural selection, 122–23
  on Darwinism, 120, 131n7
  practicality of, 121
  reality of evolutionary progress and, 128
  and Steven Weinberg, 24–27
  on teleology, 151–52
McCool, Gerald A., 36n7
McGinn, Colin, 52
meaning, in life, 109
Medawar, Peter, 161
medicine, uncertainty and evidence in, xvii
Medjugorje, 158n1
Memorial Sloan-Kettering, xviii
Mersch, Emile, 36n8
Merton, Robert K., 166
metaphysics, and being, 196
Metropolitan Museum of art, xviii
Meyer, Stephen, 132, 155, 160, 162
  on multiverse, 144–45
  on neo-Darwinism, 153–54, 157
  on sheer chance, 145–46

Michelangelo, 42
Miké, John, xx, xxxi
Miké, Valerie, xxiv ref. 3, xxxi, 239
    friendship with Pendergast, xiii–xxi
    and Pendergast Series, xxi–xxiii
Miklósházy, Attila, SJ (Bishop), xxiii
mind–body problem, and quantum mechanics, 73
modern synthesis, 155–56
Monod, Jacquer, on world governed by chance, 5
Morris, Simon Conway, on processes of evolution, 135–36
movie in-the-mind and brain, 44–46
multiverse, 144–46
mystery, 192–93
mysticism, 34
myth, 180–81

Nagel, Thomas, 162
National Academy of Sciences (NAS), 12–13, 184
naturalism, atelic, 155–58
natural selection, 114–15
    and artificial selection, 184
    evolution and, 147–59
    generation of information and, 138
    irreducibly complex systems and, 134
    new species and, 116–17
    random variation and, 117–18, 124
    See also random variation and natural selection
necessity
    as explanation for events, 138–39
    governing physical processes, 23

neo-Darwinism, 113–31, 184, 234–35
    atelic naturalism and, 157
    bases of, 115
    inadequacy of, 124
    intelligent design and, 147
    materialistic philosophy and, 137
    meaning of, 155–56
    as "modern synthesis," 115
    as "modest" Darwinism, 185
    probability of, 147
    quantum physics and, 153
    questioning of, 136–37
    teleology and, 154
    See also Darwinism; Darwinism, ambitious; Darwinism, modest
Neumann, John von, and Copenhagen interpretation, 66
neurons, and supernatural accidents, 33
neuroscience, 49–51
    as boundary condition for philosophers and theologians, 49
    limits of, 42–47
New York Botanical Garden, xviii
Newton, Isaac, 7, 122, 127, 154
Newtonian physics, 77, 123
Newton-Smith, W. H., 123
non-being
    and being, 197
    See also act of existing; being; *esse*; existence
non-reductive functionalism, 52–54
nonreligious person, 146n8

Occam's razor, 66
ocean waves, discrete entities of, 99
original sin
    cosmic powers and, xxii

Index   253

doctrine of, 170–82
myth of, 181
problem of evil and, 174–75
See also demons; evil; Satan; sin

Paley, William, 154
Pannenberg, Wolfhart
  on eschatology, 95–96
  on future as magnet for present, 106–7
Parousia, 120
participation, 198
particle physicists, 185. *See also* physics
particles, 102–3
particles and waves
  cosmic hierarchy and, 103–4
  EPRB experiment and, 103–4
  interactions of, 104
  relationship between, 62
Pascal, Blaise, 15, 263
Paschal Mystery
  overcoming of Satan and, 178
  relationship of, to Mass, 96n5
past
  ambiguity about meaning of, 107
  mode of being of, 89–90
  personal, 96n1
  as real, 87–88
  relationship to present, 88–89, 107
  See also future; present; time
pathos, meaning of, 176–77
Paul, Saint
  Letter to the Colossians, 106–7
  Letter to the Galatians, 34
  Letter to the Romans, 129, 189, 192
  on love of God, 177
  on mystery, xxix

Pauli, Wolfgang, and Copenhagen interpretation, 62
Peirce, Charles Sanders, 130n1
Pendergast Series, xxi–xxiii
  contents of Volume 2, 227–31
  synopsis of Volume 2, 233–36
Pendergast, Richard J., xxiv, refs. 5–10, 15–18
  about, 238
  Aristotelian-Thomistic philosophy of, xx
  Cosmic Hierarchy, xvi
  Cosmos, xiv, xvi, xxiii ref. 1, xxvii
  Curriculum Vitae, 237–38
  editor's account of work, xiii–xxi
  on evolution, xvi, xix
  process Christology of, xix
  process theory of Creation, xix
Penrose, Roger
  on consciousness, 50–51
  on Ghirardi, Rimini, and Weber, 72
  on Schrödinger's cat, 69–70
Pentecost, 189–90
Penzias, Arno, and low-temperature microwave background, 67
Perrin, Norman, on myth, 180, 193
philosophy
  Christian, and science, 150
  and science, 195
physicists, intellectual imperialism of, 27
physics, xxviii
  biology and, 24, 27–28
  criterion of empirical adequacy and, 120
  fundamental particles of, 233
  and living entities, 24
  particle, 100, 136–37

physics (*cont.*)
  quest for unifying theory of matter and, 7
  solid-state, 100, 136–37
Pines, David, 137
Planck, Max, 61
Plato
  "ideas" of, 198
  on knowledge, 201–2
Podolsky, Boris, on EPR experiment, 77–79
Polanyi, Michael, xvi–xvii, xx, 195, 204n4
  on human language production, 29–30
  "marginal" control, 33
  on nature of human knowing, 200–201
  recognizing faces, 4
  on science, 126
  theory of personal knowledge, xvi–xvii
Polanyi Center, 133
Polkinghorne, John, 75n3
  on Bohr and the Copenhagen school, 80
  on intelligent design, 144
  on many-worlds interpretation, 68
  on time, 89
Popper, Karl, 5
positivism, and quantum mechanics, 63
predesignation, meaning of, 140
predestination, 188–89
present
  as boundary zone, 89
  including possible future, 106–7
  influence of future on, 152
  mode of being of, 89–90
  in opposition to past, 88
  as real, 87–88
  See also future; past; time
Presse, Dom Alexis, 17–18
prime matter (Greek *hylē*), 10
probabilistic resources, 145
probability theory, 130n2, 138–43
  applied to physical reality, 113
  and estimating causes, 149
process thought, xviii–xix
purposive behavior, 151

quantum mechanics, 11, 152–53, 233
  advanced solutions of, 105
  as algorithm, 61
  and behavior of atoms, 61
  and behavior of nature, 23
  compared with thermodynamics, 77–78
  completeness of, 64
  consciousness interpretation of, 70–71
  Copenhagen interpretation of, 62–66, 152–53
  cosmic hierarchy and, 95
  cosmic tree and, 95
  Darwinism and, 152–53
  determinism and, 108
  entanglement and, 76–85
  gravitational theory and, 72
  as incomplete theory, 80
  many-worlds interpretation of, 93
  as mathematical procedure, 61
  new interpretation of, 98–110
  past interpretations of, 61–75
  pragmatism and, 64
  propensity interpretation of, 72–73
  retarded solutions of, 104–5

Index

statistical averages and, 77–78
teleology and, 95–96
transactional interpretation of, 73–75, 105

Rahner, Karl, xiii, xiv, xx, 94, 193n2, 195
  on angels, 184
  on being, 196–97
  on grace, 32, 36n7
  on human being as spirit in the world, 203
  on science, 126
  on spiritual principles, 179
  on sublation, 35n5
  on supernatural world elevated by grace, 92
  on theory of original sin, 172–73
randomness, as characteristic of nature, 64
random variation
  development of new species and, 116
  evolution and, 147–59
  generation of information and, 138
  irreducibly complex systems and, 134
  See also evolution; natural seelction; random variation and natural selection
random variation and natural selection, 124–25, 149–50, 184
  insufficiency of, 155–56
  See also evolution; natural selection
reality criterion, 78–79
reductionism
  as inadequate philosophy, 28–29
  nature of science and , 55
  particle physics and, 137
  structure of the world and, 29–34
reductionists
  analysis of living beings and, 27
  assumptions of, 41, 119
  atomistic, 22
  on consciousness, 55–57
  evolution and, 183
  on nature of intelligence, 42
  neglecting subjective experience, 30
  systems and, 22
Rees, Martin, 144–46
relativity, theory of, 11, 79, 88
religion
  as basis of ethics, 5
  science and, 5–8
revelation, divine, xxxi n4
  distinguished from theology, xxxi n4
  dynamic worldview and, xxii
  and time, 94–96
  and truths of faith, xxviii
Ricoeur, Paul, on image of serpent, 179
Rimini, Alberto, and modification of Schrödinger's equation, 71–72
Rockefeller Institute, 17
Rosen, Nathan, on EPR experiment, 77–79
Rosenfeld, Léon, 63

Sagan, Carl, 191
saints, and evil spirits, 178
Satan
  in Bible, 177–78
  defeat of, 188
  influence of, on human beings, 187

Satan (*cont.*)
  sins of, 175, 180
  See also demons; evil; original sin; sin
Saxe, John Godfrey, 18n1
Schilpp, P. A., 85n2
Schönborn, Christoph Cardinal
  on immanent design, 150
  on John Paul II not accepting neo-Darwinism, 131n11
Schoonenberg, Piet, on evil, 172
Schrödinger, Erwin, 61, 65, 76, 85n1
  on Copenhagen interpretation, 80
  entanglement and, 76–77
Schrödinger's cat, 68–69, 72
Schrödinger's equation, 66–67, 68, 70–72, 93, 102
science
  boundary conditions of, 143
  centrality of Christ and , 192
  love and, 18
  materialism and, 150
  philosophy and, 195
  purpose of, 142
  religion and, xv, xxvii, 5–8
  rise of, 4
  theology and, 8, 11
  wisdom of God and, 192
scientific theories, precariousness of, 123
scientific-technological development, 48–50
scientism, 16–18, 55
scientists
  faith of, 12–18
  mistakes of, 11–12
Searle, John R., on consciousness, 50–55
Second Vatican Council, 9, 123, 173–74

self-awareness, 45
sense objects, 64
serpent, as image of evil, 179
Shannon, Claude E., 164
Shimony, Abner, 77
sin
  consequences of, 175
  entering world, 92
  See also evil; original sin
Smolin, Lee, on loop quantum theory, 90
Smulders, P., on evil, 172
Solvay Institute, 65, 66
soul
  and body, 42, 100–101, 109n2
  brain material with respect to, 33–34
  embodied in matter, 41
  emergent properties of, 42
  formal with respect to the brain, 33–34
  influence of, 47
  See also body
souls, equal to angels, 36n6
space
  consisting of discrete quanta, 91
  existing on lowest level of hierarchy, 104
Spaemann, Robert, xviii, xxiv ref. 4
specialization
  in modern culture, 13–14
  and scientism, 18
speech, activity of, 29–30
Stapp, Henry P., 234
  on Bohr, 63, 80
  on collapse of wave packet, 73
  on interpretation of QM, 108
  propensity interpretation and, 72–73

St. Ignatius Jesuit Church, xiv, xvii
Stoeger, William, xxxi
St. Peter's College, Jersey City, 14
string theory, 90
subject, 47–48
sublation, xix, 31–34
substances, spiritual, 26
suffering, divine, 176–77
superfecundity, meaning of, 115
systems, 21
technology, rise of, 4

Tegmark, Max, on idea of multiverse, 146n10
Teilhard de Chardin, Pierre, xiii, xiv, xix, xxi, xxiv ref. 12
    cosmic vision of, xxi
    on development of man, 193
    The Divine Milieu, xxi
    on existence of evil, 174–75, 180
    "Mass on the World," xix
    modest Darwinism of, 123
teleological selection, to produce changes in species, 184
teleology, 95
    analogy of being and, 127
    cosmic, 152
    cosmic hierarchy and, 125–28
    evolution and, xxii, 50, 118–19, 148, 185
    in Pendergast's vision, xvi
    in quantum mechanics, xxii
television, consciousness and, 48–49
telic causes, 105–7, 152
telos, goal of biosphere, 126
Teresa of Avila, Saint, 34, 158n1
theists, conflict with atheists, 154
theology, Christian
    boundary disputes in, 11

    definition of, 8
    science and, 8, 150
    theorem of alternatives, 83–84
    thermodynamics, compared with quantum mechanics, 77–78
Thomas Aquinas, Saint, xv, xx, 9, 94
    on angels governing material world, 184
    on being, 202
    as best exposition of Catholic doctrine, xv
    and distinction between essence and existence, 204n2
    on divine name, 196
    and infinitive form "to-be," 199
    on material beings, 20
    on spiritual creatures, 179
Thomism, 57n3, 195
    philosophy, 196–97
    theology, 56–57
    transcendental, 197
Thompson, M. G., 77
Tillich, Paul, xxx, 55
time, nature of, 86–97
    cosmological perspective on, 94–96
    discreteness of, 90–91
    eschatological perspective on, 94–96
    events existing in, 102–3
    in Pendergast's vision, xvi
    quasi-mathematical representation of, 87
    theory of relativity and, 104
    See also future; past; present
Timone, Richard, SJ, xxxi
transcendental Thomism, 197, 202–4
transubstantiation, xix
tree, cosmic. *See* cosmic tree

Trent, Council of. *See* Council of Trent
Trinity, 235
   Pendergast's Thomistic process theory of, xix
   unity of universe with, 191
truth
   kinds of, xxvii–xxviii, 10
   known by natural powers, xxvii, 9, 10
   revealed by God, xxvii, 10
two-slit experiment, 68, 102

uncertainty principle, 78, 91
unified theory, 90
unitary procedure, as continuous and deterministic, 61
unity
   accidental system and, 100
   as consequence of love, 8
   in Creation, 7
   in diversity, 100
   human spirit and, 8
   ontological, 28
   substantial, and genuine intelligence, 39
universe
   biblical history of, 188–90
   block model of, 89–90, 93–94
   as contingent, 91
   fall of, 181
   first moment of, 96n4
   as ordered temporal and historical structure, 89–90
   rational beings in, 191
   teleological evolution of, 114
   unity of, 235
   vastness of, 190, 193n1
   See also world

variation of fitness
   meaning of, 115
   teleological, 122
Vatican Observatory, xxxi
vertices, 98–100

Watson, James
   and chemical structure of DNA, 120
   and discovery of DNA, 133
wave function or wave packet, 61
   collapse of, 62–63
   identification of, 62–63
   transformed into particle, 61
   See also particles and waves
wave packet, collapse of, 61, 66–67, 93, 102
   cause of, 71
   consciousness and, 70
   as creative decision, 73
   gravity and, 72
   on inanimate level, 70
   infamous boundary and, 68
   as random, 72
wave solutions, 74
Weaver, Warren, 164
Weber, Tulio, and modification of Schrödinger's equation, 71–72
Weinberg, Steven, 5, 24–27, 130–31n6
   and Mayr, 24–27
   on meaning, 109
   particle physics and, 137
   on universe having no intrinsic meaning, 128
Wheeler, John A., 160–61, 234
   classical electromagnetic wave theory and, 73–75
   on matter compared to clouds, 90

Whitehead, Alfred North, xv, xviii, xx, 73, 195
Whitman, Andrew, xxxi
Wigner, Eugene, on Schrödinger's cat, 69–70
Wildiers, N. M., on evil, 172
Wilson, John, on Polanyi Center, 146n3
Wilson, Robert, and low-temperature microwave background, 67
Wistar Institute, 136
Witham, Larry, 12–14, 150, 157–58, 184
world
  attaining perfection, 129–30
  governed by both chance and necessity, 23
  mystery of, 18
  See also universe

ABOUT THE AUTHOR

Richard J. Pendergast (1927–2012) was a Jesuit priest with a doctorate in physics and licentiates in philosophy and theology, who devoted his life to seeking the integration of modern science and divine revelation. His aim was to update the Christian synthesis of St. Thomas Aquinas, based on the medieval static worldview, to reflect evolution, the view of cosmic reality as dynamic process. A scholar of first rank whose research appeared in peer-reviewed professional journals, he yet preferred pastoral ministry to academic life. He deeply desired to address the general public, believers as well as nonbelievers, to offer insight into problems that may disturb the faith of the former or impede the latter's search for God. He wrote five books over thirty years, and these manuscripts are now being published in a series of five volumes, complemented by Volume 6, a trilingual reprint of his study on the teaching of the Catholic Church concerning the real presence of Christ in the Eucharist. Richard Pendergast was a seminal thinker, whose work presents a bold Christian vision—a living universe of meaning and hope.

A CHRISTIAN COSMOLOGY

The Catholic Church does not have a formal teaching on evolution at this time. But people wonder about the meaning of their lives as experienced in their own culture, which today is dominated by science. Charles Darwin's theory of evolution has raised many questions and led to diverse claims. In this work addressed to the general reader, the author discusses what has been reliably established by science, distinguishing it from interpretations of the theory guided by philosophical assumptions. Seeking a coherent picture of the world, Richard Pendergast integrates scientific knowledge with what we have in Sacred Scripture and lays the foundation of a Christian cosmology. It is the beginning of a venture for generations.

ABOUT THE EDITOR

A native of Budapest, Hungary, Valerie Miké obtained a liberal arts degree at Manhattanville College, worked at Bell Labs in systems engineering, and earned a doctorate in mathematics at the Courant Institute of New York University. She went on to participate in the introduction of mathematical techniques in medicine and pursued graduate studies in ethics and the philosophy of science. She is professor emerita of biostatistics at Weill Medical College of Cornell University and former head of the biostatistics department at the Sloan-Kettering Institute for Cancer Research. Her study of ethical issues pertaining to uncertainty in biomedical science and technology led to the notion of an "ethics of evidence"—an approach to uncertainty widely applicable to decision-making in human affairs. She has established the Ethics of Evidence Foundation, with a mission that includes publishing the work of scholars in related fields.

The motto of
The Ethics of Evidence Foundation, Inc.

All our dignity consists in thought. . . .
Let us then strive to think well;
that is the basic principle of morality.

Blaise Pascal

ABOUT THE PUBLISHER

Since 1798 Herder has been publishing works of knowledge and understanding for God's people. As the English-language heir to the renowned international Catholic publishing company, Herder & Herder continues to offer engaging books of original thinking, pastoral sensitivity, and prohetic vision.

Look for the finest in original and prophetic literature on:
Mysticism, Trinity, sacraments, Catholic thought, worldwide theology, Church leadership, and ministry and history.

www.ingramcontent.com/pod-product-compliance
Lightning Source LLC
Chambersburg PA
CBHW031600110426
42742CB00036B/260